Educating Egypt

Educating Egypt

CIVIC VALUES AND IDEOLOGICAL STRUGGLES

LINDA HERRERA

The American University in Cairo Press
Cairo   New York

First published in 2022 by
The American University in Cairo Press
113 Sharia Kasr el Aini, Cairo, Egypt
One Rockefeller Plaza, 10th Floor, New York, NY 10020
www.aucpress.com

ISBN 978 1 649 03102 0

Names: Herrera, Linda, 1964– author.
Title: Educating Egypt : civic values and ideological struggles / Linda Herrera.
Identifiers: LCCN 2021043211 | ISBN 9781649031693 (hardback) |
    ISBN 9781649031020 (paperback)
Subjects: LCSH: Education and state—Egypt. | Islamic education—Egypt. |
    Education—Egypt. | Women—Education (Secondary)—Egypt.
    Classification: LCC LC95.E3 H47 2021 | DDC 370.962–dc23

1 2 3 4 5   26 25 24 23 22

Designed by Westchester

Dedicated to Shiva and Tara

Contents

Figures and Tables

Figures

Tables

Acknowledgments

This book essentially began in 1986 when I was a study-abroad student at the American University in Cairo from the University of California, Berkeley. At the time, I lived in the Falaki student hostel in Downtown Cairo, and most mornings, would wake up to the unfamiliar sounds of drum rolls, chanting, stomping, and commands over a loudspeaker. I was disoriented and decided to ask a fellow resident, what was going on down the street? She explained, emphasizing how obvious the answer was, "It's a school." Three years later, in one of those curious twists of fate, that very school was selected as the site of an ethnographic study for my master's thesis. More than three decades after that, I revisited that study for this volume, placing it within a wider body of work and thinking on the cultures and politics of education in different eras, youth, civic engagement, and social policy, and the spectacular waves of change that have occurred in Egypt, the region, and world. I owe an enormous debt of gratitude to countless students, teachers, parents, principals, friends, and other education workers who, over the years, opened their classrooms, homes, and minds to me, guiding the direction of my research. While preparing this book, I became involved in researching and documenting a major education reform currently underway in Egypt, "Education 2.0." While this book just touches on those still ongoing reforms (hopefully another work will cover them in more detail), I am continuously reminded of the immense dedication of so many people who work in the field of education. I hope this work can be of some value to them, to students, and lay readers, and generate conversations about education policy, research priorities, and education futures, among other topics.

This volume combines original chapters with substantially revised versions of already published work undertaken between 1990 and 2021. Part 1, "Schooling the Nation," is derived from a monograph, *Scenes of Schooling:*

Inside a Girls' School in Cairo, originally published by Cairo Papers in Social Science, a division of the American University in Cairo Press (Herrera 1992). Chapter 8, "Downveiling," appeared in *Middle East Report* (Herrera 2001). Chapter 9, "Education, Empire, and Global Citizenship," is a highly modified version of "Education and Empire: Democratic Reform in the Arab world?" from the *International Journal of Educational Reform* (Herrera 2008). Chapter 10, "Young Egyptians' Quest for Jobs and Justice," was originally a chapter in the book, *Being Young and Muslim: New Cultural Politics in the Global South and North* published by Oxford University Press (Herrera and Bayat 2010). Chapter 11, "Youth and Citizenship in the Digital Age: A View from Egypt," originally appeared in the *Harvard Educational Review* (Herrera 2012), and chapter 12, "It's Time to Talk about Youth in the Middle East as 'The Precariat,'" was published in the open-source journal *META* (Middle East—Topics & Arguments) (Herrera 2017a). Acknowledgment goes to all publications and presses for permission to reprint or use portions of already published material. Regarding photos, much appreciation to my friend Dalia al-Aswad who shared her father's primary school class photo from 1930 Ismailiya (in chapter 6).

When I initially entered the world of educational research in Egypt and the region, I felt isolated. But thankfully, the field has become more robust, diverse, and a space of conviviality. I would like to thank specifically Nadim Mirshak, Hany Zayed, and Mezna Qato, who read and provided comments on an earlier version of the introduction. My colleagues and students in the Department of Education Policy Organization and Leadership and the Global Studies in Education program at the University of Illinois at Urbana-Champaign have been beyond supportive and flexible. They consistently provide a stimulating, engaging, and enabling environment to explore critical and transnational issues in education. Nadia Naqib, my editor at the American University in Cairo Press, has shown great patience and professionalism. Thanks also to Laura Gribbon and Ælfwine Mischler who worked so diligently on the production side of the book. Asef Bayat, whom I met within weeks of arriving in Cairo, has been a partner and sounding board for the better part of my life. Our two daughters, who live up to their namesakes, Shiva with the air of an eloquent and elegant poem, and Tara who channels the light of a glittering star, are sources of creativity, purpose, and strength. I dedicate this book to them.

Introduction

Educating Egypt: From Nation Building to Digital Disruption

E ducation in Egypt has unfolded in the past century with enormous success in terms of its reach and place in the collective imagination. The state and diverse groups in society have consistently leveraged education to shape identities, assert political and moral authority, and pursue ambitious visions for economic and social development. Indeed, education is such a compelling field of study precisely because of how it is intertwined in larger processes of power and counterpower, social continuity and social change, and because of its connection to the hopes, aspirations, labor, setbacks, and opportunities of millions of families and children, who make immense sacrifices to be credentialed and "educated."

This book traces the everyday practices, policy ideas, and ideological and political battles relating to education from the era of nation building in the twentieth century to the age of digital disruption in the twenty-first. The overarching theme is that schooling and the broader field of education have consistently mirrored larger political, economic, and cultural trends and competing ideas about what constitutes the "good society," the "good citizen," and the "educated person." Questions around citizenship, civic belonging, and participation in public and economic life have loomed especially large as sites of struggle and reimagining. These themes run through the book and tie its chapters together.

The book is divided chronologically and thematically into four sections: Schooling the Nation: Inside a Girls' Preparatory School (chapters 1–5); Political Islam and Education (chapters 6–8); and Youth in a Changing Global Order (chapters 9–12). Given the recent advances in digital transformation, and the uncertain educational futures made visible by the Covid-19 pandemic of 2020, the concluding section poses the question, "Is the school as we know it on the way to extinction?" The chapters draw on three decades of mainly qualitative educational research in Egypt, beginning with an ethnographic study of the everyday world of a girls' preparatory school in Cairo over the course of one academic year (1990–91). This study provided the foundation for a host of inquiries that would follow, culminating in specialized research in global policy studies in education.

This volume takes an interdisciplinary approach that draws on anthropology, sociology, political economy, philosophy, social history, and the fields of international development studies, youth studies, gender studies, and technology studies. Since new tools, technologies, and ideas are periodically infused into the education system, leading to sudden changes in behaviors and attitudes, researchers must be methodologically agile. The methodologies employed here include ethnography, oral and life histories, critical analysis of education policies, laws, and textbooks, social historical analyses, and digital social research. Ethnographic and other qualitative approaches compel the researcher to grapple with reality in all its shades and contradictions while remaining cognizant of one's own subjective positionality. These approaches do not lend themselves to tidy or grand theorization about the nature of schooling. The aim of this volume, rather, is to bring issues and social realities to the surface, raise questions, and put forward propositions for further investigation.

The Two Sides of Education: *Tarbiya* and *Ta'lim* (Upbringing and Knowledge)

Across the ages, education in Egypt and the wider Middle East, North Africa, and West Asia (MENAWA) region,[1] has been understood and practiced as the joining of upbringing (*tarbiya*) with knowledge (*'ilm*). The words *tarbiya* and *ta'lim* (the latter derived from the word *'ilm*) are often used interchangeably as synonyms for "education" or "schooling." These words, however, denote very different aspects of education and carry distinct historical antecedents.

The word *tarbiya* derives from the root *r-b-b*, which means to grow up, rear, raise, bring up, educate, or teach (children). Another form of the verb from the same root, *rabba*, means "to be master, be lord, have possession of, control, have command or authority over."[2] The word *tarbiya* harkens to a time when teachers carried societal authority and power. They shouldered the responsibility of raising children as virtuous members of their communities, according to laws and customs specifically drawn from the Abrahamic religions. Muslim thinkers such as the celebrated jurist al-Ghazali (1058–1111), and figures from Christian and Jewish traditions, viewed education as a moral process (see Tawil 2001). Education, properly performed, would serve the greater good of the society. Teachers and other adult authorities were supposed to instill virtue, good manners, and proper comportment in children, which in Arabic is termed *adab*.[3] These concepts and practices around child rearing have left a lasting impact on educational thought and pedagogy up to the present, though with modification.

With the rise of mass national school systems in the nineteenth and twentieth centuries, *tarbiya* took on more "secular" and "developmental" connotations. Teachers trained in modern pedagogic sciences were charged with bringing up children within a framework of nation building, good citizenship, and economic productivity. In other words, as societies in the MENAWA region transitioned to modern bureaucracies, and schooling became organized through a process of considerable educational borrowing from largely Western models, education professionals invariably carried notions and practices of *tarbiya* from local cultures into schools. In sociological theory, the terms "socialization" or "enculturation" come close to the meaning of *tarbiya*; however, these terms do not entirely capture connotations of "upbringing" and "*adab*" that have remained embedded in cultures of teaching and learning, even in their decidedly modified forms.

Ta'lim, on the other hand, a noun derived from the Arabic root *'a-l-m* (to know), connotes information, advice, teaching, instruction; training, schooling, education; and apprenticeship (Wehr 1980, 636). The underlying principle tying these meanings together is "having knowledge." Similar to the concept of *tarbiya*, "knowledge" carries a deep historical legacy, although it too is a dynamic category. In his magisterial study, *Knowledge Triumphant*, Franz Rosenthal (1970) traces the genealogy of the Arabic root *'a-l-m* starting with its pre-Arabic antecedents. For centuries, if not millennia, knowledge was characterized by a dichotomy between human knowledge and divine knowledge, or "wisdom."[4] Writing about the concept of knowledge in medieval Islam, Rosenthal (1970, 240) posits: "Information is the cement that holds together any human society, and a continuous process of education is necessary to assure its preservation and extension." This description refers to knowledge as a tool to ensure the reproduction of societies and the social order. However it does not account for how education adjusts to accommodate and drive new knowledges, forms of power, and changes in the social structure.

In more contemporary education systems dating to the nineteenth century, *'ilm* signifies new approaches to "scientific" knowledge and ways of knowing that could be codified, measured, quantified, and assessed: the kind of knowledge deemed essential for "modern" development and economic flourishing. Old and new knowledges and pedagogies comingle in education systems and influence each other. And as scholars of critical theory (Apple 2000; Freire 1970; Kellner 2003; Mayo 2012), feminist epistemology (Abu-Lughod 2008; Harding 1991), and postcolonial and decolonial studies (Apffel-Marglin and Marglin 1996; Borg and Mayo 2002; Leonardo 2020; Mbembe 2001; Smith 1999), remind us, time and again, knowledge is always connected, in implicit and explicit ways, to systems of power. The ongoing contests over knowledge and power penetrate debates about the content of curricula, the rules of assessment, styles of pedagogy, the economics of education, and the very purpose of education itself.

Even as modern sciences gained primacy in contemporary education systems, *tarbiya* (*parvaresh* in Persian) remained the more commonly used official term to denote "education" throughout the MENAWA region. The education ministries in Egypt, Jordan, the United Arab Emirates, Qatar, and Iran are all named Ministry of Upbringing and Education (Arabic: Wazarat al-Tarbiya wa-l-Ta'lim; Persian: Vezarat-e Amuzesh va Parvaresh). In Algeria and Morocco, the designation is Ministry of National Upbringing (Wazarat al-Tarbiya al-Wataniya), and in Syria and Iraq it is simply Ministry of Upbringing (Wazarat al-Tarbiya).[5] Education in its full sense involves the joining of *tarbiya* and *ta'lim*, even during times when the scales are tipped in favor of one aspect over the other. As historian Susanna Ferguson (2018) cogently argues with reference to mid-nineteenth and early twentieth century Lebanon, "the dyad of *ta'lim/tarbiya* marked the tension between reform and stability particularly clearly." In other words, *ta'lim* contains the promise of new knowledge, development, change, and progress, whereas *tarbiya* denotes social stability and tradition.

New Schooling Rises

The type of schooling that spread and became dominant from the third quarter of the nineteenth century has been described as "modern," "Western," "civil," "foreign," "secular," "new order," "new method," or simply "new" (see Herrera 2004, 318). Unlike indigenous schools and colleges run by religious communities and pious endowments (*waqf*), or forms of training organized by different guilds by way of apprenticeships, the new schooling was more standardized, centrally planned and monitored, and nationalistic in character.[6] It required a new professional class of teachers, administrators, and bureaucrats trained in the emerging sciences of pedagogy, education administration, and management.

The first national nod to the idea of universal "new" schooling in Egypt can be traced to the Constitution of 1923.[7] Written and ratified just four years after the 1919 Revolution, it declares Egypt a constitutional monarchy, though the country remained under partial British protectorate.[8] The constitution represents a bold rebuke to the woeful and intentional British neglect of the education of the local population. Article 19 stipulates: "Elementary education [grades one to five] shall be compulsory for Egyptian boys and girls and shall be free in public schools." In a move towards educational consolidation, Article 19 also removes autonomy from local communities with the clause, "Public education shall be regulated by law." The early nationalists and framers of the constitution understood that "education" was associated with patronage networks and practiced in loose, often questionable, and uneven ways across the country. They did not view elementary schooling as inherently positive, or a necessary asset to the national project. Article 17 sets the precedent for free education, though with a caveat: "Education shall be free *except when it breaches public order or contradicts morals*" (emphasis added). Though it would be several decades before the country would reach near universal schooling under the administration of a centralized ministry of education, the Constitution of 1923 serves as an important milestone that gave weight to the idea that *all* Egyptian children, female and male, from every ethnic and religious group, region, and background, should be educated and, at the same time, subject to state oversight.

In the 1950s and 1960s, on the heels of the Second World War and a wave of anticolonial struggles in formerly colonized lands, countries throughout the global South claimed their independence. Schools became pillars of citizenship formation in postcolonial societies. In Egypt, following the Free Officer's coup that overthrew the monarchy in 1952, a new military class came to power, led by Gamal Abd al-Nasser. The revolutionary government banned political parties and suspended the Constitution of 1923. The subsequent Constitution of 1956 maintained previous guarantees of free schooling for all Egyptians but added new language, asserting the state's dominion over the population's civic, moral, and intellectual education. According to Article 49, "Education is a right for all Egyptians guaranteed by the state.... The state especially takes care of the development of the people civilly and intellectually and morally." The revolutionary government used all methods at its disposal—soft power by means of schooling, mass media, and culture (mainly music and films),[9] and hard power in the form of the repressive arms of the state, the police, intelligence, and army—to fashion a society for a new Egypt.

During the Nasser years, public education was administered by a centralized state bureaucracy. Scores of Egyptians, particularly from rural and urban poor areas, became first-time school-goers. Their ability to access schools and earn educational qualifications led to high levels of social mobility. However, at the same time, non-Arabs and non-Muslims found themselves newly marginalized in a system that institutionalized discrimination and narrowed the definition of what constituted "Egyptian."[10] Throughout the 1950s and 1960s, large portions of religious, ethnic, and linguistic minority communities in Egypt, including Christians, Greeks, Jews, Italians, Syrians, and Armenians, left Egypt as many of their properties and businesses were sequestered, and their schools nationalized and Arabized.[11]

Nasser's government (1956–1970) also famously brought al-Azhar University (est. AD 972) and its network of Azhari schools under its control. With the Law of al-Azhar of 1961, the government set out to weaken the Muslim scholarly class (*ulama*), who had long enjoyed social prestige and economic power. These religious clergy controlled vast amounts of property and wealth through the *waqf* system of religious endowments. They had enormous influence over the education of Muslim children through their networks of primary schools and mosque-based Qur'anic classes. Despite efforts in later decades to reassert their political and economic standing (Eccel 1984; Zeghal 1996), Azhari institutes came to be widely perceived by the rising middle classes as schools "of last resort." Government policies perpetuated their lower status by, for example, requiring Azhari schools to admit students who failed in the general public schools.[12]

The pan-Arab project of the Nasser era would experience a precipitous demise following the Arabs' crushing military defeat in the 1967 war with Israel. After Nasser's death in 1970, his vice president Anwar Sadat (1970–1981) assumed the presidency. Sadat's government turned away from Nasser-era ideologies of state socialism, Arab nationalism, and Third Worldism, in favor of pursuing more free market "Open Door" (*Infitah*) economic development policies. While embracing economic liberalization, the new government also pivoted towards social conservatism and instituted Islamic law (*sharia*). Like Nasser before him, Sadat marked his epoch with a new constitution, the Constitution of 1971. In a departure from the previous constitution, it codified fidelity to Islam and the Muslim scholarly class. Article 2 stated: "Islam is the religion of the State and Arabic its official language. Islamic law (*sharia*) is the principal source of legislation." Sadat also lifted Nasser-era restrictions on Islamist groups, most notably the Muslim Brotherhood, in an effort to offset the growing leftist opposition in the country. He thereby emboldened the Islamist current in the country, a move that would later backfire.

The articles relating to education in the 1971 Constitution combined Islamic identity and cultural conservatism with free market capitalism. The constitution reaffirmed the state's commitment to free, universal, compulsory schooling at the primary stage, but added a new condition: "Religious education shall be a principal subject in the courses of general education" (Article 19). Article 18 covered the political, economic, and developmental imperative of education, stipulating that the State is responsible for supervising every stage of schooling "with a view to linking all of them to the requirements of society and production."[13] These dual positions reveal the state's attempt to advocate for cultural continuity while promoting change through engagement in a global economic order.

Sadat famously signed the Camp David Accords with Israel in 1978, an act largely applauded by the international community but controversial at home. People within Arab societies largely espoused nonnormalization with Israel because of its treatment and disenfranchisement of the Palestinian people. Nevertheless, Camp David led to Sadat being the first Muslim recipient of a Nobel Peace Prize,[14] and Egypt becoming the largest recipient of US development and military aid after Israel. Trade and international investment in Egypt experienced a boom. Multilateral and bilateral finance institutes including the World Bank, International Monetary Fund (IMF), United States Agency for International Development (USAID), and other development agencies within the Organization for Economic Cooperation and Development (OECD) countries became more influential players in the country's path of economic and social development, including the education sector.

Sadat's diplomacy with Israel and alignment with the Islamists tragically and violently led to his demise. On October 6, 1981, during a parade commemorating Egypt's military victory in the 1973 Arab–Israeli war, Muslim extremists marching in the procession assassinated the president. When Hosni Mubarak, Sadat's vice president, came to power, he had to negotiate his predecessor's complicated legacy. Mubarak (1981–2011) embraced economic liberalization and tried to walk a middle road as a regional power. Unlike his predecessors—and his successors following the January 25 Revolution of 2011—Mubarak did not attempt to reshape society with a new constitution but continued on the course already set by Sadat. The 1971 Constitution was updated and ratified in 2007, though the articles pertaining to education remained unchanged. On the heels of Sadat's assassination and the escalation of radical Islamist movements (see chapter 6), national security became an even more dominant feature of the state machinery. Yet many other groups and individuals were also vulnerable to the state's repressive system, from labor organizers and the full spectrum of the opposition, to people who did not fall in line with Mubarak era cronies' demands. Educational institutions across all levels were subject to policing and surveillance, in part to stop them from becoming zones of recruitment to illegal Islamist organizations. However, policing of schools and universities was also carried out to quell political engagement and activism of all sorts, and curb behaviors at odds with the intentionally vague category of "public morality" (see chapters 6 and 7).

With the geopolitical realignments after the fall of the Berlin Wall in 1989 and the supposed dawn of a new world order, the education sector in Egypt swayed to the tremors of the times. If the 1950s to 1970s represented the postcolonial era—a time when schools and universities were involved in forging the developmental Arab state and economy by cultivating "the future of the nation," its young productive citizens—by the 1990s education was turning into a profitable sector of the economy and an opportunity for investment. Subsequently, a new business class comprised of the ruling oligarchy, Islamists with connections to the Arab Gulf, and a new class of western-oriented entrepreneurs made their fortunes in the booming consumer and service sectors. These ranged from cars, real estate, and telecommunications, to private hospitals, kindergartens, schools, universities, and study centers.[15]

It was at this point, during the ascent of the Mubarak regime in 1990, and amidst a changing global and regional order, that I stepped into an Egyptian government school for the first time. Little did I realize then that research into schooling would lead me toward inquiries into politics and geopolitics, Islamist movements, youth cultures, online activism and revolution, the politics of international development, digital transformation, and the collective effects of all these issues on education futures.

Researching the Unfolding Drama of Education

This book moves between the local and the global, the micro and the macro, as it examines the broad social forces that drive educational practice, ideas, and change. These levels of observation bring into view the constant interplay between structure and agency. Among the main questions the work addresses are these: How have different interest groups—including foreign governments and entities, multilateral organizations, social movements, the private sector, civil society, and youth themselves—been forces for educational change? What happens when education actors harbor fundamentally different views about the purpose of schooling, the role of the citizen, and the character of the collective "we" in society? How do new educational ideas, policies, modes of financing, technologies, and practices emerge, to what ends, and to whose benefit?

This book is divided into four sections. Each one reflects different time periods, themes, foci, and methodological choices. Part One, "Schooling the Nation: Inside a Girls' Preparatory School" (chapters 1–5) is an ethnography in the tradition of cultural anthropology, carried out between 1990 and 1991. At the time, I was a master's student in anthropology/sociology at the American University in Cairo and the program required an original thesis. Influenced by the writings of the renowned anthropologist Margaret Mead and the work of social psychology around human development and life stages, I had an interest in learning about Egyptian girls at the stage of adolescence (see Mead 1928 and 1930). Additionally, as a student of Middle East studies, I had long been an avid reader of the rich and revered traditions and institutions of learning in the region. I originally considered conducting a study of the women's section of al-Azhar University, or of girls in Azhari schools, but did not necessarily want to focus exclusively on Islamic institutions. I opted instead to explore "modern" state schooling, which was supposed to be more inclusive and comprise laboratories of citizenship and civic life. Schools were widely seen at the time as microcosms of the nation, sites of political socialization fundamental to the nation-state project.[16] There was no ethnographic record of the everyday life of a contemporary government school in Egypt, which made the undertaking all the more appealing.

Unbeknownst to me at the time, this ethnography would become a snapshot of national schooling at the end of an era, a time overlapping with the close of the Cold War and the opening to more aggressive forces of globalization. Chapters 1 to 5 document the everyday workings of a school, paying attention to the human dramas and struggles therein, and the extraordinary amount of organization, effort, and work exerted by numerous dedicated teachers and other education workers in order to keep the system running. These descriptions show how the education system is dependent on a high degree of legal and administrative regulation, yet at the same time is shaped by human factors such as the principal's leadership style, the attitudes and life experiences of members of the school community, the condition of the built environment, and the spirited students who breathe life into the space.

Looking at the life of that school today, certain aspects seem dated, such as the analog, low-tech way of organizing everyday life, a style of corporal punishment that was more widely accepted then but would be frowned upon today, and an earnestness about the enterprise of schooling, which has been shaded with more cynicism in recent years. Yet other features are as relevant today as they were in the past, such as the obsession with examinations and grades, the importance of the "hidden curriculum" in understanding the reproduction of power and ideology at school,[17] teaching to the test, competition for private lessons, forms of cheating and gaming the system, population pressure and stress on the built environment, and power struggles that take place at the different levels of the administrative system. Above all, this ethnographic account provides a reminder of the immense labor and high hopes so many families place in their children being schooled, and the struggles of all involved to manage the system with its angels and demons, its promises and its perils.

Part Two, "Political Islam and Education," (chapters 6–8) emerged from an urgent desire to understand how groups and movements use the institutions and technologies of state power to try to forge alternatives to it. I had been living in Egypt since 1986 and witnessed firsthand the intense Islamization of society and escalation of conflict between militant Islamists and the security state. During this time, some schools were becoming supposed ideological breeding grounds for radical ideas and recruitment, making the entire education sector a matter of national security. At the same time, education markets were opening as part of a state-led drive towards privatization. A new category of for-profit private schools, private Islamic schools (al-madaris al-islamiya al-khassa), combined schooling with lifestyle aspirations, business with politics, and upward mobility with piety. For my doctoral dissertation at Columbia University's Teachers College,

I wanted to continue building my knowledge through grounded ethnographies, while incorporating perspectives from social history, politics, and political economy. Fortunately, I was able to get permission to access three private Islamic schools from 1996 to 1999.

In the chapters of Part Two, I describe some of the unique rituals connected to these private Islamic schools, and the state's reaction to them. I also discuss the ways in which they represented experiments in counternationalism. This section, while containing a good deal of original ethnographic detail, is heavily supplemented with media reports, legal cases, minutes of parliamentary sessions, and other secondary source materials. I seek to understand what was actually new about this "new Islamic education," and what was a continuation of older patterns. The middle school and high school students I came to know at the private Islamic schools proved extraordinarily insightful. When I was confused and at times oblivious about what was happening at the school, they would set me straight and explain the subtext of what I was observing. Chapter 8, "Downveiling," came directly out of conversations with students (some of whom appear in Figure 1), who were laser-sharp analysts of their schools and the power dynamics therein.

Part Three, "Youth in a Changing Global Order" (chapters 9–12), came about as "youth" and youth subjectivities in relation to a knowledge economy became foci in international development interventions, similar to "women" and "gender" in the 1970s and 1980s. The "knowledge economy," also called "knowledge society," became the development orthodoxy in the latter decades of the twentieth century (see Mazawi 2010; Powell and Snellman 2004). This framework favors technologically oriented and market-driven approaches to education and learning. It has manifested in the prioritization of STEM subjects (science, technology, engineering, and mathematics) over humanities and the arts, privatization over education as a public good, and investment in educational technologies over parallel investments in people and local communities. It has also infused a logic of competition and entrepreneurship into multiple aspects of social life.

In Egypt and other countries of the MENAWA region, democracy and related concepts—human rights, active learning, civic participation, gender empowerment, global citizenship, and entrepreneurship—were international policy mantras mapped onto education (see chapter 9). Many efforts were made to integrate these concepts into school curricula and to support civil society's nonformal education programs as avenues towards

1. In the classroom in a private Islamic school, Cairo. Author center. 1996.

democratization. Then, in the aftermath of the September 11, 2001, terrorist attacks on the United States, global attention was suddenly paid to "Muslim youth," who became the objects of the US-led "war on terror."

This section takes "Muslim youth" and "youth" as key categories. It explores the relation between youth, education policy, citizenship, and global politics using two methods: critical discourse analysis of international development reports and policy documents (chapters 9 and 12), and life history interviews with young people (chapters 10 and 11). The chapters highlight the dissonance between the voices of Egyptian youths who articulate their struggles, aspirations, and ideas for fair social policies, and the oftentimes out-of-touch and ideologically driven policy prescriptions about what young people need and should do.

Chapter 12 turns to Egyptian youth and citizenship in the digital age. The bulk of research and theorizing on youth and digital media have largely come out of the global North. However, Egypt provides a compelling and prescient case of digital disruption and change. There is no denying that in our current digital age, in this Fourth Industrial Revolution, children and youth are coming of age and learning and exercising citizenship—communicating, socializing, deliberating, and doing politics—in fundamentally different ways compared to previous generations. But to what ends? Chapter 12 ponders civic engagement in the digital age from the point of view of the young tech-savvy generation in Egypt who participated in the January 25 Revolution of 2011.

The study is informed theoretically by the sociology of generations and methodologically by biographical research with high school and university students, with a focus on "communication biographies." The social media platforms and communication methods they used provided incredible opportunities for networking, organizing, and creating memes and a host of artistic content, but at the same time were rife with risk. The platforms were easily infiltrated and surveilled, crowded with bad actors with nefarious aims, and owned by foreign corporations incentivized by profit, to name just some of the darker sides associated with digital communication. Still, during that moment in history, young, wired youth took their citizenship and civic education into their own hands and collectively tried to create an alternative society that was fairer, more inclusive, experimental, and participatory.[18]

The concluding chapter, in Part Four, brings education to the current era. Just as in previous epochs, when new governments attempted to reorder society through drafting constitutions and long-term development plans, so has been the case with the government of Abd al-Fattah al-Sisi (2014–present). This postrevolution, or "counterrevolutionary" government as detractors call it, is attempting to steer Egypt in a radically futuristic direction. Among its more ambitious undertakings—along with building a new capital and up to thirty-four new "smart cities" in the desert from the ground up[19]—has been to build a "New Education System," or "Education 2.0." The new government's broad commitments to education can be found in the Constitution of 2014 (the third constitution produced after the January 25, 2011, Revolution), which goes into more detail than previous constitutions. It lays out government expenditures on pretertiary education (at least 4 percent of gross domestic product) and devotes articles to technical education (Article 20), academic independence (Article 21), teachers (Article 22), scientific research (Article 23), Arabic language, religious education and national history (Article 24), and illiteracy (Article 25).

The actual reforms toward the "New Education System," or "Education 2.0" are moving fast and furious in different directions.[20] At the primary stage, they involve building an entirely new curriculum framework and supplying books that support multidisciplinary, interdisciplinary, and activity-based learning. Whether or not this new framework has been changing classroom culture, teacher pedagogy, and learning remains to be seen and requires investigation. The most far-reaching changes in education have to do with the digital transformation of the sector. By any measure, some remarkable and pioneering digital initiatives have emerged in connection to the reforms.[21] The Egyptian Knowledge Bank (Bank al-Ma'rifa al-Misri) (EKB), a massive online library that provides high-quality peer-reviewed resources in three languages, rivals and surpasses top-tier research university libraries. The EKB also contains portals for all preuniversity stages, from kindergarten through twelfth grade, with multimedia materials corresponding to the curricula. All secondary school students have government issued tablets and can access a wide range of learning materials on the EKB and other platforms. At the time of writing, the EKB is free of charge and accessible to all 100-million-plus citizens and residents in Egypt. Moreover, access to the EKB extends to other countries in the Arab world and Africa through special agreements.

Efforts to reimagine, update, and redesign the education system have been led by Dr. Tarek Shawki, minister of education and technical education (appointed 2017). An engineer by training, Shawki is a former director of the UNESCO Regional Bureau for Science in Arab States (2008–2012) and chief of the section for ICTs in Education, Science and Culture (2005–2008).[22] As someone who has been an evangelist for technological innovation in education and culture, the minister exhibits techno-optimist inclinations. A "techno-optimist" or "techno-utopian" believes in the power of technological solutions to redress social problems and create improved, more efficient, and more prosperous societies. Techno-optimists tend to take an ahistorical approach to social policy, meaning that they do not necessarily see a problem with imagining society as a blank slate on which to map development visions and plans.[23] More importantly, there is little recognition of the darker and dystopic sides of digital futures. Media theorists, social scientists, philosophers, and science fiction authors, among others, have pushed back against ideas associated with techno-utopianism. Douglas Rushkoff (2019), for instance, argues in *Team Human* that digital technologies are eroding human communities and human freedoms.

The concluding chapter is a rumination on the future of education. It reviews three factors that are upending the Egyptian education system: a runaway shadow education system and continuous innovations of educational entrepreneurs; the attempt by the post-2014 government to build a new education system that involves, among other things, digital transformation by way of injecting it with a number of digital tools, platforms, and learning technologies; and the Covid-19 pandemic that opened the way for a hybrid model and normalized distance learning. It asks if schooling as we know it, the model born out of an earlier industrial revolution, is on a life support system gasping for its final breaths of air? And if so, what is on the horizon to replace it?

Among the objectives of this work are to take stock of major education trends in Egypt, the region, and the world in the past half century, reflect on what merits preserving and strengthening from the past, what needs to be relegated to history, and what might be imagined totally anew. Questions about civic belonging, and the ideological consequences of new ideas and visions, loom large. These times require immense imagination, evidence, and consensus building as we charge ahead in uncharted territory toward education futures.

Part One

Schooling the Nation: Inside a Girls' Preparatory School

1

An Ethnographer's Orientation

Summary: It is extremely difficult to get the necessary security clearances to conduct qualitative research in Egyptian schools, but gaining access is just the beginning. This chapter describes how an ethnographer enters the world of a girls' preparatory school (sixth to eighth grade) in Cairo in 1990–91, and recounts the early, awkward encounters with members of the school community. Over time, and with the help of the principal, a group of teachers, and the students, she slowly learns to navigate the environment. She comes to understand the school as a microcosm of the nation, where performances of citizenship, power, hierarchies, class, and gender dynamics, are on full display.

The First Day of School

On a bright fall morning two weeks into the 1990–91 term, I was nervous and full of anticipation for my first day of school. I would be spending a good part of the next nine months at an Egyptian government girls' preparatory school, in order to produce an ethnography of its everyday life.[1] Wishing to dress for a part I had little idea how to play, I cobbled together a loose and long outfit that I thought might help me "blend in." It consisted of a long-sleeved white button-down blouse, a striped cotton skirt that went down to my ankles, and tan loafers with no socks. I tied my unruly hair back in a ponytail and slung an oversized black leather briefcase over my shoulder. Looking back, this get-up made me look entirely conspicuous.

I arrived early to the security office of the American University in Cairo (AUC) in Tahrir Square. Mr. Amr was waiting in his neatly pressed powder blue uniform. He opened the top drawer of his desk and pulled out a white envelope that contained my long-awaited research permit. As if setting my eyes on a holy relic, I asked if I could see it. He carefully unfolded

2. Falaki School, Cairo. 1990. (Photograph by Linda Herrera).

the long single sheet of paper, adorned with an array of official stamps in indigo, black, and red. I stared in awe. For nearly two years, I had traipsed through countless security offices of the ministry of education, state security, and local district offices, on a quest for this permit. By some miracle, and surely with behind-the-scenes follow-up from AUC, the permit had now materialized.

To my enormous relief, Mr. Amr announced that he would accompany me to the nearby selected school to introduce me. We headed down Mohamed Mahmoud Street, crossed Yusuf al-Gindi dodging honking taxis and whizzing bikes, and stepped over the curb of Falaki Street, where we could hear girls chanting in unison from beyond the cement fortification. We walked a few paces down the tree-lined street and stopped in front of the main wooden gate. As Mr. Amr reached for the brass knocker, I muttered, "I hope they let us in." He reassured me, "Don't worry, we have the paper from the government (*al-hukuma*). They can't say no."

Someone on the other side cautiously unlatched the door just enough to allow us to squeeze through. Two girls sat on a small bench behind a rickety wooden table. They were wearing red caps and red arm bands with the words "*al-hukm al-dhati*" written on them in white Arabic script. *Al-hukm al-dhati*, which means "self-rule," was instituted in the years following the July 23 Revolution of 1952, when the public school carried the revolutionary mission of cultivating citizen-students for the ambitious project of building a new, independent nation. It was meant to give young people a sense of duty to country, responsibility in running its institutions, and experience in self-rule. *Al-hukm al-dhati* performed a range of tasks from taking morning attendance and reporting absences to the social worker, to running errands for teachers and administrators. These largely consisted of bringing them chairs, delivering papers, and ordering tea (the school janitor maintained a kettle in a storage area, and provided tea and sugar on a metal tray for twenty-five piasters per glass). Their greatest responsibility was to secure the gate by keeping watch over who entered and exited the school.

The two girls asked for our IDs and jotted down our details in a mammoth rectangular ledger. They inquired as to the purpose of our visit, and then one of them stood to escort us to the principal's office. We crossed the unpaved courtyard to the central building, an old villa with the original stone engravings of ribbons and bouquets of flowers across the upper windows, signs of bygone splendor. The school's administrative offices were spaced across the ground floor, with the classrooms on the second floor.

In built environments, space is organized in a way that signals power, status, and the internal rules of hierarchy. In this ground-floor corridor of offices, a room to the left was flanked by two *al-hukm al-dhati* officers who stood at semiattention on either side of the door. This room was unmistakably the power center. The wooden plaque on the wall read "*al-mudira*," The Principal. Our guide cleared her throat from behind the threshold, and announced, "Abla, these are the visitors from the American University." *Abla*, a Turkish word to denote respect for an older sister, entered the Egyptian lexicon during the Ottoman period. Students referred to female teachers and other female staff as *Abla* as a sign of respect and closeness, as if the school represented a kind of national family.

With a curt wave of the hand, the principal gestured for us to enter. Abla Adalat was a handsome woman in her mid-fifties, with stern green eyes and a cream headscarf pinned tidily around her head. She sat behind a long sturdy wooden desk upon which sat a cup of tea, an ashtray (the principal smoked), and a manila envelope. She possessed an air of imperiousness mixed with impatience. Already at this early hour, she was holding court with several people vying for her attention.

Mr. Amr stated our business, explaining that I was a researcher from AUC and that the government had approved my request to conduct a study of Egyptian education by observing her school. She looked somewhat weary and replied, "I will need to see the permission letter," which he duly handed over. Abla Adalat examined the paper, frowning. Once reassured of its authenticity, she placed it in her top drawer and said in a completely deadpan voice, "Welcome" *(ahlan wa-sahlan)*. She gestured for us to take a seat on one of the wooden chairs lined in a row against the side wall.

Without missing a beat, she continued a heated conversation with a disheveled man who I later learned was Mr. Samir. He served in dual roles as school secretary and accountant. "Why isn't there a chair in each classroom for the teacher?!" she demanded. Agitated, he insisted that it was not his fault and not his job to provide these things. Raising her voice, she retorted, "It is your job!" They continued in this vein, hurling accusations, recriminations, and threats at each other for a full seven minutes. I timed it. As Mr. Samir left the room grumbling, Abla Adalat sighed deeply.

As if aware she was playing a leading role in an unfolding drama, she turned to me and explained that she had only been at this particular school for two weeks: "I came here and found the school in complete disarray. It will take about two months for me to get things running properly, God willing. Little by little, order will come."

Her manner with students often assumed the air of a strict disciplinarian. A girl from *al-hukm al-dhati* stood before her to dispatch a message, shifting her weight from side to side and flailing her arms in the air as she spoke. Abla Adalat turned to the social worker, Abla Azza—who had been sitting on the couch poring over some charts for over an hour—and lashed out at her. "Is that what you teach these girls? To stand anyway they want when they're talking to an adult?! You have to teach them to stand straight with their arms at their side in a nice way. Things have got to change around here!" Just minutes later, another student approached, placed her elbow on the principal's desk, and began speaking with eyes cast down. The principal shouted abruptly, "Stand up straight! Now keep your arms at your side." The girl's cheeks turned a shade of crimson and she mustered the courage to continue. She instinctively lifted her arms, gesturing emotively with her hands. The principal commanded, "Keep your hands at your side!" The girl left the room on the verge of tears. The next student received similar treatment. In quick succession, a fourth student entered the room and Abla Adalat could not bear it any longer. She took one look at the girl and, pointing her index finger towards the door, roared, "Get out!"

Over the next three hours a stream of visitors, ranging from parents, students, workers, and teachers to administrators, delivery people, and government inspectors, passed through the open office door. No sooner did the principal begin a sentence with one person, than another would lean over the desk and interrupt her to ask a question, state a problem, or request an official stamp or signature. "I will be with you next," she would say, gesturing with her hand for the person to wait. The flow of human traffic picked up even further after the 11:30 a.m. recess, when a string of students entered to turn in items they had found in the courtyard. "This hair clip was on the ground, Abla." "I found twenty-five piasters." "Someone's tie fell off." Glancing down at the growing collection of lost-and-found items, Abla Adalat let out a long sign and shook her head.

Meanwhile, Mr. Amr edged out of his seat and stood up. He addressed the principal and asked politely if he should accompany me to the school the next day. "No, no," Abla Adalat answered. "It's not necessary. I know her now. She'll be fine." He excused himself and we said our goodbyes. Abla Adalat leaned over and asked in a muted voice, "What do you intend to do here at the school *exactly*?" I had thought a lot about how to answer this question and gotten some practice during various security office interviews. I explained in broken Arabic that I was interested in the history of education in Egypt, since the time of Gamal Abd al-Nasser, but that there was very little information about the actual day-to-day running of Egyptian schools. I wanted to document the everyday workings of a school as way of better understanding the education system. Since this school was specifically a girls' preparatory school, it could also provide insights into the education of girls during the stage of adolescence.

Not entirely convinced, she asked, "Why was *this* school chosen for you?" I answered very straightforwardly that it was chosen because my contact at the Ministry of Education, to whom I was introduced through a contact at the American University in Cairo, knew the school's former principal. In addition, I had requested a school near my home, since I had a two-year-old daughter whom I dropped off in a local nursery school while I was out, and this school was just a twenty-minute walk. She seemed reassured, and replied, "At your service."

I took this opportunity to ask for some basic information about the school: the year it was established, famous graduates, the history of the villa, and so on. The principal admitted that as a newcomer herself, she did not yet know a great deal about the school's history, and indeed would like to learn along with me. She called different people to her room—the librarian, the social worker, and a few senior teachers—and we were able to cobble together some information.

The original owner of the villa was a nineteenth-century astronomer, al-Falaki Bey, the name then given to both the school and the prominent downtown street on which it is located. At some point, probably in the early 1970s, an Egyptian oil company had bought the villa. Not long thereafter, the Egyptian government had entered into a permanent and irreversible rental contract with the company to turn the villa into a school. In this period, scores of villas throughout Cairo and throughout Egypt were being converted into schools to accommodate the growing student population, and to fulfil the country's constitutional duty of providing universal schooling for all Egyptians. The villa, located on prime real estate just one block from Tahrir Square, was worth millions of Egyptian pounds. Despite the owner's legal attempts to get out of the rental contract, the courts ruled in favor of the government. The rent on the property was set at a fixed sum of eighty Egyptian pounds per month, which in 1990 amounted to roughly twenty-four dollars.[2] There were at that time 1,066 students enrolled in the school, a villa originally built to house a single, grand family.

Having made some progress on the school's history, it seemed like a good time to take my leave. In truth, I had been furtively jotting down snippets of observations and needed time to flesh out my notes, in order not to lose the vivid details. I stood up and thanked Abla Adalat and told her I would return the following morning. She said I would need to present her with a detailed research plan. I said, "Of course" *(tab'an)*, I had a document that I had already prepared and presented to the security offices. We said our goodbyes and I smiled at her with genuine gratitude for letting me take refuge in her office for these several hours.

Occupying a place on a chair in the principal's room was the best newcomer's orientation I could imagine. As visitors passed through the office on that first morning, some paused on seeing me. One visitor looked me over from head to toe, and asked Abla Adalat—knowing full well I was not—"Is this a new teacher?" She responded, "No, she's a researcher." This response was usually met with either raised eyebrows, or a somewhat skeptical "hmmm." As I later realized, being seen by the principal's side by a stream of people connected to the school gave me an air of legitimacy. It would help open doors with teachers in the coming days and months.

I stepped out of the villa into the warm musty air of the courtyard where a physical education class was in session. The students kicked up dust as they performed their exercises. Stepping back onto the street, I watched the formidable wooden doors close behind me. Just hours ago, the world beyond those doors had seemed so impenetrable. Now, my head was spinning with voices, faces, scenes, and images of an entire world. I rushed around the corner, pulled out my notebook, and frantically wrote down my observations from this first encounter.

The Ethnographer's Dilemma

I arrived at the school at 7:45 the following morning, just in time for the morning assembly, which in Arabic is called the *tabur* (see chapter 2). A few spirited girls whizzed by me, giggling, and said, "Good morning, Miss." I stood tucked in a corner set back from the main entrance, and waited until the ceremonies were over. When the bell rang at 8:15 a.m. sharp, everyone marched off in lines, military style, to their classrooms. I had not actually thought through where to go on day two. Not sure what to do with myself, I headed over to the principal's office. She was the only person I knew up to this point.

The door was closed and the two *al-hukm al-dhati* girls who stood guard gave a sign that I should wait. We could hear Abla Adalat shouting from behind the door, followed by cracks of a stick contacting flesh. Two girls emerged from the office rubbing their palms, with heads lowered as they cried quietly. Within moments of the door opening, people began streaming into the office. I stood outside on the threshold looking in tentatively, and if truth be told, felt rather intimidated. Abla Adalat caught my eye and said in English, "Good morning, come in." She extended her arm to the same chair from the day before. I sat there in silence, awkwardly jotting down observations in my notebook from time to time. After three-quarters of an hour, she finally leaned over to me and asked smiling, but with understandable impatience, "What do you need?"

I did not exactly know what I needed but I had to come up with an answer, and fast. I asked if I could meet a teacher, maybe an English teacher, who could show me around the school. She nodded and called out, "Come here, *al-hukm al-dhati*." A girl rushed over, eager to help. "Go find any English teacher and bring her here." The girl asked nervously, "Which one, Abla? One from Year One, Year Two, or . . . ?" Abla Adalat cut her off, annoyed, and repeated, "I said ANY one of them. I don't care which one. I just want an English teacher." The student returned about five minutes later with a teacher, tall and pale, in her mid-to-late twenties, wearing a black abaya. I had the sense from her all-black outfit and her sad, exhausted eyes, that she was in mourning. Abla Adalat said, "Abla Mona, this is Abla Linda, a researcher from the American University. I want you to show her around." Based on the startled expression, I could see this was clearly unwelcome news for Abla Mona.

We headed up the central staircase, with its deeply indented white marble steps. I admired the faded grandeur of the curved wooden railing, and the exquisite stained glass windows at the top of the steps. I tried to strike up a conversation with Abla Mona about how the villa had some beautiful details, but she was in no mood for chit-chat. She led me to the left of the staircase to a square wooden table in the hallway, which I learned was the English teaching staff corner. A teacher was leaning over the table, rapidly marking a pile of student notebooks. Abla Mona introduced us, and after a quick "*ahlan wa-sahlan*" (welcome), the teacher continued her work. Abla Mona ordered the nearest girl from *al-hukm al-dhati* to bring me a chair, a precious commodity perennially in short supply. When the bell rang, Abla Mona and the other teacher excused themselves and headed off to their classes.

Alone in the empty hallway, I looked around aimlessly. I opened my briefcase, took out a newspaper from the previous day, and reread it. At the end of a seemingly interminable class period, four teachers approached the table. The oldest one was in her late thirties, physically imposing with dyed chestnut hair and blond streaks. She looked at me with some hostility. She announced, asserting her unmistakable dominion over this territory, that she was the senior English teacher.

Every conceivable space on the school grounds, each hallway, corridor, closet, was carved up as a territory for a unique cluster of teachers. I quickly understood that within the school there were a number of micro-communities, each with its own order, power structure, and place in the overall hierarchy. I was in the language teacher territory, where the English and Arabic tables were positioned side by side in the corridor. Among the English teachers, Senior Teacher Abla Fatma ruled. I picked up on her authoritarian streak and knew that as long as I was under the patronage of the English teachers' table, I had to go through Abla Fatma for any requests. The junior teachers appeared afraid of her, and would not want to undermine her authority. Abla Fatma had already heard about my presence in the school and asked what I wanted with the English teachers. I started explaining my research to her in English, but soon realized she did not understand what I was saying. From time to time, she would shake her head exaggeratedly and say in a loud voice, "Yes. Yes."

During my first week at the school, I would wander over to the English teachers' table after the *tabur*, due to a lack of options at that time more than anything else. They tolerated me, but I knew I would have to scout out more welcoming places to spend my time. Sometimes I would sit alone in the library to write up my notes. The librarian was kind and accepted my presence. However, when the space filled up with classes, I had to move and find another spot.

Feeling the need to "act like a researcher," beyond just jotting down observations, I asked Abla Fatma if I could do some brief interviews with her and the other English teachers. She agreed, but only after getting the green light from Abla Adalat. I came up with a preliminary questionnaire about teachers' educational background, extracurricular language exposure, their work/life balance, and their views on the examination system. I also started observing their English classes. The level of English instruction was poor, though I did not comment on it to anyone. My interest was more in pedagogy and the classroom dynamics. Abla Fatma took the initiative to introduce me to a few Arabic teachers at the neighboring table. For the next couple of days, I accompanied different teachers to their Arabic and English classes. I would usually sit in the back corner of the classroom in a chair provided by the girl serving that day for *al-hukm al-dhati*, take out my notebook, and jot down observations. These initial classroom visits allowed me to become familiar with the rhythm of a class session, and with certain pedagogic norms and rituals.

The Breakthrough

When I turned up yet again at the English table at the end of the week, Abla Fatma acknowledged me with one of her annoyed comments, something along the lines of, "You're back again?" "Haven't you finished yet?" or "Really? You want to see more classes?" Desperate to expand my horizons away from the language teachers' colony, I asked her if she could introduce me to a mathematics teacher. She sighed deeply and said, "At your service." She lifted her ample body from the chair and led me slowly down the stairs to an area behind the courtyard. There was a large table with nine mathematics teachers gathered around it. She announced as I stood awkwardly by her side, "Excuse me. This is Abla Linda, a researcher. She would like to attend a mathematics class. Does anyone have a class the next period?" A few teachers looked up at me, slightly bewildered. A man in his mid-thirties, well-groomed and with impeccably ironed clothes, stood up and said nonchalantly, "She can come with me." We chatted on the way to the class and I mentioned my husband and daughter. He stopped in his tracks and said, "You have a daughter, really?" From that point on, his demeanor with me was more formal and curious.

After class, we walked back to the mathematics table. I thanked him and turned to make my way back upstairs to the English table. A junior mathematics teacher, a recent university graduate, caught up with me on the stairwell and said in a hushed voice, "Excuse me, but I've heard you're a researcher, conducting a study on education. What exactly are you doing?" I explained with my now well-rehearsed summary. He said with a tone of sincerity and earnestness, "My name is Mahmud. If there's anything I can help you with, just tell me. Really, anything at all. I graduated from the Faculty of Education and my father worked in education all his life, so I have a good background in the topic." Not wanting to miss this opportunity and apprehensive about returning to the language tables upstairs, I answered, "Actually, are you free right now? I do have some questions about the school." He answered in the affirmative and we headed to the library. I pulled out my notebook and asked about the everyday routine of the school and the basic administrative structure. When I did not understand some explanation or description, I asked him to write it out in Arabic, which he did with great patience and detail. I would later go over the written passages with an Arabic teacher and translate them. To this day I am indebted to Ustaz Mahmud for taking me under his wing and being so generous with his knowledge and time.

The following morning, I passed by the mathematics table and asked Ustaz Mahmud if I could attend his class. His colleague, a buxom woman in her late thirties, chortled and exclaimed in a loud voice, "Mahmud, I think Linda likes you! What do you think? It's a good chance for you!" She laughed boisterously. I was mortified. The teacher whose mathematics class I had attended the previous day jumped to my defense and said, "No! She's married and has a daughter." The woman immediately stopped laughing and said in a surprised voice, "Is that right? But you look so young."

With all eyes on me, I seized the moment to satisfy their curiosity, get ahead of the gossip, and allay their suspicions about having a foreign researcher from the American University in Cairo poking around their school. I confirmed that I did indeed have a daughter and asked if they had any other questions they would like to ask me. Here's more or less how that, and similar interrogations throughout the coming weeks, unfolded:

"Yes, I'm married for three years now. How old am I? I'm twenty-six. My daughter? Her name is Shiva. She's almost two years old. Where is she now? She's at an Egyptian nursery school across the street from our home. I live in Garden City. I dropped her off before walking over here. No, my husband is not American. What is he? He's Iranian. Yes, he's Muslim. Yes, he's Shi'i." Eyes raise, extremely wide, accompanied by some gasps. "He's from Iran and his family is Shi'i, that's normal there, isn't it *(mish kida walla eh)*?" Some of them chuckle. "Yes, I grew up Christian." More eyes raise. "Why haven't I converted to Islam? That is between God and me. Why don't I look American? Because my father's family is originally from Spain and Mexico and my mother's family is from Lebanon." To this I hear random "ooh, good people the Lebanese. . . . So she's an Arab." "My husband's work? He's a professor of sociology at the American University in Cairo. Which county is better, Egypt or the United States? Well, there are things in Egypt that are better than in America"—they smile—"and vice versa. What's better in Egypt? The amazing history, the people and their great sense of humor *(dammuhum khafif)*, the films and soap operas, the Nile. Egypt really is the mother of the world *(umm al-dunya)*." This crowd-pleasing line never ceased to draw some smiles. Saved by the bell, the cross-examination ended. The teachers stood up to go to their classes and one of the senior mathematics teachers asked if I wanted to observe his class. I agreed with great appreciation.

Even as I got to know more teachers, I continued to face a major problem, namely where to sit and how to spend my time. A mundane but real dilemma was the scarcity of seating, and I did not have a designated chair. Many teachers tasked students with carrying their chair back and forth between the classroom and their faculty table. When I arrived at a table, someone would often feel obliged to give up his or her chair or stop their lesson preparations and grading to politely chat with me. I did not want to disrupt their work or take their seat, and needed to find an alternative plan.

I came up with a solution. After the morning *tabur*, I would attach myself to one of the class lines and march with the students to their classroom, where I would spend the day. On entering the classroom, I would ask the homeroom teacher—the one designated to inspect the class during the *tabur* and keep track of attendance and classroom needs—if I could join the class. If she or he hesitated, I would quickly add, "I have the principal's permission." I would normally sit in the back corner, sharing the bench desk with one or two students. The girls could not have been more delighted to have me join them. As my presence in different classes became more regular, the girls competed to get me to sit next to them and called out, "Abla, Abla, sit here, sit here!" I often remained with girls from the same class during the midday break. Students often insisted on gifting me chips and biscuits from the canteen, bought from their meager pocket money, despite my pleas that they should not. We sometimes left school together and walked toward our respective homes in a pack, until reaching the crossroad where we would split up—the girls in the direction of district Abdeen, and me to Garden City.

Orienting myself toward the students had many advantages. They were affectionate and welcoming, enjoyed someone showing such interest in their views, and were keen to express and talk about their lives and the school. Some of them were exceptionally sharp, perceptive, and discerning. These girls of eleven to fourteen years drew my attention to the deeper inner workings of the school. They pointed out power conflicts and strained relations among administrators and teachers. They talked about and debated together issues of fairness at school, and had a lot to say about teacher ethics and behavior. Nothing and no one escaped their notice.

A Delicate Balance

Within a few weeks of being at the school, I had learned the names of a majority of the teachers and was on friendly terms with many of them. They often invited me to sit at their tables or take part in their conversations. When I started conducting formal tape-recorded interviews (which required a separate research permit from the Ministry of Education), their interest in my research grew. Teachers would approach me and ask, "Don't you think what I have to say is important?" or "When were you planning to get around to interviewing me? I have a free period after the break if you like." The research process progressed more steadily, though it was never entirely smooth sailing.

Not everyone was comfortable with my presence, and I had to dodge some tricky encounters. For instance, one afternoon a male teacher with an uneven long beard cornered me in the hallway. He berated me for American support of Israel and then steered the conversation to Islam. He declared, "I find it very strange that you haven't converted to Islam knowing your soul will be eternally damned." He then started to say something about the (Christian) infidels, at which point I took my leave. It was rumored, not surprisingly, that this teacher had fundamentalist leanings, and some whispered that he was a member of one of the illegal Islamist groups. Another incident involved the district mathematics inspector, an elderly man who visited the school once per month. He would often chat with me when he had finished checking the teachers' lesson plans to practice his English. One afternoon, on learning that my husband was from Iran, he shouted in a playful tone, "What?! You're married to a Shi'a??! Get out of here! Get out of this room!" Everyone, including myself, laughed at his ballsy performance. But a joke can reveal an underlying attitude, and I did not want to wade anywhere near the waters of sectarianism.

On the subject of religious identity, a group of female Christian teachers sometime sought me out. They felt they could trust me, even though they admitted they found it unusual that I was married to a Muslim man. They wanted their voices as Christian teachers to be part of the research record. We would occasionally huddle in a quiet corner where they recounted incidents of subtle and unsubtle forms of discrimination. For instance, they pointed out how Christian teachers were bypassed for promotion, whether

3. Friends at Falaki School, Cairo. Author second left; Abla Adalat center. 1991. (Photograph by Linda Herrera.)

by the school principal or district supervisor, and were convinced that this was the result of anti-Christian discrimination. I heard similar complaints expressed by other teachers over the years. They also directed my attention to how Christian students were sometimes unfairly excluded from the coveted positions in student government, or were not selected to represent the school in competitions, despite their high grades and ranking first in their class.

Religion and minority rights are highly sensitive political topics. While I tried to understand the place of religion or sectarianism in the life of the school, and listened to grievances with concern and empathy, I did not actively pursue this line of inquiry in interviews or conversations. I was exceedingly aware of the fragility of my position and the limits of doing research in a security-oriented state with fairly clear red lines. Not only did I not want to get expelled from the school or put my husband or family in danger (he was Iranian after all, in a country with strained relations with Iran, and we were sure our phone was tapped and he was under surveillance), but I was also cognizant of the golden rule of research ethics, "do no harm." I avoided issues that I thought could put members of the school community at risk. For these reasons, when thorny issues around religion and politics surfaced, I listened and took note but did not initiate or intentionally probe these topics.

Fortunately, I did not have to navigate the cultural and political landmines alone. A group of five teachers had taken me under their wing. They took a keen interest in my research and opened my eyes to many salient issues around the school. While anthropologists might refer to this inner circle as "informants" or "interlocutors," I prefer to call them my supervisors, *mushrifin*, and also my friends. My peers in age, these teachers patiently, carefully, and generously oversaw my work, just as the senior supervisors did for them. They helped me compile questionnaires, advised on the best way to pose questions, directed me regarding which interview points I should and should not cover, helped me gather statistics on the school community, reviewed my notes, and evaluated my progress. Thirty years later, I remain eternally grateful to Abla Siham, Abla Amina, Ustaz Mahmud, Ustaz Ali, and Ustaz Emad. I could not have done this work in this detail without their support and guidance.

2
Schooling Citizens

Summary: How do schools manage the responsibility of oversee-ing and safeguarding the civic, scientific, and moral development of children? How much of what transpires at a school is the result of central planning, regulations, and ministry oversight, and how much is contingent on the efforts and management style of school leaders? To address these questions, we draw on two key sources: observations from the morning assembly *(tabur)*, a national ritual that takes place in all schools as a performance and enactment of citizenship; and a series of interviews with and about the principal, a formidable figure who reigns over this microworld of the school.

The *Tabur*

Every morning at 7:45 in cities, towns, and villages throughout Egypt, resi-dents can hear the military-like march rising from the walls of their local schools, signaling the start of the *tabur*, which literally means "the lining up." The morning assembly brings together the entire school community, the body politic, in a ritualistic performance of nationalism, discipline, and community building. The *tabur* requires a high degree of coordination and planning. This allocated time provides the school community with the opportunity to gather, inspect the students, make announcements, share national news, and pay tribute to God, country, and each other. It also allows teachers to showcase their top students and provide them with opportunities for public speaking.

A musical ensemble consisting of five students kicks off the morning's rituals from their place atop the front steps of the villa, which serves as a stage. The drummer carries her instrument from a leather strap around her neck and beats out the first measures of a military-like march. Two accor-dion players and two xylophonists take their cues and join her. Students rush into single-file lines, eight for each of the three years of the preparatory stage, making a total of twenty-four lines. The homeroom teachers take their positions at the helm of the row of their designated class.

The gym teacher with the most seniority, Abla Iman, oversees the straightening of the lines, the first phase of the *tabur*. Dressed in a gray scarf and ankle-length gray dress, she picks up the microphone. Her already powerful voice is amplified by the speakers, which are set at full volume. She starts the military commands: "School at attention!" Those girls not yet in place run over to their assigned line. Like army cadets, these students are expected to stand upright with chin up, chest out, shoulders back, stomach in. The next command is, "Space yourselves out." Students stretch their arms so that their fingers touch the shoulders of the person in front of them. The teacher then calls out, "At ease!" This is the cue for everyone to move their left foot out in alignment with their left shoulder and interlock their thumbs behind their back. Abla Iman continues with the next drill, "Attention! At ease! Attention! At ease!"

At this juncture, teachers inspect their class lines, walking up and down the rows to ensure the lines are straight. With just one exception, all teachers carry wooden sticks of different dimensions and thickness. The most common shape is an oblong plank of wood of about a foot and a half long. The second most common hitting instrument is a thin cane. When a girl stands in a way that distorts the symmetry of the line, her teacher might shove her inside the line, or whack her on the shoulder until she rearranges herself. When the teachers finish their inspections, they retake their positions at the front of their class lines.

The principal inspects the rows from her perch at the top of the steps, and shouts to a group on her right side. "Year Two, look at yourselves.[1] What a disaster! Straighten up!" She then scours the courtyard and yells, pointing to a girl, "You, in the third row. Move over to the left. Now everyone, take a step forward." She pauses for a moment and asks, "Who's talking?!" She points an accusing finger and says, "Yes, you in the back. I want to see you in my office after the *tabur*. Now everyone, stand up straight, straight!" Using her body as a model of correct posture, she commands, "Raise your chins, shoulders back. No more of this slouching and sloppiness." She scans the girls, dressed in a sea of gray skirts, white blouses, and black shoes. Her gaze lands on the color red. A student is wearing a red hair clip, red necklace, and red nail polish. Her skirt and shirt are heavily crinkled. The principal shouts to the homeroom teacher at the head of the line. "Abla

Sawsan, what is that girl in front of you wearing? Is that supposed to be a uniform? Bring her to me immediately after the *tabur*." She turns forward, with an intimidatingly stern expression, and reprimands the entire student body. "You have all got to respect yourselves and your school. You should not come here after throwing on just anything. Your uniforms must be neat and clean, not looking like they came out of the garbage! This will not be tolerated!" Frowning deeply, she shakes her head in disapproval before passing the microphone to the religion teacher. She remains in place with her hands firmly locked behind her back.

The religion teacher, a stout man wearing a long gray robe and short white turban with red skullcap *(taqiya)*, introduces Nagafa, his student from Year Two whom he chose to perform the morning's Qur'anic recitation. She has been silently practicing for several minutes on the stage, moving her lips with her eyes cast upward. She steps to the center of the platform, visibly nervous. Her uniform skirt is too large, and the waist is folded over and fastened with a large safety pin, probably a hand-me-down from an older sister. She begins the verse, her voice cracking. She stumbles on a line and repeats it until she gets it right. When she finishes, she leaves the stage, shaken.

The next portion of the *tabur* is dedicated to news and announcements. Each day a subject teacher from a different class takes responsibility for this segment, which lasts about five minutes. Students often express excitement when it is their class's turn and tell me, "Be sure not to miss the *tabur* tomorrow, Abla. Our class has prepared something really special." On this particular morning, a science teacher selects two short articles for her students from Year One to read. The first item is news about the year's Nobel laureates in chemistry and physics: this is a way to bring news of the world into the school. The second reading is from the semiofficial newspaper *al-Ahram* about President Hosni Mubarak's meeting with a visiting dignitary. At this point in the *tabur*, the girls are beginning to get restless, and many are shifting their weight from side to side, breaking the at-ease pose to fan themselves as they are standing without shade under the morning sun.

The national anthem is next on the program. The band starts playing the familiar tune, "Biladi, Biladi, Biladi" ("My Country, My Country, My Country," its music composed by Sayyid Darwish). In a disinterested and routine way, everyone faces the flag and begins to mutter the words "My country, My country, My country, You have my love and my heart." Their singing is lackluster and entirely out of sync. The principal looks out at them, shaking her head with an expression of disbelief. She thunders forward and thrusts out her hand for the band to stop. "You disgrace this national song! I can't make out a single word with all your mumbling. You are singing this for Egypt, for *Egypt*, our country!" Her tone softens as she instructs them to repeat the words after her and proceeds to take them through the entire anthem, word by word, verse by verse. When they finish, she announces, "We're going to try this again. Sing the words as if you mean them, clearly and with pride." Her intervention is effective. Students sing out the words at the top of their lungs, with spirit and enthusiasm. She nods her head in approval and gives the signal for the next teacher to proceed.

The mathematics teacher Ustaz Mahmud steps up to the microphone and bids everyone a good morning. He announces that there will be some construction work in the school and certain areas will be off-limits. He then proceeds to read names from a list that the social worker hands him. These are of students who performed at the top of their classes in the end-of-month examinations. Finally, he reads the names of five students, selected by the social worker and homeroom teacher, who will serve the following day as *al-hukm al-dhati*. He reminds them to report to the social worker in Room 103 to get their assignments, which will be either the main gate (2), the principal's office (2), or social worker's office (1). He then offers them congratulations, as it is a badge of honor to be selected to serve as *al-hukm al-dhati*. As it turned out, that institution of "self-rule" was being phased out and this was its last year. An inspector from the local governorate explained that it was ending because students needed to prioritize studying and should not miss class time. In any case, he thought, students of this age couldn't handle real responsibilities and would only make a mess of things.

The final portion of the morning *tabur* is dedicated to group exercises, which conclude with everyone marching off to their classes. The band plays the same military march, and the gym teacher takes her place to keep time, shouting, "One, two, three, four!" The girls stomp their feet four times, clap their hands four times, and shout out in unison, "Long Live the Arab Republic of Egypt" *(Tahya Gumhuriyat Masr al-'Arabiya)*. They repeat this sequence four times as they pivot 90 degrees to the left each time, returning to their original position facing front on the fourth repetition. With over one thousand girls in a fairly confined space, there is the inevitable bumping into each other and stepping on one another's feet. But considering the space constraints, the exercises proceed quite smoothly. The girls continue marching in place while a second gym teacher on the ground orchestrates their exit, moving her arms like a traffic officer to the right, sideways, and straight ahead, as lines march off in all directions to their classrooms.

Instilling Punctuality

Early in the year, the *tabur* was regularly interrupted by students arriving late. The principal found this lack of punctuality unacceptable and came up with two punitive measures. First, she instituted a "tardy fine" of twenty-five piasters, the normal sum of a student's pocket money, to be paid to the school in the event of tardiness. Students with no pocket money were exempted from paying the fine. Second, she appointed a group of teachers to guard the main gate in the morning, to prevent any latecomers from entering during the *tabur*. Students had to wait until it was over and meet their fate, which was usually a caning on both palms.

Some mornings, the principal stood at the gate herself, her back to the line of girls accumulating at the school entrance. One day, a well-dressed father accompanied his daughter to school five minutes late. He approached the principal and politely and deferentially tapped her on the shoulder, introduced himself, and made an excuse for his daughter's tardiness. Abla Adalat simply nodded her head without a word and extended her arm backwards, indicating his daughter should stand in line with the other girls. He shrugged apologetically to his daughter and left her on the verge of tears. On another day, nearly fifty tardy girls had accumulated at the gate. When the *tabur* ended, the principal ordered them to stand in a long single-file line across the length of the courtyard. She appointed the gym teacher to dole out their punishment, a strike on the palm of each hand with a long wooden stick. Standing upright with her hands behind her back, she called out to the teacher, "Hit them harder, harder!" Not satisfied, she took the stick and hit the last ten girls herself. One girl whom the principal recognized as a frequent latecomer, received double the hits on her palms. The girl rubbed her hands together between blows as silent tears streamed down her cheeks. The principal waited, stone-faced, holding her stick up in preparation for the next whack. She commanded the girl to go to the end of the line and wait her turn for a second round of punishment. The second time around she hit with far less force.

The girls sometimes found sympathetic staff to help them sneak into the school late to circumvent their punishment. One morning, as I approached the school ten minutes after the start of the *tabur* (thankfully

I was not subject to punishment), I watched as three girls ran up the street breathlessly. The school's cleaner or maid, affectionally called the "dada," was keeping watch at the gate with strict instructions not to let anyone in. One girl asked her nervously, "Is she going to beat us?" The maid shrugged and replied, "Maybe." Another girl held out her hands and said, "Oh no! My hands hurt me so much from last time. You know we come all the way from Bulaq and the earlier bus was so crowded, we couldn't get on it." The maid, clearly sympathetic to their plight, opened the gate a crack, and when the coast was clear, gestured for them to quickly run in. They zipped along the side of the courtyard to safety. On surveying the scene from the gate, I caught the principal glancing at them, but she let them pass as if she had not noticed.

As the term progressed, the principal sometimes shifted tactic by appealing to students through kindness and maternal emotions. One morning, after launching into a harsh diatribe about the unacceptable behavior and lack of respect students showed for the school, she changed her tune completely. She switched into a lengthy and emotional monologue about her deep and sincere feelings for the students. In a gentle tone, she said, "I never had any daughters of my own, so I consider you all as my own. I love you as if you were my daughters. I want you all to be simple, good girls. That's why it's so important to me that you act in the right way." She continued to explain that even though her tactics might appear harsh and overdone at times, they were for their own good. She insisted, "You may not realize it now, but everything I do is for your benefit." Her vigilance paid off, for a month into the term there were only occasional latecomers. Still, the principal kept watch at the gate from time to time to remind everyone she was watching.

Students talked, gossiped, and constantly evaluated the principal's behavior. Most of them accepted that if they broke the rules or acted badly, they deserved to be punished, but they disagreed on the degree of punishment. The principal regularly resorted to corporal punishment in the forms of twisting a girl's ear, punching her shoulder, or whacking her palms with a stick. One girl said, "She's good for the school, but she hits too hard." Another student noted, "It's good that she's strict, but she really scares us."

In a conversation with a group of second-year students, one girl pointed out that the principal could not be a real role model because she smoked, wore boots, and wore pants under her dress. She viewed these practices as improper for a Muslim woman. Her classmate disagreed, arguing that the principal wore a headscarf, was dedicated to her work, and morally upright. She viewed her character as exemplary.

A girl in third year, who had experienced the regimes of two previous principals, saw a dramatic change in the school for the better. She explained:

> This year the teachers come to classes on time. They're never late because they know the principal will shout at them and replace them with another teacher. Last year, we had a principal who didn't care about being on time or the order of the school. The one before him was even worse.

Most students agreed that they benefitted from having a strict principal, and acknowledged she was working to raise the level of the school. This in turn would increase students' chances of success and promotion to the secondary stage, and of course, the big dream of many of them to go to university.

School Leadership

There is a popular saying among Egyptian educators: "A school is only as good as its administration" *(al-madrasa hiya al-idara)*. This idea can be taken a step further and altered to "A school is only as good as its principal." The principal is the most senior person in the school, possessing a great deal of authority over its everyday running, and setting the bar for behavioral standards and management. However, she does not have authority over appointments, the curriculum, the examination system, or the timetable. These are all managed and coordinated at the ministry level and overseen by local education authorities.

In 1990, the official duties of the principal, as stipulated by the regulations of the Ministry of Education, were as follows:

> The school principal or director assumes full responsibility for taking decisions concerning his (her) own school. The Ministry and Directorate of Education cannot interfere with his (her) work except with regard to checking the correct implementation of laws and regulations during school visitations. In this capacity, school principals perform the following tasks:
> • Assign technical and administrative tasks and issue the necessary directives for implementation and follow-up;

- Supervise arrangements for the beginning of the school year and the preparations for holding examinations;
- Monitor the implementation of rules, regulations, instructions, schedules, and syllabi according to approved plans;
- Preside over school board sessions and approve the executive measures;
- Supervise the work of his (her) subordinates, give those who break the rules advice to correct their behavior, grant emergency leaves, suggest the promotion and transference of school staff, and allow them raises as incentives. (National Center for Educational Research 1986, 16).

On arriving to her new post in September, Abla Adalat found the school in a state of "near anarchy." She immediately made plans to overhaul the school in every way possible and bring order to the chaos. She explained:

When I came here, I found serious disorder among both the faculty and the students. They showed a basic lack of respect for the school and for all its rules. My first job was to instill a feeling of responsibility in people, to give the school an identity as a place of knowledge, not some open space where people come and go as they please. No! A school has to run according to a system. It has classes, curricula, and order. When the system works, it translates into results.

Abla Adalat was the highest-ranking person in the school as its principal, and at age fifty-five, the oldest person among the school staff. She had worked in education for three decades and believed in the power of education to lift society and raise the life chances of girls (see chapter 3). When she was a student herself, she had been at the top of her class and had dreamed of pursuing a career in medicine. However, her father, a general manager in the Ministry of Justice, would not allow her to attend medical school because it was coeducational and, in his opinion, an unsuitable environment for his daughter. At that time, she felt she could not challenge his authority, and so agreed to pursue her second passion, music.

Abla Adalat enjoyed a long career as a music teacher in Cairo. Her first post was as a music teacher in a girls' preparatory school in 1959. She taught for fifteen years before being promoted to First Teacher, the highest level a teacher can reach before being transferred to the secondary level. She received her next promotion seven years later in 1981 to the position of vice principal of a secondary school. In 1986, when she got promoted to the top job of principal, Abla Adalat requested a leave of absence to take a position at a girls' school in an Arab Gulf country for four years, in order to earn a good sum of money that would go far in securing her financial future. On returning to Egypt in 1990, the ministry appointed her to her current post as principal of Falaki School, which she referred to in the possessive, as "my school" (madrasti). After working for thirty-two years, Abla Adalat was eligible for retirement, but did not want to stop at what she considered her peak. As a widow with two grown sons, she had the time to fully devote herself to her calling in education and knew she had her work cut out for her. She talked about her strategy to get the school in good order.

> My first priority was to strike at the disorder by any means. I needed to show everyone that the school had a leader with a conscience, someone who cared for them, not someone indifferent [like the previous principal]. I needed to be vigilant and supervise everything. I knew that after instilling a sense of responsibility in the teachers, even if I had to do it by force, they would eventually perform their duties to the fullest, even when someone wasn't standing over them to push them.

To lay out the new ground rules under her leadership, the principal held two all-staff meetings early in the term. Her first priority was to crack down on private lessons, a practice that was officially "illegal" but rife, as these lessons provided essential supplementary income for many teachers. Her second priority was to tackle the high teacher absentee rates. She entreated them to understand the need to teach with consciousness, to respect punctuality, and cautioned them that if they missed their classes, their pay would be docked.

The new principal was the topic of endless conversation among teachers and students who debated her management style, character, and dress. They held mixed opinions, but whatever their stance, there seemed to be a consensus that Abla Adalat was trying to raise the level of the school which others had neglected for years. Teachers spent a lot of time in the first months comparing her management style to that of the previous two male principals. A female teacher who had been at the school for three years explained how the school had changed:

> Last year, no one respected us teachers. You would see the girls talking and joking with male teachers. Their heads were full of thoughts definitely not related to their education! The girls wandered in and out of the school at different times and wore anything they wanted with their uniforms. The teachers showed up late for their classes if they showed up at all. This year the school looks more like a proper school. It fits my idea of what a school is supposed to be. It's clean, it's orderly, it's a place where I feel I want to work. Before, I didn't feel like working.

A junior science teacher, who had transferred to Falaki School from another school in Cairo, commented:

> I used to teach in a school with a very bad male principal. I was afraid of being stuck in an awful profession. After coming here and finding such strong leadership, a school run with order (*nizam*) and discipline, I saw another side of teaching. When you have a strong principal, the teachers and students working with her will also be strong. I've seen another side of education here and think I will stay in this profession for the rest of my life.

Some teachers, however, preferred the more relaxed style of the former principal. A male teacher complained that Abla Adalat was not sympathetic to their problems. Their job was really hard, as they had to deal with overcrowded classrooms, low wages, and students' low levels of education. He resented her stringent rules and high expectations and recalled the former principal with fondness:

> The last principal was so kind and friendly to all of us. He spoke with us softly and slowly and was sympathetic to our problems as teachers. He tried to make things easy and comfortable for us. This principal goes around yelling all the time, humiliating us in front of our students. And she doesn't like to see us rest. As soon as someone takes a break, drinking tea or just relaxing, she finds something for us to do. I go home exhausted!

A group of female teachers brought up another side of Abla Adalat, her approachability and sense of humor. They sometimes went to her for advice and spent time with her after hours. One teacher explained, "She's like a mother to us. We can talk to her about anything." Another teacher nodded in agreement and added that she has a wonderful sense of humor. Whatever their personal preference regarding her leadership style, a science teacher summed up the general sentiment regarding their new principal with the statement, "If the captain is weak, the ship will sink. We don't have to worry about sinking ships around here!"

Renewing the Built Environment

The previous two principals were not only lax when it came to maintaining order, they also neglected the physical grounds. The main building was dilapidated, unkept, and lacking in certain basic amenities. Many light fixtures and desks were broken, windows cracked, and the plumbing clogged. Abla Adalat firmly believed that a rundown and neglected physical environment stunted learning and repelled the community in it, whereas a clean and orderly school had the opposite effect. She elaborated:

> I can't stand anything dirty. When I came here my immediate priority was to start cleaning up the school for the sake of the girls. A clean school provides them with a comfortable and pleasant place to study, and gives them a sense of respect for learning. If the school is dirty, they'll throw papers on the floor and abuse it. But if it's clean, they won't do that.

This sense of community she was trying to foster was essentially about civic and social belonging.

> The student must not feel that since the school is supported by the government, it's not hers. No, the girl should think, "This school is mine because we pay taxes and the government bought all our supplies from those taxes." They should have a sense that the whole school and everything in it belongs to them. They should take care of it as if it is their own.

The principal's first priority was to "light the school for the girls." She started with the five basement classrooms. These classrooms each contained a single bulb that dangled from the ceiling. The lighting was so dim that students could often not make out the writing on the blackboard. These classroom caves, dark and poorly ventilated, crammed in up to fifty-five students each. "How can a girl develop a love of learning and how can teachers take pleasure in their work in such an environment?" she asked.

School repairs required resources. Every school had access to an annual maintenance allowance of LE 500, provided by the Ministry of Education. This paltry sum barely covered the school's most basic needs. Reluctant to apply to the Ministry for additional funds because of the bureaucratic hurdles involved, and the likelihood of a negative response, the principal appealed instead to the neighborhood council, which had its own budget for local projects. Her application for funds was accepted. A representative from the council oversaw all repairs, hired the workers, ordered the supplies, and handled all financial aspects of the project.

An assortment of electricians, carpenters, foremen, and construction workers streamed through the buildings and interrupted classes. Either Abla Adalat or the school secretary accompanied them as they surveyed the light fixtures, counted and measured broken windows, inspected the desks, and measured the walls. Their first priority was to upgrade the voltage capacity and repair the broken lights. The second priority was to repair or replace the desks, which were in a dreadful state of disrepair. The desk benches held up to three students each. Many of them had broken tray tops which students kept in place by balancing them on their knees. The trays often collapsed in the middle of class when a pupil so much as leaned down to write something. Another problem was the supply of smaller desks intended for primary school children. Students at the preparatory level had to cram into these desks and would sit uncomfortably for the entire day.

During the coming months, the carpenter's assistant would appear at random times at a classroom carrying a desk on his back. He would swap out the old desk with a new one to the delight of the students. The first few times, the teacher would pause the class to allow everyone to celebrate the exchange and express their congratulations to each other on the new desk. As the visits became more frequent, they became part of the normal routine. The teacher would nod for the carpenter to enter, and carry on the lesson without a pause.

During the mid-year break, the workers repaired the second-floor classrooms. Their walls were dull green and off-white and covered in pock marks from nails, thumb tacks, and scribblings made over the years. The refurbished classrooms felt fresh and clean. A committee was formed to oversee a reallocation of offices and classrooms to make better use of the space. The principal's office moved to the defunct computer room, defunct because no one paid the LE 30 fee to take computer lessons. The faculty tables for mathematics, Arabic, and social studies were consolidated in the principal's former office, turning it into a teachers' lounge. The green reception furniture that was crammed in the principal's old office was moved into the center of the main hall, which allowed visitors to sit there comfortably as they waited for an audience with the principal.

At one point, a massive bulldozer rolled onto the courtyard. The thunderous roar of its engine caused students to rush to the windows and peer outside to see what was causing the commotion. During the recess, hundreds of girls streamed into the courtyard and rushed toward the bulldozer. The presence of the hulking machine in their schoolyard caused them to squeal in delight. Some girls, so mesmerized by the sight, could not resist running their hands over the dusty metal. Their teachers immediately rushed over, waving their sticks, and whacked them on their backs or shoulders, until they cleared the area.

The bulldozer chugged toward its first target, the steps leading to the main villa that served as the stage for the *tabur*. It slowly devoured the steps on which a flagpole carrying the Egyptian flag stood fluttering in the wind. The flagpole teetered and fell. A teacher commanded the driver to stop, so that she could climb and rescue the fallen flag. By the next morning, piles of rubble and pieces of iron gate had accumulated in a mound in the main courtyard. Barefoot workers rolled a wheelbarrow around the scene of devastation, collecting wreckage and throwing it onto the growing pile. From time to time, they would start a controlled fire to reduce the debris, sending clouds of smoke up toward the classrooms, where lessons continued uninterrupted.

For weeks thereafter, classes were held to the sounds of drilling, banging, and nailing, which echoed and boomed throughout the building. Teachers shouted above the commotion, lecturing from the middle of the room so everyone could hear them. At times, the electricity was switched off and classrooms were pitch dark except for the beams of natural light that entered through window grates high on the walls. The hallways were strewn with bags of cement, supplies, and fragments of plaster, which generated dust and made circulation very cumbersome. Everyone did their best to help each other climb over debris to exit and enter their classes. The students and teachers showed a remarkable flexibility and tolerance during the period of construction. They did not complain, but rather expressed the need to be patient, as these temporary inconveniences would soon materialize into a better school that would benefit not only all of them, but future generations.

3

Educating Girls

Summary: Basic education is compulsory and free for both girls and boys in Egypt; however this does not mean that their experiences are equivalent. This chapter shows how, at a particular place and moment in time, teachers and school leaders abided by a tacit set of gender-specific disciplinary and pedagogic practices. It reviews the home economics framework, a subject required for all girls at the preparatory stage at that time, to illustrate how gender ideals were enshrined in the formal curriculum. Finally, through classroom observations we see the interplay between the official curriculum and hidden curriculum, where attitudes and performances of social class and status surfaced.

Future Mothers, Wives, and Workers

The idea that all boys *and* girls in Egypt should attend school first found expression in Article 19 of the Egyptian Constitution of 1923. The Article reads, "Elementary education [grades one to five] shall be compulsory for Egyptian boys and girls and shall be free in public schools." Each successive constitution includes articles on universal education for children of both sexes. Advocates for girls' education as early as the third quarter of the nineteenth century argued that educated girls were essential for the nation because they were responsible for raising Egypt's children, its citizens and future generations.[1] From the 1950s and 1960s, in addition to their roles as mothers of the nation, girls were also valued for their future contributions to the country's economic productivity, or their "human capital" potentials. Article 11 of the 1971 Constitution of Egypt (amended in 2007) conveys the dual roles of females: "The State shall guarantee the proper coordination between the duties of woman towards the family and her work in the society, considering her equal status with man in the fields of political, social, cultural and economic life without violation of the rules of Islamic jurisprudence."

At Falaki School, the range of education professionals and any adult working in the school including the cleaner and guard, considered it within their right, and indeed their duty, to bring up girls in ways suitable to prevailing cultural and social mores. However, there were no hard and fast rules about how to manage the upbringing *(tarbiya)* part of education. When asked, adults would make vague references to raising girls in ways compatible with a Muslim majority, Arab, Eastern, conservative society. School staff oversaw students' behavior through a mix of consensus, conformity to context specific practices, class sensibilities, and adherence to dominant—if largely unexamined—ideological and political norms which found expression in the hidden curriculum.

In Loco Parentis

The school served as a space of political socialization and integration into middle class urban society. The adult authorities served as a kind of extended family who assumed familial roles; they acted *in loco parentis* (in the place of parents). The language of family permeated all forms of school life starting with the title frequently given to women teachers of "Abla," a familial term to denote a big sister. It was common to hear members of the school community using metaphors of the family, likening colleagues to mothers, fathers, sisters, and brothers, and students to daughters and little sisters. As illustrated above, the principal appealed to students by equating them to the daughters she never had. She was forthcoming about her obligation to raise the girls in all dimensions: moral, intellectual, physical, psychological, and civic.

> My most important priority is to raise the level of the girls scientifically, intellectually, and morally. I need to implant values and morals in them, to teach them to follow the correct rules of society so that they can grow up correctly, with stability. A girl has to learn respect. She has to learn to be clean and to talk and dress correctly. She has to learn how to handle herself, to deal with any person regardless of whether they're older, younger, or her peer. These are the very basics.

In the year 1990, a large proportion of girls were first generation school-goers. Within this school, 60 percent of mothers had no formal education. They were unfamiliar with their daughters' routines and did not know how to prepare them for school life. Teachers stepped in to play parental roles for this group of first generation girls who were pioneers in their families.[2] Their very act of leaving the house and crossing parts of the city to attend school represented a shift in the girl's place in public life and similarly imbued teachers, at least theoretically, with caretaking responsibilities. As one female teacher remarked:

> The very fact that a girl can go out of the house every day and walk to her school without a brother or father, then meet friends and different kinds of people there, provides her with an opportunity my generation would never have dreamed of. When I was growing up, people would have said that it's not proper for a Muslim girl to go out unaccompanied for any reason. But now, attitudes about girls have changed, largely due to the acceptance of education.

The principal, who had spent thirty years working in girls' preparatory and high schools, was the parent-in-chief. She set the tone for how to raise her female students.

> The girl is female by nature. God gave her certain gifts which she must not downplay but learn to use and respect. A girl is a girl. A boy is a boy. The two sexes must be aware of their distinctive characteristics and not be merged into one.

She elaborated further:

> We have to treat the girl as a future woman. We must teach her how to respect her femininity, how to act as a female, how to become a wife, how to become a housewife. We have to prepare her for how to treat her husband and raise her children, the future generation. She must learn how to become a successful woman in life, to harmonize work in the home with work outside it. She has to know her limits, which are different from those of a man. God created the differences between the two sexes and we must nourish them.

The principal placed a high priority on regulating the girl's body, dress, and comportment. These priorities translated into measures to enforce the proper school uniform. Students were expected to arrive to school with a clean uniform that consisted of a few simple components: an ironed white button-down blouse, a gray skirt that fell at or below the knee, white socks, and black shoes. The three main grooming rules were simple: the hair should be pulled back neatly, the nails had to be cut short, and no makeup was allowed. Certain items were expressly forbidden, including high heeled shoes, nail polish, colored hair clips, decorative hair bands, short skirts, and any dangling earrings and necklaces.

Each morning, the homeroom teachers inspected the girls' appearance and wardrobe. If a girl was found to be in violation of the rules by, for example, wearing makeup or nail polish, or having unbrushed hair and an unwashed face, the teacher would send her to the nurse's room to clean up. If the problem was that the student was wearing nonregulation or inappropriate clothing (such as a short skirt), she would be sent home to change her clothes, and might have to pass by the principal's office first.

The principal justified the school uniform policy in clear and unequivocal terms:

> The student must act her age. She must primarily be interested in knowledge and learning, not her looks. She should take care to maintain a pleasant, acceptable way of looking. She should be decent and very simple, not crass. A girl shouldn't wear funky clothes. Should she wear the clothes of a thirty-year-old woman? Is she thirty? No, she is twelve years old. The uniform should be clean, the socks clean. And her hair, should it be frizzy with fancy hairdos at the age of twelve? No! If she does this now, what will she do when she goes to university? And what will she do after she finishes university?!

The principal carried out spot inspections of different aspects of the uniform. One day she inspected the length of skirt hems, another day the focus was on blouses and whether they were ironed and buttoned high enough to cover the bust area. Yet another day, she focused entirely on the color of the girls' socks. One morning in the fall, the inspection was specifically on hair color. The principal ordered all girls with light shades of hair, whether blond, reddish, or light brown, to remain in the courtyard after the *tabur*. Twelve girls stayed behind and formed a single line. One by one the principal had them lower their heads as she dug her hands into each girl's scalps to examine her hair roots. She was looking to see if anyone had dyed their hair. She discovered four guilty heads and proceeded to punish the offenders by punching them on their backs while shouting about how shameful (*'ayb*) and improper it was for girls of their age to alter their innocent appearance. She finished by caning each girl forcefully on their palms. They all left the courtyard in tears, heads lowered.[3]

The next campaign targeted inappropriate jewelry. The principal gave a rousing speech at the *tabur* one morning about how excessive displays of gold not only accentuated differences in wealth but were "unsuitable for children." The only gold jewelry students were permitted to wear at school were small earrings in the form of posts or small hoops. Some girls continued to live dangerously and took pleasure in flouting the rules. They concealed gold necklaces under high-collar blouses and clandestinely showed them to their classmates. Other girls wore gold rings and on seeing the principal or a strict teacher would quickly remove them. Teachers were ordered to confiscate dangling earrings, gold chains, rings, and bracelets. They handed these items over to the principal who locked them in her top drawer with a tag carrying the owner's name. One day, the principal became so angry on seeing a student wearing a long gold chain that she ripped it off her neck, causing the girl's skin to tear slightly and bleed. Parents had to come to the school themselves in order to collect these precious items, and when they did, they too received a firm scolding.

The war on gold caused quite a stir. A number of teachers who normally supported their principal's strict measures complained that this time she had gone too far. The policy would prove short-lived, as it ended up bringing a scandal to the school. A student's gold bracelet that had been confiscated went missing. The girl's outraged parents filed a police complaint accusing the school management of stealing student property. Not wanting more trouble, the principal abruptly put an end to the policy of confiscating jewelry.

Disciplining Girls

For the most part, teachers genuinely believed that punishment carried pedagogic benefits. Throughout many months of classroom observations, certain disciplinary patterns emerged. A teacher considered it their right and even duty to punish a student if she answered a question incorrectly, did not complete her homework, talked during a lesson, arrived to class late, forgot her workbook or supplies (in art or sewing for example), or showed disrespect to the teacher by not using "Abla" or "Ustaz" before the name.

Teachers used a mix of techniques to mete out punishment, from embarrassing and shaming the girl in front of her classmates, to corporal punishment which normally meant a caning on the palms or a punch on the shoulder or back. Some of the other less commonly used but tacitly sanctioned punishments included making a girl stand holding her arms up for five minutes to half an hour, or sending her to the corridor with a paper attached to her back with the word "stupid" written on it.

When asked about the differences between teaching girls versus boys, a number of teachers spoke about consciously adjusting their discipline strategies according to the student's gender. A male teacher echoed the sentiment of many of his fellow male colleagues when he explained:

> The major difference between teaching girls and teaching boys is how we approach punishment. Girls can be punished more verbally. A teacher just basically needs to embarrass her in front of her classmates. This does not work with a boy. He has to be beaten and beaten harshly. The [adolescent] boy feels that he's grown up and on the same level as the male teacher. He won't respond to a mild punishment. As boys grow older and stronger, the [male] teacher begins to worry that they might hit back, so at that stage he must change his tactics.

Verbal punishments not only had the effect of shaming and embarrassing a student into submission. The tactic could also be a shunning mechanism, signaling to other girls to stay away from that person. A female Arabic teacher explained why she found this approach effective:

> The best punishment for girls, which differs from that for boys, is to attack them psychologically. Maybe I'll say something that will upset her, make her feel like she's not good. This would be an instant punishment and also serve as a warning for other girls to stay away from her.

All teachers, with just one exception, the science teacher Abla Marwa, carried a stick and used it at least occasionally. Teachers spoke about how hitting was an especially efficient form of punishment during a class lesson. In the words of a male mathematics teacher:

Hitting is the easiest way to punish someone. It saves a lot of time for the teacher who doesn't want to think about other ways of dealing with a problem. I personally hit according to the degree of the offense. If the student does something serious, I'll hit her four or five times on the palm. Because she's a girl I'll hit her gently, not harshly.

Class discrimination and favoritism appeared to run deep. Those girls most subject to humiliation tactics and the harshest physical punishments were first-generation students from poorer social backgrounds. Even though teachers for the most part saw themselves as doling out discipline in a fair and measured way, many teachers engaged in observable discrimination against the poorest students. A female teacher summed up the class bias when she explained:

The problem with government schools is that there are girls from different social backgrounds. You can't trust them. Some of the girls may steal, have bad morals, and bad families. I sent my daughters to a language school where I knew they would be with girls at their level. Thank God, they're both at university now.

For their part, students held firm opinions about corporal punishment and the disciplinary norms. These girls had grown up in public schools during the 1980s where hitting was the norm. When asked what they thought about this practice, they expressed mixed feelings. Some argued vehemently against it, asserting that hitting was wrong and out of bounds. One student remarked, "Parents should decide on their daughter's punishment, not teachers. Anyway, when we get hit at school it always gives the opposite result." She meant that hitting made them hate the subject, resent the school, and develop overall negative feelings about school learning more generally. Another girl who rarely got hit and was from a family representing the professional middle class, disagreed. She echoed the logic of her teachers by saying, "Sometimes hitting works for students who will only study if they're punished first. If it brings them better results, it's worth it." Even with this high tolerance and acceptance of corporal punishment, when I asked students who they considered the best teacher in the school, they consistently named Abla Marwa. It was no coincidence that she was the only teacher who did not carry a stick, never hit students, and practiced a pedagogic style of positive reinforcement (see chapter 4 for descriptions of her classroom). However rare, they recognized and valued a pedagogy in which they felt respected and experienced a joy of learning.

Inside Home Economics

If the hidden curriculum revealed informal and context specific ways of discipling and reinforcing norms, the formal curriculum captured the ways in which gendered knowledge was codified. Home economics (*al-iqtisad al-manzili)* was a required course for all female students at the preparatory level until the mid-1990s. For the purposes of getting a clearer picture of this subject, and seeing the dialectic between theory and practice, curriculum analysis is combined here with classroom observations. This is because analyzing formal curricula alone does not allow us to understand how a subject is received among its intended audience. Although home economics was not included in the national examinations and therefore was not part of the student's overall grade point average *(magmu')*, it was a required subject for which students met once a week for two consecutive periods.

Home economics covered topics deemed essential for the girl's transition to her assumed impending role as a wife and mother in a nuclear family. The course was divided into applied and theoretical sections, and organized around five modules: childhood and family relations; home administration and family economics; the home, its furniture, and tools; food and nutrition; and clothes and textiles. The topics progressed from first year, when the student was eleven or twelve and entering adolescence, to second year, when she was expected to experience a spike in growth and physical maturity. According to the school nurse, most girls started their menstrual cycle by the end of the first year or in the second year. The second-year curriculum took up more-adult issues such as family planning and home medical care, and provided instruction on advanced cooking and sewing. The third-year syllabus presupposed that marriage was utmost on the girl's mind and prepared her to make the leap from being a schoolgirl to a wife and mother. Below is an edited and abridged translation of the official home economics curriculum framework for years one to three at the preparatory stage.

Home Economics Framework: Preparatory Stage

Year One
Childhood and Family Relations
Students of the age of eleven or twelve learned that they were leaving childhood and entering a new life phase, adolescence. During this stage of budding maturity, the girl realized the importance of the family and participated more fully in family life by taking on extra responsibilities. She needed to understand that at this age, she started to emit body odors when she perspired, and was supposed to wash herself in a way that eliminated such body odors. Overall, she was taught to be more aware of her body, maintain high standards of personal hygiene, regularly wash her face, and groom her hair. The girl at this age must also be more selective in choosing her friends, and understand that she cannot trust just anyone.

Home Administration and Family Economics
Girls had to start getting used to the idea that one day they would become wives and mothers and run their own households. They needed to acquire certain skills to prepare them for their future responsibilities including preparing for a family, understanding the importance of household budgeting, living according to their family's financial means, and performing household duties with efficiency.

The Home, Its Furniture, and Tools
The students learned how to furnish, decorate, and clean their own rooms. They also learned how to select and maintain home appliances like ovens and washing machines. Finally, they were instructed in how to set a dining table properly, with plates, glasses, cutlery, and serving platters.

Food and Nutrition
This segment covered information on nutritional needs, with emphasis on how to select meats and vegetables in the market, and how to recognize the signs of malnutrition. The girls also had

academic lessons on how to boil, fry, and grill different foods. In the actual applied cooking lessons, students prepared simple oriental sweets and half-cooked or frozen foods.

Clothes and Textiles

Students learned how to wash, iron, and care for cotton material. They were also instructed on the parts of the sewing machine and the iron. In the applied lesson, students learned how to sew pillow covers, laundry bags, and kitchen towels. They also learned how to work with buttons and lace as well as how to add decorative flourishes to their clothes and household items.

Year Two
Childhood and Family Relations

This module stressed that girls should not deviate from cultural and social norms and should always "handle certain situations in accordance with the customs of family and society." They learned about family planning in marriage and that having a small family would lead to better health and higher standards of living. The practical lessons were on first aid and treating minor wounds and burns.

Home Administration and Family Economics

Students received tips on how to shop in a smart, economical, and respectable manner. They learned how to dress for shopping and the importance of their appearance, how to discern between wholesale and retail shops, and the pros and cons of different payment options, whether cash, credit, or installment plans. Finally, they learned how to read different kinds of sales tags.

The Home, Its Furniture, and Tools

The students received instructions on how to furnish every room in a house and how to select and care for kitchen appliances, to make minor electrical repairs, and stock a medicine cabinet.

Food and Nutrition

This section focused on Egyptian cooking and ways to prepare meals for families. The girls also learned how to plan the different courses of a meal—the main dish, salads, drinks, and desserts—and how to estimate and determine proportions for each course. For the applied component, students used the kitchen in the home economics room to make typical recipes using different ingredients such as beans, fish, meat, and vegetables. Among the dishes they cooked from scratch were baked fish and macaroni with béchamel sauce.

Clothes and Textiles

These lessons dealt with undergarments and proper clothing for sleeping. For the in-class sewing lesson, girls learned how to draw and cut out a pattern, select appropriate material and thread for different articles of clothing, and use a sewing machine. They also learned the basics of knitting.

Year Three
Childhood and Family Relations

This module dealt with family planning, furnishing a home, and preparing balanced meals. As in second year, it continued to stress moral character, and in particular, "the importance of holding onto good traditions and staying away from the wrong ones." It also provided guidelines on how to prepare for marriage, with instructions on how to determine the dowry and plan for the wedding. Additionally, girls learned about caring for the sick, with guidelines on how to take and record a temperature, techniques for applying cold compresses, and ways to sterilize sheets and change a patient's clothing.

Home Administration and Family Economics

This segment provided information on scientific thinking in decision making about the household and family. It included a lesson on how to weigh up the pros and cons of homemade products versus store-bought ones.

The Home, Its Furniture, and Tools

Here, students received guidelines on how to select home equipment and appliances, with specific mention of the pressure cooker, freezer, refrigerator, and vacuum cleaner. They also learned details about the requirements for weekly house cleaning, and tips for decorating the home and arranging furniture to allow for ease of movement.

Food and Nutrition

This segment focused on fowl as a food group and included information on its nutritional value and what to look for when purchasing fowl. It also addressed the different kinds of starchy food and their nutritional value. In the applied lessons, girls learned how to preserve foods through freezing, salting, and drying. They also learned about how to use yeast in baking, and received lessons on preparing and wrapping food for trips.

Clothes and Textiles

In the in-school sewing lessons, students made simple house clothes and learned how to attach finishings such as pockets, ruffles, and buttonholes. They also learned how to use an iron during sewing, how to care for hand-sewn items, and the characteristics of synthetic materials.

If we unpack the hidden curriculum or the ideological underpinnings of the home economics framework, we find a recurring message around maintaining traditional gender roles while embracing a changing middle-class consumer culture. In other words, home economics represented a framework of managed change. The imagined household was one in which girls had their own rooms, the kitchen was stocked with modern appliances and consumer goods, and meals were taken at a dining table with cutlery and other accoutrements. From a class perspective, the course was disconnected from the lives of the majority of the population, and certainly the community within this school. An in-school survey revealed that 83 percent of students lived in apartments with one to three rooms, and 70 percent in households of five to seven people. None of these 83 percent had their own bedroom, and few took meals at a dining table with full cutlery, though many households were accumulating basic appliances like refrigerators. The norm within this milieu was to share meals at home in a more traditional setting around a low round table. However, the fact that home economics did not reflect the lived reality of students from predominantly urban poor and lower middle-class sectors was perhaps beside the point. It provided an aspirational vision of what it meant to be part of the rising educated middle classes, by painting an idealized portrait of an up-to-date traditional woman who could manage a respectable modern household.

The Curriculum Comes Off the Page

The lesson plans for home economics were short on specifics and allowed individual teachers space to interpret the guidelines and decide on which aspects to emphasize. Some teachers, with more conservative leanings and with less energy, focused more on morality topics, such as the importance of respecting parents and maintaining good traditions. Others spent more time on applied skills in the arts of homemaking. Abla Salwa, the senior teacher for home economics, held a BA from the Department of Home Economics at Helwan University and took homemaking to a high art. She lectured the girls with the aid of detailed diagrams about the importance of deep cleaning. She assumed that most of the students were not living in home environments with high standards of hygiene and saw herself as carrying the mission of raising their standards. She explained:

> After marriage, the girls should be prepared to do all the housework. Maids are expensive now, about a hundred pounds a month, and most people can't afford them. I teach the girls how to clean out the refrigerator and clean out gas cylinder. These are things a mother doesn't expect of her twelve-year-old girl, but she must learn them nevertheless.

Abla Salwa was passionate about the culinary arts and supervised all the cooking lessons. She wholeheartedly believed that cooking was key to a girl's future success in life, and devoted as much class time as possible to cooking. She explained:

> All girls should learn how to cook. Even if a woman has a successful career and is happy with her employment, if she doesn't know how to cook and take care of her family, her whole life will be destroyed.

The actual cooking lessons took place in the home economics room, which resembled a science lab. It was equipped with countertops, gas burners, faucets with running water, and cupboards supplied with all the necessary aluminum cooking supplies. This space accommodated up to 150 girls a day, and was itself in need of a thorough deep clean. Portions of the countertops and floors were caked in grime, and the cupboards and other structures were in a state of disrepair, with missing hinges and handles, and some exposed wires.

During the cooking lessons, students stood around the three long tables arranged in a U shape. They wiggled into any space that would allow them to lean forward, rather than stand back in a second row. Cooking lessons were divided into two parts. Part One involved cleaning, preparing, and cooking the food. Part Two was the written lesson with the recipe and cooking instructions. The students were responsible for maintaining the kitchen, washing appliances, and cleaning up after each session.

On one particular spring morning, a cooking class of second-year students proceeded as follows. Abla Salwa opened the refrigerator and removed four whole fish wrapped in newspaper. A total of forty-five girls crowded around to get a good view. She placed the fish at the head of the center table and took out a knife to remove the fish scales. She explained, "Now girls, fish is full of protein and much better for you than meat or chicken. If you ever have a cold or flu, just eat fish." She paused to show the class how to decapitate the fish's head from its body. A few girls giggled or feigned expressions of horror. She momentarily left the table to get a pair of scissors, whereupon one girl picked up the fish by its tail and swung it in the face of the girl standing next to her. Other students reached out to poke and prod at it. The girl hurriedly returned the fish to its place when Abla Salwa returned. One girl looked especially disgusted and kept making exaggerated faces. The teacher asked her if she had a problem. The student brazenly claimed that she didn't think these fish were fresh. The teacher, in defensive mode answered, "I swear to you. I bought all of them last night at the market. You don't expect me to go buy them at seven this morning, do you?"

As she took a knife to cut open the fish's stomach, she called out to the school cleaner Nadia to bring her a baking tray. Nadia, a plump and elderly woman who had worked at the school for over ten years, also served as Abla Salwa's assistant. As Abla Salwa proceeded to gut the fish, while pointing out the fish's anatomy and the importance of cleaning it properly, she called out to Nadia, "Run over to the store and buy some cumin and lemon. Be quick, please!" After the demonstration, Abla Salwa took the remaining three fish and distributed them in a somewhat haphazard fashion at different points around the table, to give the students a chance to prepare them.

The excited girls grabbed the fish from each others' hands. The students became boisterous and snatched each other's knives. The teacher suddenly pounded her fist on the table and shouted, "Stop it, you donkeys!"

Whoever happened to be holding a fish at that moment got to continue with scaling and gutting it. A small group formed around each fish, and other girls on the outskirts of each small group lost interest. They started chatting with each other or simply zoned out of the lesson altogether.

Nadia reappeared from the store carrying the ingredients wrapped in newspaper. Abla Salwa set to work stuffing the fish as she explained how to mix the spices. On finishing the preparations, she placed the tray in the oven and opened her purse to remove a carefully wrapped bar of soap. Soap was a luxury item, and there was no soap in the home economics room, nor in any of the bathrooms for that matter. Anyone who wanted to wash their hands with soap had to bring their own supply. She walked over to the sink and thoroughly washed her hands and arms. Then she returned to her place at the head of the table to begin the written part of the lesson. There was no blackboard in this room, so Abla Salwa dictated to the class. The girls took out their notebooks and wrote out the list of ingredients, oven temperature, and cooking time.

As Abla Salwa was dictating the recipe, and with twenty minutes left in the class period, the sewing teacher Abla Nabila entered the room. She greeted her colleague with a kiss on each cheek. Abla Salwa asked Nadia to prepare them tea and left the lesson to sit with her colleague. She didn't give the class any instructions: she just left them mid-lesson. Nadia put a kettle on the burner and took the opportunity to have a cup of tea herself. She sat with the two teachers as they chatted about the prices of food, their various ailments, and medications they were using. Each woman pulled out sandwiches from their purses, indicating that this was a prearranged break. They continued their conversation sipping tea and eating sandwiches while the students did their own thing—reading, chatting and joking in small groups, or simply waiting idly in place. When Abla Nabila finished her snack, she stood up and left the room. Abla Salwa finished the final portion of the dictation until the bell rang for the morning recess. She reminded the girls to return to the room during the last five minutes of the break to taste the fish, which was to be fully cooked by that time.

Halfway into the break, four girls ran into the home economics room, pulled the fish from the oven and began devouring it. Soon after, four more girls arrived and hovered over the tray, competing to get a share. They laughed playfully and pushed each other about, oil dripping from their fingers. Their teacher looked up from her chair completely unfazed and ignored them. Several girls wandered into the room at the designated time and looked with disappointment at the picked-over fish carcasses strewn across the tray.

On a different day, a third-year class made stuffed green peppers. The teacher removed the food from the oven and asked the girls to pass forward their plates, which she had distributed with forks earlier, so that they could taste the dish. Not a single student budged. She asked them again, but they remained still. Just one girl offered her plate and began timidly eating. This was one of the two girls who had assisted the teacher earlier in the lesson by washing the vegetables, chopping the herbs, and stuffing the green peppers. This girl looked tired and weathered. Her uniform was ragged and stained, her body small for her age, and she had several long scars on her face. Her appearance and comportment showed not only that she was from a poorer background than her colleagues, but also that she led a life of hardship.

When I spoke with the girls after class to get their feedback about home economics, most were dismissive because it was not a graded course. When asked if at least they learned some recipes and cooking tips, they generally replied that their mothers, not the school teacher, taught them how to cook, and that they were attached to their mothers' ways. One girl declared, as her classmates nodded in agreement, "Cooking class is a waste of time." Another girl chimed in, "We really don't learn anything. It would be more useful if we took carpentry like in the boys' schools, but they insist on giving us cooking." When I asked a group of girls why they refused to taste the food prepared in the lesson, the ringleader among them explained, "Our mothers told us never to eat any food outside of the house, including at school. It's not clean." Another girl added, "You can see the food they use is disgusting. It's not washed properly. And those two girls kept handling it with their dirty hands. It really makes you lose your appetite."

The topic of cleanliness, and lack thereof, came up frequently in these conversations. The state of the room stood in sharp contrast to the lectures about the need for strict hygiene and techniques for deep cleaning. On one occasion, the principal entered the room to inspect the kitchen. She opened the cupboard and surveyed the items with an exaggerated expression of revulsion. She carefully lifted a food grater covered in rust and asked accusingly, "What's this? What's this doing here?!" Maintaining an expression of utter disgust, she dangled the grater high above the garbage and released it to the sound of a crack. She berated the teacher and her assistant, shouting that it was unforgivable for them to use such rotten supplies at a school. Didn't they realize they could poison the girls with these old, rusted things? Abla Salwa attempted to argue back, saying something about her lack of a budget, but the principal cut her off and refused to listen. She then sat down and sighed. Turning to me she said, "Sometimes I'd like to kill them, but with my hands, not with that rusty old thing." She and the other women, who moments ago were tensely arguing, burst into laughter. The principal left, shaking her head.

The students were keenly aware of social disparities within the school community, and of their place in its social order. These differences were amplified through the subject of home economics. In theory it was supposed to raise schoolgirls to aspire to an ideal of middle-class girlhood and womanhood. In practice, however, girls from poorer backgrounds would end up doing a good deal of the tidying and work, as if they were being socialized to be the cleaners or serve the members of the higher social classes. The middle-class sensibilities implicit in the home economics framework thus played out in a manner that accentuated class differences and set students apart.

4

Teachers of the Nation

Summary: Teachers are often idealized in Egyptian society as the souls of the nation. In actuality, they harbor many grievances and often appear as the scapegoats for the ills of the education system. Teachers work in highly challenging conditions that include low pay, second jobs, declining status, high-density classes, and under-prepared students. This chapter offers a snapshot of teachers' lives, attitudes, and struggles and shows how their working conditions impacted classroom pedagogies. Though the vignettes are from a specific time and place, they offer insights into enduring aspects of the "teacher problem."

Serving the Nation

A common message amplified in semiofficial newspapers, television talk shows, presidential speeches, and any national media that covered public education, was that teaching was an act of patriotism. The teacher was someone who supposedly entered the profession out of selflessness, national service, their love of country, and love of God. Whatever their motivations, noble or otherwise, it was an indisputable reality that teachers were not making a livable wage and were suffering from the effects of the decline in their social status.

As Ustaz Emad, a junior science teacher, observed: "Before the mass production of teachers which began at the end of the 1950s, a teacher was a true person of knowledge, well versed in all subjects. We can say that teaching was one of the most prestigious professions. That's not the case anymore." Teachers are at the heart of the education system and have been accorded the enormous task of elevating the nation's generations. Yet the reality has been that they hold an exceedingly paradoxical position in Egyptian society. Public school teachers often work in highly difficult circumstances for notoriously low wages. As the population of the country has grown exponentially, from 20 million in 1951 to 55 million in 1990 (when this study took place), to 104 million in 2021, the government has struggled to sufficiently expand and update the educational infrastructure, and to keep up with teacher preparation needs.

At the time this ethnographic study was conducted, the majority of teachers were graduates of faculties of education. Most of them landed in the teaching profession by default. In a survey of teachers at the school, only 9 percent of them indicated teaching as their first career choice. Others had aspired to join faculties such as engineering, architecture, and biology, but did not achieve the required score on the university entrance examination, the Thanawiya 'Amma, and ended up by default in education colleges. A mathematics teacher remarked, "I really wanted to be an engineer, but my grades weren't high enough. I had no other choice but to enter the Faculty of Education." Whether arriving to the teaching profession by choice or through lack of other options, the low salaries combined with declining social status cast a shadow over their professional lives.

Ustaz Emad was a second-generation science teacher. He had wanted to be teacher from the time he was a child, to follow in the footsteps of his father, Ustaz Mohnes. He recalled walking with his father and feeling proud as people greeted him with such respect and appreciation. When his students caught a glimpse of his father on the streets, they would stop what they were doing and fall silent in respect. Shopkeepers saluted him with honorifics: "Hello, Basha." "How are you today, Engineer Mohnes?" Neighbors greeted and approached him with affectionate handshakes and also turned to him for advice, seeing him as a trusted person who could mediate disputes. Ustaz Emad did not experience the same treatment whatsoever. He explained,

These days our society has really low regard for teachers because it has become materialistic. People think those with money are better, that they're higher class. Just look at the university entrance exam. The subjects that need the highest grades are engineering and medicine. If you follow the list of subjects by ranking, you need to go all the way down until you get to education. The teacher gets the lowest salary. What is fifty or sixty pounds? It's very little compared to other fields.

A social studies teacher who dreamed of becoming a teacher since the time she was a child felt let down by her society and government: "I was surprised to find that the society looks down upon the profession as something trivial and insignificant. I partly blame the government. They mistreat us by giving us the lowest salaries of all the professions."

One of the art teachers, a fresh graduate from the Faculty of Interior Design, lamented the reaction of friends and classmates on hearing she was a teacher in a public school. They would express surprise and sympathy and exclaim, "A teacher? Can't you find a better job than that?" Or they might reply, "Why don't you go into something in the private sector?" She could have found work in the private sector and earned at least ten times her teacher's salary of LE 60 per month, but her parents did not want their unmarried daughter to work in an office far from home, out of fear for her safety and reputation. When they saw an advertisement for an art teacher in a nearby school, they pressured her to apply. After working two years as a teacher, she found it hard to adapt to the environment. "Teaching wore me out," she explained. "I went home every day with a headache from all the noise everywhere. I couldn't get used to the inefficiency of the system, the shortage of supplies, the budget arriving late, the lack of space." After two years in the classroom, she left the school for a desk job in the Ministry of Education.

A Volunteer Profession?

The government sets the salary scale for all employees working in the public sector. The amounts are determined according to seniority and credentials. Within the school, the principal is the senior-most person and top earner, followed by the vice principal, senior teachers (also called first teachers), junior teachers with university degrees, the senior secretary, junior secretaries, the nurse, social workers, junior teachers with degrees from a technical secondary school, and finally the custodians, who may or may not have completed primary school.

As the table below indicates, the highest salary before bonuses was LE 216 per month, and the lowest one was LE 35 per month.[1] To put these numbers in context for the time, in 1990 a kilogram of meat cost LE 11. A very modest two- to three-room flat in Cairo, which a couple would need to secure before marriage, required LE 10,000–15,000 key money, plus a permanent fixed rate of rent in the range of LE 50–100 per month. Round-trip transportation on the bus was 30 piasters, and a breakfast or snack of

Table 1. Egyptian Ministry of Education monthly salary scale (in LE), 1990–91

Level	Starting salary	Ending salary	Annual increase
Excellent	216.92	—	—
High	140.00	207.75	6.25
General manager	125.00	197.00	6.00
First	95.00	179.00	5.00
Second	70.00	164.00	4.00
Third	48.00	139.00	3.00
Fourth	38.00	107.00	2.00
Fifth	36.00	82.00	1.50
Sixth	35.00	67.00	1.50

tea and *ful* (fava bean) sandwich ran about LE 1. Teachers who relied on their teaching salary alone could neither satisfy their basic needs, nor plan for the future.

When asked how teachers were expected to live on their salaries, the principal offered the official line about teaching being akin to national service, a volunteer profession. She explained, "Anyone who volunteers to work in the teaching profession must give a hundred percent regardless of the salary. We know the salaries are low compared to the cost of living, but everyone here accepted this and must work in a way that satisfies his conscience and his God. If someone claims that he's not going to work properly because of the low salary, is that a good excuse? Should we stop all education because the ministry is poor?" Nevertheless, in private, the principal was keenly aware that the low wages were a problem. She was especially concerned about the situation of single men trying to prepare for marriage, and female and male teachers with family responsibilities. She herself was a widow who had to raise two sons on a teacher's salary.

Teachers were resourceful, and they found different ways to manage life on a limited salary. Their preferred income-generating activity was to work after hours giving private lessons. This option was open to teachers of mathematics, English, Arabic, social studies, and science, the subjects that carried weight for the overall grade *(magmu')* (see chapter 5). Other teachers, especially men, worked second jobs in whatever work they could find, from construction and taxi-driving to different forms of service work. A large proportion of teachers also joined an informal savings' cooperative known as a *gam'iya* (plural, *gam'iyyat*). Teachers would self-organize and contribute a monthly sum to a common pool. The contribution could range from LE 20 to LE 100 per month. Each month, one person would receive the entire sum which would allow them to put a down payment on a big household item, pay a debt, or plan for a wedding or holy pilgrimage, whatever cost they needed to cover. There were different *gam'iyyat* at the school, and some teachers participated in more than one.

Depending on their life situations and access to additional income, some teachers managed better than others. For instance, Abla Nagwa, a forty-year-old science teacher with two daughters under the age of four, was widowed the previous year. After seventeen years of teaching, her salary was LE 137. Her monthly rent was LE 70, and she was just scraping by between her low salary and her husband's modest pension. She arrived at school each morning in mourning clothes of a black ankle-length skirt, a faded black blouse with a black lace collar, and a black headscarf decorated with white beads. Her voice was faint, as if speaking required her to muster her limited reserves of energy. Her daily routine left her exhausted as she described:

> I wake up at 5 a.m. to get myself and my girls' things ready for the day. I wake up my small daughters at 6 a.m. to prepare them for the daycare center. I walk them over and drop them off before taking a bus here to the school. I leave the school immediately at 1:30 p.m. and reach them at 2:30 p.m. We go home and I prepare lunch and clean the house. It's impossible for me to give any private lessons or do private tutoring after school. Who will care for my daughters if I'm not there? No one. But thank God. One must thank God for everything.

Abla Nagwa always arrived at her class well prepared. She carried a stick but rarely needed to use it, as the students feared her. Whenever she entered the room, they immediately fell silent. She did not begin each lesson like most other teachers with a greeting or pleasantry, but with an order: "Empty your desks and sit up straight." She would walk slowly to the board and write out different formulas, pausing to explain each one. Occasionally she asked after a long, exhausted sigh, "Do you understand, Year Three, or shall I repeat it again?" No one dared ask her to repeat anything. At the end of each class she would utter a curt "*al-salamu 'alaykum*" and carry her fatigued body to its next destination.

For some teachers, the strains of the job combined with the low salary caused them to leave the profession. A twenty-seven-year-old music teacher, living at home with her parents and engaged to be married, earned LE 74 per month. She had hoped to put aside money for her marriage, but barely managed to get by from month to month. She remarked, "I would like to take some of the burden off my fiancé who is saving to prepare our flat, but most months I don't even have enough money for the week's transportation costs. Without a contribution from me, I know it will take years before we can marry, but I just don't know what I can do." Were it not for her two brothers who worked in Saudi Arabia and bought clothes for her, she admitted she would have only one outfit to wear for the entire year. For her, having brothers earning good incomes in an Arab Gulf country meant she had some kind of security. She expected they would help her in the future, for without them, her family would slide into poverty.

In conversations about work/life balance with female teachers, some of them said even though their teacher's salary was paltry, it provided them with some degree of independence, especially in the context of marriage. This applied more to teachers who lived near the school and could walk to work, avoiding transportation costs. One teacher explained that she was frugal and knew how to stretch her salary to the maximum. She did not want to rely on her husband for all of her needs, and felt that too much financial dependence could cause problems in the marriage.[2]

The Art of Teaching

"Teaching is an art and not anyone can be a teacher. Not anyone can give. Some of the staff certainly are not meant to be teachers, but they're the only staff I have."

—The Principal, Falaki School.

Teachers at the school performed their jobs along a spectrum ranging from excellent to abhorrent, with most of them somewhere in the middle. To get a sense of the qualities that made an exemplary teacher, I regularly asked students about their favorite teachers, and two names came up time and again: Abla Marwa, a senior science teacher who had been teaching for two decades, and Ustaz Zaki, a mid-career mathematics teacher.

Abla Marwa stood apart from her colleagues in two distinct ways: first, she was the only teacher at the entire school who did not own a stick and she never resorted to corporal punishment; and second, she did not believe in private lessons. She believed that through skilled teaching and the right time management, she could achieve everything she wanted in the classroom. She considered the classroom a place of equity and equal opportunity for all students. As a first teacher, her teaching load was lighter than her junior colleagues. She taught fourteen periods per week as opposed to a full load of twenty to twenty-five periods per week.

In a typical class session, Abla Marwa entered the room and wished the girls a good morning or afternoon. She began each class as a kind of review and asked students to recall what they had covered in the previous lesson. She would then ask a series of questions about the last lesson and reward correct answers by saying, "Bravo," "Very good," or "I see you've studied well." As she introduced new material, she would pause frequently to ask if the class had any questions. If someone hesitated, she would encourage them with a comment like, "Don't be shy. I'm sure it's a good question," using classic techniques of positive reinforcement. The lab space and resources were limited, but she would do her best to demonstrate a point with an experiment. One afternoon after explaining a lesson, she turned off the lights and invited everyone to come closer. The girls excitedly moved their desks forward, their curious eyes sparkling in silent anticipation. Abla Marwa lit a candle, held it in her left hand and pulled a ping pong ball attached to stick from her pocket. With her props in hand, she explained in a low steady voice, the relationship between the earth and the sun and the appearance of day and night. She spoke to a rapt audience. Even with all the challenges, Abla Marwa displayed a positive attitude about her profession saying, "The greatest thing about being a teacher is seeing your students grow up and become successful, achieving something great. I feel that I contributed to that success." To keep order in her class, she drew on techniques of positive reinforcement, experiential learning, and patient communication. Most other teachers drew on more traditional punitive measures to keep order and respect in their classrooms.

A second beloved teacher was Ustaz Zaki, a thirty-three-year-old who taught mathematics. He was one of the few teachers at the school who had actually chosen the teaching profession. He explained, "My uncle was a teacher and I always looked up to him. I wanted to be one too." Ustaz Zaki was a highly dynamic, skilled, and engaging teacher, and students considered themselves incredibly lucky to be assigned to his classes. He often walked into the class without any notes or book, yet he came fully prepared. He always looked dapper and professional with his clothes meticulously pressed.

One morning after briefly greeting the class, Ustaz Zaki wrote out a problem on the blackboard. "Who can solve this?" He asked, inviting the class to the challenge. The girls took a few moments to study the problem, and then a few became excited, raised their hands enthusiastically by snapping their fingers and shaking their wrists. He pointed to a girl in the middle of the room. She stood up and talked through the solution while Ustaz Zaki wrote her instructions on the board. When she finished, he asked the class whether or not it was correct. When they replied in the affirmative, he agreed and said to the girl, "Bravo. Sit down." He then asked, "Is there anyone who still doesn't understand this?' He waited a few moments, looking out to the room to give anyone a chance, and said, "No one? Okay, then we'll move on." When he turned his back to the class, he spoke in a higher, more exaggerated voice to keep their attention. He filled the blackboard with bold lines, arrows, and formulas, then turned to face the class and remarked, "Now remember, we learned this last week. This is how we apply it." He swung his arm back to the board and let the chalk crack down hard as he brought the lesson to its conclusion. The class was absolutely rapt. He combined a high level of showmanship with clear exposition of the lesson. When he stopped to scold someone for talking or otherwise not paying attention, he would do so only briefly to redirect her attention. He praised students for their good work, but not excessively, and he interspersed his lessons with jokes, but paused only briefly to allow for the laughter, before returning to more serious matters of the lesson.

During the last five minutes of class, he checked the day's homework. He paced slowly up and down the aisles, surveying the notebooks, a stick in his left hand. He stopped intermittently with comments. "A hundred congratulations, I see you finally got a suitable notebook," he said with playful sarcasm to a student who smiled. Then, grabbing the notebook of another girl he asked in a disapproving tone, "Is this the correct way to draw the lines? No, this is wrong!" and tossed the notebook back on her desk. To another he said, "Bravo, very well done." He then stopped at the place of girl whose notebook was closed, a sign that she had not done the homework. Without uttering a word, he waited as she stood up and extended out her hands. He struck each palm once with the stick and continued pacing down the row without saying a word. After checking the last notebook, he uttered a brief *al-salamu 'alaykum* and briskly left the room.

Ustaz Zaki's salary was on the low end of the scale at LE 80 per month because he did not have a university degree. After obtaining his preparatory school certificate, he had enrolled in a teacher training institute which allowed him to teach in primary school. He returned for further certification and was promoted to teach at the preparatory and secondary stages, a move that would give him access to the lucrative private lesson market. As a star teacher of an important subject, his services were in high demand and he even had a waiting list.

As was the norm at that time, he met four students together at a designated home, and each cluster made up a group (*magmu'a*; plural *magmu'at*). He charged LE 100 per group per month for two meetings of an hour per week (each student paid LE 25 per month), which was the going rate for a mathematics tutor in a government preparatory school. Ustaz Zaki understandably did not want to reveal how much income he earned through private lessons, and when asked responded, "Why do you want to know? Are you from the tax office?" However, one can do a simple calculation taking into consideration that he taught twelve groups that each paid LE 100 per month for a total sum of LE 1,200 per month. Put differently, he made fifteen times his government salary by giving private lessons.

His earnings were high, but he also worked extremely long days. He explained: "I leave the house at 6 a.m. and return at 8 p.m. exhausted. I eat dinner, watch a little TV, and collapse. I hardly spend any time with my wife." But he was grateful for the income because, as he relayed, "I have a family, a baby on the way, and am the eldest of five. I must help my father by contributing money to my brothers and sisters. So thank God the work is there." Among his monthly expenses were the LE 40 for his own sister's private lessons in Arabic and science. He also admitted to having a weakness for nice clothes, and said, "I must buy a new piece of clothing every month." He was easily the best dressed teacher in the school.

Classrooms of Corruption and Violence

Any school could contain teachers entirely unsuited to the profession, individuals who by any measure should be nowhere near children. Here we present the profiles of two teachers whose behavior represents the corruption of the profession and part of the reason for the erosion of trust between schools and families. The first example is of a teacher who neglected her duties and coerced students into taking private lessons with her through physical and psychological abuse, a practice that came to be called Forced Private Tutoring, or FPT (see Ille and Peacey 2019). The other example is of a teacher temperamentally unfit to teach who used excessive violence on students.

The senior English teacher, Abla Fatma, entered her class wearing a tight-fitting orange dress with leggings and flip flops *(shibshib)*. She faced the class with a frown, clutching a thick stick. The girls stood up and recited in unison in English, "Hello, Abla Fatma, it's nice to see you." Their teacher scowled back and pointed her stick accusingly at a girl who was whispering to her neighbor and shouted. "You, donkey! Shut up!" She then gave the command, "Sit down class."

Still frowning and tapping the stick against the palm of her left hand, she menacingly asked, "Who among you has not brought back your exam paper signed?" She scanned the silent class and repeated the question, but in a louder and more threatening tone. "I asked, who among you forgot to bring back her signed exam paper?" Two girls hesitantly stood up.

"Come here," the teacher ordered, motioning them to the front of the class. She raised the stick over her head and waited for the first girl to hold out her hands, palms upward, and cracked the stick down hard on each one before doing the same thing to the second girl. She then shouted, "Go sit down, you idiots!" They returned to their desks as they rubbed their welted hands together.

"Now," Abla Fatma continued turning her lip up in a disgusted way, "who else hasn't brought back the signed exam paper? You had better tell me now before I check myself, because believe me, you will really be sorry then!"

A frail girl, much shorter and thinner than the others, with unbrushed hair, sunken eyes, and shabby clothes, fearfully approached the teacher. She was trembling. The teacher lifted her stick and as she began her strike, the girl quickly drew back her hands. Abla Fatma gave her a vicious look and yelled, "Put your hands out!" The girl fearfully complied, and her teacher smashed the stick down on each palm. With tears streaming down her cheeks the girl, hunched over, returned to her desk.

After doling out these punishments, the teacher finally started the instruction and ordered the girls to open their workbooks to the day's lesson. She paced the room and stopped abruptly beside a student and said with feigned horror, "What's this?! You wrote in the answer to the work we're supposed to do in class. Don't you know that's work for the class-room, not for the house? Get up in front of the class, you disaster *(musiba)*. Get up there! Who else has prepared the classwork at home?" A girl quickly began erasing faint pencil marks in her book as the teacher screamed at her, "You animal! Get up here too!" And the next round of hitting began. Completing class work at home in advance of a lesson was a sign that the student was receiving support after hours with the subject, most likely with a private tutor.

The teacher then went to the board and wrote out some English vocab-ulary words and told the class to silently read the passage in their books for the duration of the class period, paying special attention to the new vocabu-lary. When someone broke the silence, she shouted abuses and smacked them with her stick. Certain students, however, could talk or breathe freely in the class with impunity: those who took private lessons with her. This teacher drew on a sadistic arsenal of hitting, insulting, and psychologically abusing students to bully them into taking private lessons with her. She also deliberately wasted time during the class period so that students would need private lessons to make up for missed instruction.

Abla Fatma was a university graduate from a Faculty of Education English department. She was thirty-five years old, unmarried, and had been at the school for ten years. In an interview I conducted with her just weeks after this classroom observation where she knew I had been pre-sent, she gushed about how she loved working in education and had always wanted to be a teacher. She said she considered herself a big sister to all the girls. When I asked about her views on hitting, she exclaimed in a surprised and feigned sweet voice, "Hitting?! Oh, no! I would never hit the students. This could make them hate the subject and hate me too. Oh no, hitting is certainly not the answer." To the question about whether or not she gave private lessons, she replied shaking her head and clicking her tongue, "No, no, no. Absolutely not. My salary is 131 pounds a month, thank God. I live a simple life with my mother and I must go home and stay with her after school."

Her fictitious statements echoed societal idealizations of the teacher as someone who was like a big sister, loved the profession, and would never harm the students. Abla Fatma was notorious among students and teachers for the high number of private lessons she gave, despite her evident weak-ness in her subject. A third-year student explained:

Abla Fatma is the worst teacher. She insults and hurts the girls who don't take lessons with her and treats the girls who take private lessons with her very nicely. She gives them higher grades in the monthly exams, even though their level is lower than other students. Anyway, they can't improve their English with her because she is too weak in the subject.

Abla Fatma managed to circumvent any punitive consequences from her supervisors. Her behavior seemed to fall within the range of "acceptable," although her supervisors would not have observed the worst of it, nor necessarily been aware of the extent to which she abused her position to coerce students into taking private lessons. The students were too fearful to even report her. The school absorbed and accommodated such teachers, even as most colleagues frowned upon such practices.

Another teacher notorious for his excessive use of violence was the art teacher Ustaz Husayn. Unmarried, in his mid-twenties, and a graduate from a vocational secondary school, Ustaz Husayn was not shy about expressing his contempt for the job and disdain for the students. One afternoon, on hearing the sound of the long buzz that signaled the start of the fourth period, Ustaz Husayn leaned back in his chair in the art room to check the schedule taped to the wall. He saw a large X by his name for the fourth and fifth periods indicating he had a double class. As his colleagues rushed across the courtyard to reach their classrooms, he stayed firmly in his chair and coolly said, "The girls need to take a little rest." He lifted a cup of tea to his lips and fired up a new cigarette. He finally pushed himself slowly from his chair and sluggishly walked across the room to the dusty tape recorder on a wall shelf and pressed play. On hearing the first measures of a much beloved Farid al-Atrash song, he exclaimed as if in ecstasy, "Ah Farid, sing to me." He closed his eyes and filled himself with more tea, smoke, and song. Half an hour passed before he stood up and said, "Well, I had better go see what the girls are doing." I was the only other person left in the room at that point and was scheduled to attend the class. He sighed and gathered a pile of uncorrected student booklets, picked up a broken stick, and turned to me asking, "Are you coming?"

As we walked down the corridor toward the classroom, we could hear shrieks and what seemed like mayhem coming from the unattended classroom. He gave out a long sigh before opening the door. Several girls gasped on seeing him and the entire class stood up at attention and said disjointedly, "*Al-salamu 'alaykum.*" I quickly slipped to the back of the room and squeezed into at a desk in the corner.

He ordered everyone to sit down and be quiet and then settled down behind the table at the front of the room. He took a red pen and began marking the booklets. The class remained relatively quiet for about thirty seconds before the students started chatting with each other. He looked up and shouted, "Eh, what's all the noise about?" He pointed to two girls sitting directly in front of him and commanded, "You two, stand here in front of the class." He held his forehead in his left hand and tried to continue his work but could not concentrate. He banged his fist on the table and yelled, veins bulging from his forehead, "Enough! Enough! Didn't I say to be quiet!" He stood up in an agitated state and started poking different students with his stick in a random way. "You! Get up there. I will punish you when I'm good and ready." He pointed at a girl in the second row and she nervously pleaded with him, "I swear Ustaz, I wasn't talking, believe me." He cut her off and yelled, "Listen to what I tell you!" Without warning he whacked her hard on her shoulder. She screamed, and her reaction provoked him further. He continued striking her arms as she begged him to stop. "Ustaz, stop, stop!" After about the fifth strike he said, "Okay, if you want to stay in your place, go ahead." He left her sobbing, her head buried in her arms.

By this time, eight victims stood at the front of the classroom awaiting their punishment, a few silently weeping after witnessing his violent outburst. He stood in front of each girl, the stick up in position, and each one held out her hands without protest. Each girl returned to her place sniffling. With nine girls crying, and the first girl sobbing loudly, he began the day's lesson.

He cleared his throat to get into teaching mode and said, "Today we're going to learn how to draw a leaf." He picked a dusty leaf from the windowsill and held it up. He tried to continue with a calm demeanor and steady tone, but he was still tense following the violent episode. He picked up the chalk and started explaining in a perfunctory way how to draw the outline and interior veins of the leaf, but then abruptly stopped and lashed out at the sobbing girl. By this time, other students had surrounded her in an effort to comfort and calm her by rubbing her back and stroking her hair.

The teacher stopped the lesson and lashed out at her, "Will you just stop it!" She cried out, "But Ustaz, it's really bad." She got up from her place and showed him her forearm, heavily swollen and discolored. "It's nothing," he flatly replied, though he was taken aback when he saw her arm close-up. She returned to her desk, her head down and her back shaking with sobs.

He finished the lesson and instructed everyone to take out a notebook and draw a leaf without talking. He returned to correcting the booklets. A few minutes later, a girl eagerly approached his desk to show him her drawing and asked if it was correct. "Yes, that's fine," he replied distractedly. Another girl appeared at his desk, and then another, until a crowd of some ten girls were shoving their sketchbooks at him saying, "Look at mine, look at mine!" He slammed his stick on his desk and shouted, "Enough! Go back to your seats!"

The class continued in this disorderly way through the end of the period. He was clearly shaken by his own violent outburst, and as we walked across the courtyard back to the art room he said dejectedly,

> I want to explain something to you. I'm tired, really tired. I work here for 60 pounds a month. Sixty pounds. I can't give private lessons because I'm an art teacher. With my salary I can't even afford clothes or food for the month. So, what do I do? I beat the girls. But it's no use. They still don't behave. So, I beat them more. In the end, I'm not happy, and they're not happy either.

He stopped walking and held out his hands to show me how they were rough and calloused.

> Look at these hands. Are these the hands of an artist? No, they're the hands of a worker. In order to eat I work in the afternoons in a factory doing any odd job, lifting, carrying, anything at all. And I'm supposed to be a teacher. A teacher! Huh! I'm just fed up.

Three weeks later Ustaz Husayn beat a girl in the same class to the point of breaking her arm. The following day, the girl's father stormed into the school in a fury yelling, "Where is he? I'll beat him myself and show him what it's like." Ustaz Husayn was nowhere to be found. He had been absent for three days following the incident. The father complained to the principal and demanded he be punished. The next thing we all heard was that Ustaz Husayn was transferred to a boys' school.

The Demise of the Teacher?

Public opinion had been turning against corporal punishment, and in 1990 the practice was banned by administrative order. However, as in most matters, it would take time for the practice to catch up with the law. From this point on, parents had the right to file a police report against teachers for abusive behavior. The court reviewed cases and passed sentences for offenders, ranging from prison terms, stripping teachers of their credentials, or requiring the Ministry of Education to pay compensation to victims' families. In a famous case in 1990, a boy's family sued the Ministry of Education after a teacher beat their son in the face with a stick, causing him to lose his left eye. The court ruled for compensation to be paid to the family.

If a parent filed a complaint directly to the school but did not involve the police, it fell on the principal to determine the appropriate punishment. In such cases, the Legal Affairs Department at the district level would get involved. Due to the labor laws, it was extremely difficult to terminate a teacher's government contract. The principal had the authority to dock the offender's pay, withhold benefits, delay a promotion, or recommend a transfer to another school. The most effective way of purging a teacher from the system was to transfer him to a faraway or remote area, which he would likely refuse because it would involve entirely uprooting his life. These transfers were in essence a way of forcing corrupt and violent teachers out of the profession.

The reality was that the low salaries combined with difficult working conditions, the challenges of reaching a work/life balance, and other factors, gave rise to a host of pressures, abuses, and distortions in the system. These problems and challenges were only exacerbated by the ubiquity of private lessons, a topic we will turn to in chapter 5.

5

Grade Fever

Summary: This chapter lays out the relationship between high-stakes testing on the one hand, and pedagogic styles, social relations within the school, and the enormous shadow education system known as private lessons *(durus khususiya)* on the other. It also discusses the elaborate rituals around testing and the immense organization needed to prepare for, administer, and grade examinations. Finally, it reviews how population pressures and the need to pass students through the system leads to political decisions, as opposed to performance indicators, to promote students from one level to the next.

Magmu' Mania/Grade Fever

Each year when the examination season approaches, families throughout Egypt exhibit a collective state of anxiety. They talk incessantly about the high-stakes tests and their hopes that their child receives a high grade, or *magmu'*, for the year. The word *magmu'* is derived from the Arabic *jama'a* which means "to add up or combine." Parents and their students begin to obsess about the *magmu'* in primary school, but it becomes more intense at the preparatory stage when families invest more in private lessons, in the hopes that their child or children will perform well enough to enter the university track. During the secondary stage, in the lead-up to the university entrance examination, the Thanawiya 'Amma, a veritable *magmu'* mania overtakes society. The *magmu'* determines the faculty that the student will join in university, and the faculty is tied up with profession, status, and income; in short, it is associated with future livelihoods and life chances for success. Many dreams of becoming a doctor or engineer are shattered by as little as a few points, and sometimes even a fraction of a point in the *magmu'*. One student summed up its overpowering weight when she said, "We are so afraid of the *magmu'*. It is our future. It is everything!"

Table 2. Distribution of the overall grade at the preparatory stage, 1990

Subject	Points
Arabic language	60
Social studies	60
Mathematics	60
Foreign language (English or French)	40
Science and health	40
Art	20
TOTAL	280

In 1990–91, only 30 percent of preparatory graduates were admitted to university-track secondary schools, which meant that the stakes were extremely high. Those who did not reach the cutoff grade had the option of moving to a lower status technical-track high school.

In each year of the preparatory stage, the *magmu'* consisted of 280 points, distributed as shown in table 2. Not all subjects were included in the *magmu'*. Religion, music, home economics, physical education, and other extracurricular offerings at boys' schools such as carpentry and agriculture, were graded on a pass/fail basis. The teachers of these subjects were not in demand for private lessons, with the possible exception of religion, for which families often brought a shaykh or religion teacher home to train their child to memorize the Qur'an.

The education system's reliance on high-stakes testing opened the way for what has been called the "shadow education system."[1] A vast system of regulated and unregulated lessons permeated all corners of Egyptian education. In an attempt to keep education equitable, schools offered low-cost after-school group lessons called "*magmu'at*" for two hours per week per subject. This practice dated back to 1952, and was revived by the education Law No. 49 of 1986 (see National Center for Educational Research 1991). Teachers had the option of teaching two after-school group lessons per term and were paid according to the number of enrolled students. The group could not exceed twelve students and most teachers would not agree to teach a group under eight students. These extra lessons were essentially a system of overtime pay. The student paid a fixed fee of LE 6 per month per subject and the sum was divided as follows: 80 percent to the teacher; 15 percent to the school; and 5 percent to the education governorate in which the school was located. Teachers earned LE 4.80 per head, and with a maximum of twenty-four students in two group lessons per term, a teacher could earn an additional LE 115 each month. Although modest in relation to what private teachers could earn in the unregulated market, the option was still attractive for some.

Female teachers in particular liked the convenience of in-school group lessons, since the alternative would be to travel from house to house, or set up their own homes for private lessons. An unmarried female science teacher, who lived with her parents, explained her situation:

> As a girl, I can't just go to anybody's house and my father doesn't want me to bring students into our house. He says that when he's at home he wants to relax and be comfortable without students coming and going. He tells me that when I have my own home, I can do what I want.

She used the extra money from the group lessons to join a savings cooperative.

Of the nineteen teachers who gave group lessons at school, fourteen were female. Four of the five male teachers had fairly lucrative private lesson gigs outside the school, and their earnings from the in-school group lessons were paltry in comparison. They explained that they gave the after-school lessons as a kind of social service to support the students from lower incomes. However, as in many instances, you get what you pay for. Students often complained that the class sizes of twelve for group lessons were too large, and that some of the teachers were just there for the extra income. For students with the means, the outside private lessons were the far more desirable option.

Unregulated Private Lessons

"Private lessons," explained the principal, "now this is a big problem. But if God ordains a teacher a certain amount of money from private lessons, it will come. But he must first do his work as a class teacher in a way that satisfies God."

Every year the Ministry of Education sent a memorandum to all schools reminding them that private lessons were forbidden by law. Every year the number of students who took private lessons continued to rise exponentially. According to an independent study of a sample of second-year preparatory school students in 1991–92, 75 percent took private lessons of some sort, whether the after-school group lessons or the unregulated external private lessons.[2] The potential income from private lessons attracted many people to the teaching profession. As a mathematics teacher stated very clearly, "It's only by giving private lessons that I can stand this profession. Without them I would have quit this job and looked for something else to do."

Private lessons were officially banned for two key reasons. First, they placed financial burdens on Egyptians who had the constitutional right to a "free education." A study from this time found that urban households spent 20 percent of their expenditures on private lessons per child at the primary stage. The proportion would have gone up for every successive stage. Even struggling and impoverished families put aside money for private lessons. For instance, Nawal, a third-year preparatory school student, lived with her widowed mother and five siblings in a one-room rooftop dwelling. Her mother's life had been hard, but she hoped for better days for her daughter. Nawal worked in a pastry shop after school for LE 50 per month and contributed her earnings to a family pool. With the approval of her mother, she set aside LE 10 each month for her own private lessons. Her mother encouraged her to study hard to get into a secondary school, but she was skeptical that Nawal would make it.

> I don't think she'll finish her education. I want her to finish university, but I don't think we'll have enough money for it, considering all the money it will take for private lessons to reach that stage and get a high enough *magmu'*. But God is merciful and will help us.

The second reason for the ban on private lessons was because they opened the floodgates of corruption. Private lessons generated enormous profits and distorted the teaching profession in fundamental ways. It was common to hear parents and pundits adopt a language from organized crime to describe what was happening with private lessons. The term "private lesson mafias" was an especially common phrase (see chapter 9).

Apart from corrupting the bond between teachers, students, and their families, private lessons also threw teachers into a ring of competition. While teachers generally behaved congenially with each other, just under the surface they engaged in all kinds of backhanded behavior stemming from competition. For instance, after greeting his colleague in a perfectly friendly manner one morning, a mathematics teacher turned to me and whispered, "He's trying to steal my students." He explained:

> Last week when I was absent he took over my class. He asked a few girls to solve problems at the board. Each time he would make a comment like, "Who taught you that absolutely stupid way of solving this problem? That is the most idiotic logic I have ever seen." He knew very well I was their teacher. The truth is, I have more private students than him and he wants to get some of my students by tricking the girls into thinking I'm not a good teacher. But they understand these tricks.

In another instance, a French teacher became furious when she discovered two students in her class were taking private lessons with a teacher from another school. She took revenge by harassing and beating them in class. Still other teachers deliberately wasted class time or left out essential parts of the curriculum in an attempt to force students into making up lost material in private lessons. Even teachers who initially rejected these practices eventually succumbed to them. A recent graduate from the Department of Social Studies of an education faculty confessed:

> The problem with being a teacher is that the government doesn't care to provide us with a decent living. We can't cover our basic needs. We're under a lot of pressure and many of us have psychological problems. We don't want to live in a dishonest way, but find we have no choice. We end up doing some things in order to survive. We force our students to take private lessons with us.

The shadow education system exists and thrives in an environment where examinations are sacrosanct. Private tutors act as high priests and priestesses who prepare students to enter the temples of examination rooms, where futures and life chances are determined.

With a Little Help from Your Friends

The school year is punctuated by examinations. Though all of them carry weight, not all examinations are equal. In the course of the academic year, the school administered six monthly examinations graded by the class teacher, and two ministry mid-year and end-of-year examinations. The latter two accounted for 80 percent of the overall grade, whereas the six monthly examinations, combined with marks for in-class work, attendance, and discipline, covered the remaining 20 percent. Students did not depend merely on examination preparation to excel, but also on support from each other. They sometimes devised elaborate cheating schemes, and other times simply asked a classmate for help during the examination.

The day before the end-of-month examination for November, a second-year student nervously collected her books to bring home for a long evening of study. "I'm so worried," she explained, "This year isn't like last year when we could rely on our classmates to help us during the exam. Not at all! With our new principal, no one will dare look to their neighbor for any help. I really have to study hard." On the morning of the examination, the *tabur* was brief. Students rushed off to their classrooms to settle in for the first examination, which began at 8 a.m. In a first-year classroom, dimly lit and at full capacity, girls sat nervously in anticipation of their science test. Two Arabic teachers were assigned to proctor the examination, one dressed entirely in pink pastel, from her headscarf to her long skirt, the other wearing bright yellow. Their clothes were a splash of color in the drab green and beige room.

Both teachers warned the class sternly against cheating. The teacher in pink was clearly in charge. She instructed everyone to take out a blank piece of paper from their notebooks. At that point, the senior science teacher passed by the room, curtly greeted the teachers, handed them a photocopied pile of examinations, and dashed off to the next classroom. Facing the class clutching the examinations, the teacher in pink commanded, "Write your name and class on the tests as soon as you receive them. Is that understood?! Your name and class." She then proceeded to hand out the examination papers while warning them to keep their eyes on their own papers.

The students, packed two to three to a desk, struggled to fit their pencils, papers and scrap paper on their communal desk trays. They wiggled and contorted their arms until they landed on a position that would allow them to write. Some of them inevitably glanced sideways. Ms. Yellow took a seat at the front of the class while Ms. Pink paced the aisles holding a thick stick. The two teachers had a coordinated system of communication. At one point, Ms. Yellow called over her colleague and whispered in her ear. Ms. Pink proceeded down an aisle and stopped before a girl and asked her colleague, "This one?" When she got the affirmative, Ms. Pink lingered in front of the girl with a disgusted expression. The girl froze and stared down at her paper. Ms. Pink give her a hard slap on the back and warned her, "Look in front of you!"

For the first half hour, Ms. Pink paced the room vigilantly, but gradually became visibly tired. She walked to the front of the class and leaned against the door, since there was no extra chair for her. From my view from the back of the room, I could see the students keeping careful watch over the teachers. When they found an opportunity, they quickly signaled to a classmate for help, or looked over another's shoulder. Even with two proctors, there was constant surreptitious communication between the students.

One student broke the silence when she stood up and asked, "Excuse me, Abla, but this question on carbon . . ." The teacher in pink cut her off sharply, "I'm an Arabic teacher. I don't have the slightest idea about science." Ten minutes later, another student stood up to ask for some guidance and the teacher brushed it off saying sarcastically, "You are free to do whatever you want with it." She then pointed the stick at someone and shouted, "If you talk again, I'll beat you! Is that clear?!"

Meanwhile, the principal was making her rounds to all the classes. When she charged into the classroom for a surprise inspection, the girls let out a collective gasp and the teachers jumped to attention. The principal stood erect, her hands clasped behind her back, and announced in well enunciated classical Arabic, "No one should ask any questions. Everything on the paper is very clear. You must answer all questions on your own and not with anyone else's help. Is this understood?!" When she finished her message, she paced the length of the classroom as the students nervously continued to write.

Not all proctors were so vigilant. Some teachers sat in the front of the room disinterested as students spoke freely to one another or left the room for long periods of time. Some teachers openly helped students with the answers, even by writing out answers on the board. Other teachers shouted at the students and beat them for the slightest infraction. Whatever the proctor's style, the monthly examinations were a far looser affair than the high-stakes Ministry of Education equivalents.

Administering High-Stakes Examinations

The ministry's mid-year and end-of-year examinations required many days of preparation. The principal appointed members to two special committees that oversaw all logistics and assured the integrity of the examination and grading process: the Organizing Committee, or *Lagna*, and the Discipline and Control Committee that went by the name of *Control*. These committees worked in close coordination. The *Lagna* compiled the examination schedule, whereas the *Control* checked the information and made large color-coded posters with all the key information including the class, subject, date and time of the examination, and the room number, and hung them in designated areas around the school.

The designated headquarters of the *Lagna* was the art room, which became off-limits for all other forms of work. When three art teachers gathered in a corner of the room during *Lagna* preparations, the principal drove them out shouting, "What do you think you are doing in here? Get out right now! I don't want to see another teacher in the *Lagna* again!" The room contained a number of long wooden tables which held voluminous ledgers, filled with information about room assignments and scheduling.

The *Control*'s room was even more secured. It had a padlock and sign on the door that read, "Forbidden to Enter." The *Control* oversaw the most sensitive part of the examination process, namely the handling of examination papers and grading. The team assigned a code number to each student and made a small individualized identity card for them to carry around during the examination, so that they could identify their correct seat. All examinations were blind-graded and only the *Control* had access to the key to the student's real identity. This elaborate system was designed to mitigate against any cheating and tampering with the grades, and was a sign of the lack of trust between the ministry and the teachers. Only the school principal and the members of the *Control* had access to the enormous ledger—roughly two feet in length and one foot in width—where they recorded grades from the entire year's examinations and calculated the student's *magmu'*.

Classes essentially ceased to function eight days prior to the ministry examinations. Although students were officially supposed to attend school, few actually turned up, and teachers stopped reporting absences. On the day prior to the examination, students were forbidden from entering the school. Unlike the monthly versions, only one student was allowed per desk during these ministry examinations, and the *Lagna* designed a system to spread out the students throughout the school, utilizing all available spaces including hallways, entrance areas, and activity rooms. They secured all examination areas with barriers so that no one could plant any cheat sheets. A special scrubbing committee was charged with cleaning and sanding down all desks, since the wooden desktops were full of engravings, doodles, and stickers, and could potentially have cheat notes on them.

4. Ustaz Ali of the *Control* Committee recording examination grades, Falaki School, Cairo. 1991. (Photograph by Linda Herrera.)

On the first morning of the end-of-year examinations, the mood was somber and tense. The *tabur* was scaled down to its bare essentials: the Qur'anic recitation, national anthem, and an announcement about the examinations. A science teacher stood at the microphone and read out each room number and the names of students who would be in that room. The girls marched off to their examination rooms, while the principal stood guard at the entrance to take note of any latecomers. A teacher rushed through the gate at 8:55 a.m., just five minutes before the 9 a.m. starting time, and the principal scolded her with a rough, "Where have you been?! Get to your room immediately!" The teacher apologized and ran off to her destination.

Meanwhile in the *Control* room, committee members were busy counting out examination papers and placing them in large manila envelopes. A representative from the Ministry of Education delivered the papers in the morning to minimize any chance of their being leaked. The *Control* sealed each envelope with an official ink stamp to reduce the possibility of any tampering with their contents on their way to the classrooms. Only first teachers were allowed to pick up and later deliver the completed examination booklets to the *Control* room.

On receiving the completed examinations, the *Control* worked in utmost secrecy behind locked doors and under pressure. An assembly line of three *Control* members handled each booklet. The first one pulled off a perforated paper at the bottom of the examination sheet that contained the student's name and code number. The second person, using a rubber stamp with rotating numbers of the sort used in libraries to stamp return dates in books, imprinted the examination paper with a numerical code and stamped that same number on every sheet so that it could be matched to its author after the booklet was corrected. The third person checked that the stamp on the perforated paper corresponded to the number on the examination paper.

Two members of the *Control* inspected each examination booklet page by page, front and back, for any signs of cheating or surreptitious communication with the class teacher. They searched for unusual symbols, code words, torn pages, or other idiosyncrasies. For instance, it was common for students to write at the top of the page, "In the name of God, the most beneficent and merciful." If this phrase appeared at the bottom of the page, for instance, it became suspect. This might be taken as a code for a teacher to recognize the student's identity and adjust her grade. When possible, the *Control* inspectors would erase anything resembling an identifying mark, but when this was not possible because, for instance, of ink markings, a tear on the page, or imprints of a name as the result of a student pressing especially hard with the pencil, they were put in a special pile. Only senior teachers were allowed to correct these suspicious booklets.

On the eighth and final day of examinations, teachers came to the school to do the grading. They arrived at noon, and were not allowed to leave the school grounds until they completed the entire batch of examinations. Some of them remained at the school until 9 p.m., which was especially taxing for those with families. The first teacher placed all graded booklets back in an envelope and delivered them to the *Control*, where each coded examination paper was matched back to the student's name.

The work of the *Control* resumed by sorting all the examinations by year and in alphabetical order by student. A row of teachers, each one holding the examinations of their subject, waited for each student's name to be called, starting with A (*alif*). The first name was "Abir Abd al-Mustafa." If the sorting had been done accurately, all her examination booklets would be at the top of everyone's pile. Each subject teacher would then read the grade: "Science, 12.7," "Arabic, 10.3," and so on. Invariably, some papers were out of order, which meant that everyone waited until the teacher located the correct booklet. There was some margin of error allowed, since a number of girls had similar if not identical names. The chair of the *Control* alone was responsible for recording the grade in the massive ledger which contained the names of every student.

The Politics of Passing

The chair of the *Control* tabulated the final results and duly reported the dismal outcome to the principal: 70 percent of first year students had failed both the final examination and the year. The school administration had expected a high fail rate after receiving the new cohort of students in the fall. A little under 25 percent of incoming students (109 out of 429) had arrived functionally illiterate. They had been passed up the ladder from primary school despite their lack of preparedness. The school sorted the weakest students—as measured by their results in the final year of primary school—into remedial classrooms known as the "French classes." These students took French as opposed to English as their second language, because, for some reason, French was considered less demanding. Roughly two out of six classes per year were designated as French classes. The energy and the mood in these rooms differed considerably from the mainstream classes. Girls were less responsive, slower overall, and often antisocial. They likely suffered from a combination of malnourishment, abuse, and cognitive and physical challenges. Teachers had neither the tools, time, nor know-how to deal with students with special needs. It was no surprise that this group did not have the wherewithal to manage the examinations and their school-work. However, 45 percent of students in the mainstream classes also failed the year, which pointed to the much larger systemic problem of a vastly underperforming education system.

In principle, any student who failed their examinations had the opportunity to retake them in August. In the previous year, roughly 50 percent of students who retook their examinations still did not pass. The high failure rates caused serious educational management problems. On receiving the report of the 70 percent failure rate at the school, the ministry official responsible at the district level insisted that students be promoted to the next year regardless, to make room for the incoming students who had already been assigned to the school. He instructed the principal to appoint a special committee of senior teachers to adjust grades so that students would be bumped up from a failing grade to a passing grade. In other words, he asked the principal to form a committee to falsify the grades.

The principal and her team of dedicated teachers had exerted tremendous effort and care to ensure a fair examination process. They had worked long hours and done their best to abide by the rules and proper procedures. Now, at this final stage, they were being told to doctor the books. The principal protested, and vigorously. She wanted to find a solution that would actually address the problem. She proposed to organize rigorous remedial courses and provide students with the requisite support to pass the examinations on their own merits. She spent a week negotiating with the local education office, but her efforts were in vain and she was outranked by the senior ranking official. Although he was sympathetic to her arguments, he too was under pressure from his superior at the ministry who was adamant that all first-year preparatory students be promoted to second year to make space for the larger incoming class. In the end, the principal had little choice and reluctantly appointed the committee to change the grades.

The process of preparing for, administering, and grading examinations took a heavy toll on the staff. During the eight-day period, members of the examination committees in particular had gone above and beyond the call for service. They arrived at 8 a.m. and sometimes stayed as late as 10 or 11 p.m. The last three days were especially exhausting and demanding. This select group of the brightest and most diligent teachers had started the examination period with a sense of purpose, commitment to high standards, and integrity. The endless work of checking and rechecking papers, stapling, detaching, sealing, stamping, and recording was onerous. As a result, when they had to witness their hard work being reversed with the falsification of grades, they became utterly demoralized.

This same group of teachers, who normally came to school impeccably dressed and immaculately groomed, now arrived unshaven and disheveled, with crinkled and stained clothing. Teachers who otherwise interacted with their colleagues with warmth and courtesy were short tempered and snapped at each other. But this stage of acrimony was short lived. When teachers from the committees returned after a few days' break, to close up and return the school to its original order, relations were restored. The teachers shook hands and kissed each others' cheeks (women with women and men with men), patted each other on the backs, joked about the ordeal of the past week, and, yes, commiserated about the results.

The chair of the *Control* who oversaw the initial recording and then rerecording of grades visited the principal to report the final results. The school's pass rate, after tampering with the results, was over 99 percent. Abla Adalat could not contain her frustration and sadness. She cried: tears literally flowed down her cheeks. She cried for the many girls who would never receive the support they needed to lift them out of a state of functional illiteracy. She cried at her own, albeit forced, complicity in the bureaucratic farce of setting up a system to ensure a rigorous and honest process, only to then fabricate examination results. Her dreams of transforming the school environment, of changing the lives of the more than a thousand girls under her watch, of molding them into great women and citizens, were thwarted at so many junctures. Even with all her energy, power, determination, leadership, and resourcefulness, she could not find a pathway to effectively work within the system.

The system was overburdened, sagging under the weight of population stress, bureaucratic inertia, and a real lack of vision for how to raise the level of the vulnerable students. Education had become professionalized and technocratic, a matter of managerial procedures and obsessed with numbers: test scores, pass rates, enrollment rates, numbers of buildings and classrooms, and ratios. In the process of reaching quantitative indicators, the system had lost sight of education, of nurturing its young citizens, of building an educated society that addressed the actual needs, the diversity, and the range of talents of its young citizens. After returning to Egypt with the determination to raise the level of education, Abla Adalat felt defeated. All the goodwill and effort in the world was not enough in the end to sustain her. The system had broken her. By the end of the year, she started making plans for early retirement.

The wheels of schooling would keep turning. The summer would come and go. A new batch of students would arrive. Teachers would prepare their lesson plans, and the classrooms, hallways, and stairwells would be brimming with new friendships, gossip, exhaustion, dreams, struggles, and all the hopes and fears familiar to adolescent girls. The pundits would continue to argue and debate about how to "fix" the problems of education: high density in classrooms, run-down facilities, the scourge of private lessons, untrained teachers, unprepared students, corruption, violence in schools, extremism in schools, a packed curriculum, cheating, and so many other issues that would remain staples of public discourse around the education system.

This school was one of millions around the world, and yet it contained within its walls something universal. I arrived at the school that first day nervous, a stranger, a student researcher with little experience and many questions. Everything initially seemed so unfamiliar and impenetrable. But in the ensuing months, with the patient, thoughtful, and sometimes tough guidance of a group of energetic educators, and with the warmth, openness, and perceptiveness of the students, I ended up being the one getting the education. My time at Falaki School would prove to be formative in ways I could not possibly understand at the time. I learned the importance of humility in the endeavor to learn and make sense of the world. I grew to understand our debts and responsibilities to those who open their lives, struggles, and worlds to us. And so, I end this ethnographic account of a school, part of the world community of schools that brought me back countless times to my own parochial school in San Francisco, six thousand miles and many years away, with gratitude to the teachers of the past, teachers striving in the present, and teachers of the future.

Part Two
Political Islam and Education

6

The Islamist Wave and Education Markets

Summary: 1990s Egypt was a decade of intensified conflict between the state and Islamist groups. Ideological and political battles extended deep into the school system, which caused the new minister of education to reorient education as an urgent matter of national security that required vigilant oversight and intervention. This chapter examines the Islamist current in education going back to the Muslim Brotherhood's founding in 1928. It shows how contests over the hearts and minds of the country's children had been underway for decades but intensified in the 1990s as economic liberalization policies opened the way for more privatization in the education sector and allowed for the entrance of new players.

The National Security Minister

In 1990, the sitting Minister of Education Dr. Ahmad Fathi Sorour (1986–1990) was abruptly transferred into the role of Speaker of Parliament, the second-highest-ranking office in Egypt. He was urgently needed to replace the former Speaker Rif'at al-Mahgub, who was slain in Cairo on October 12 at the hands of Islamist militants. This was the highest-profile political assassination since October 6, 1981, when President Anwar Sadat was gunned down by Islamist militants during a military parade. President Mubarak duly appointed Dr. Husayn Kamal Baha' al-Din as the new minister of education. He entered the cabinet in the midst of national and regional unrest, with active conflicts in Afghanistan, Iraq and Kuwait, Palestine, and other countries. It was also the start of the post–Cold War period, which brought about realignments in the global economic order. The new minister would oversee major sector changes toward the internationalization of the curriculum, the introduction of new technologies, and general policy changes in the direction of educational privatization and liberalization.[1] Minister Baha' al-Din's greatest legacy, however, was arguably in how he managed the education sector during a time of heightened conflict with Islamist militancy.

Early in his tenure, Baha' al-Din raised the alarm that schools and universities had been slipping dangerously out of the state's control and into the hands of extremists. He argued that Islamist groups and individuals had been infiltrating schools to indoctrinate children and youth and recruit them into their movements. The state had to do everything in its power to take back schools, which were becoming, in his words, "hatcheries of terrorism." The minister and President Mubarak coordinated a message about education. They made the case that education should no longer be viewed as part of the service sector like healthcare, but as an integral component of the country's national security apparatus, akin to the military. Yet, at the same time, they argued, education should be viewed as a vital component of the economic ecosystem. In 1997, Baha' al-Din wrote:

> We should be very firm in confronting this problem because we are living in a developing country which needs numerous investments to assist with building a stable environment for business ventures. . . . The first aspect of a new educational policy is that education is an issue of national security. . . . The use of the term "national security" was for a long time equivalent to military power, the shield that protects the nation from all the external threats. This term changed in the period after World War One and before the end of the Cold War, when experts, politicians, and high-ranking military officers realized that national security is broader than mere military power. . . . Education, rather than military might, has become the lever for international competition.[2]

The minister was sending a clear message that extremism and terrorism were not only an ideological threat to children's development and safety but were fundamentally bad for business. Egypt adopted the new post–Cold War orthodoxy of neoliberalism, in which the education sector was subsumed under the knowledge economy. Sociologists Powell and Snellman define the knowledge economy as

> production and services based on knowledge-intensive activities that contribute to an accelerated pace of technological and scientific

advance as well as equally rapid obsolescence. The key components of a knowledge economy include a greater reliance on intellectual capabilities than on physical inputs or natural resources. (Powell and Snellman 2004, 201)

In keeping with the prevailing discourse of the time that economic liberalization went hand in hand with political liberalization, Baha' al-Din further elaborated that Egypt was committed to "spreading American values" and sailing with the "winds of democracy, freedom and human rights" (Baha' al-Din 1997, 58).[3] The trouble was that the political environment in Egypt was far from liberal and conflicts inside the country were escalating, which led to a deeper reach of the state's security apparatus.

1992 would go down as Egypt's most violent year since Sadat's assassination. The underground Islamist group al-Jama'a al-Islamiya (commonly shortened to "al-Jama'a")—in its quest to destabilize the Mubarak government and establish an Islamic state—attacked tourists, assassinated the "secular" writer Farag Foda, killed police and security officers, and in the first sectarian massacre in about ninety years, gunned down thirteen Christians in a village in Upper Egypt (Human Rights Watch 1993). The government came down hard with arrests and new "antiterrorism legislation" which gave security forces even broader powers than they had under the Emergency Law. On the education front, more information was coming out that Islamist movements and actors were embedded in schools and universities. The new minister was expected to respond to this crisis, and fast.

Many voices from the press and policy circles questioned the suitability of Dr. Baha' al-Din—a medical doctor who specialized in pediatrics—for the office of education minister, especially in this time of crisis. His two previous positions had been chairman of the Department of Children's Medicine (1988–91) and director of the New Children's University Hospital in Cairo (1991). However, looking further back into his past, Baha' al-Din had proved himself as a loyalist over successive regimes, starting with that of President Gamal Abd al-Nasser (1956–1970). As a student, Baha' al-Din had joined the Youth Organization (Munazzamat al-Shabab) established during the Nasser era, and was promoted to its secretary general in 1965. Indeed his predecessor, Fathi Sorour, had held the same position. In 1968, Baha' al-Din became secretary general of the Department of Professionals in the Socialist Union and had a reputation as an ideological watchdog, someone who ensured that people held the party line. He would go on to become the longest serving minister of education in Egypt's history, holding the post for thirteen years, from 1991 to 2004.

Even though Baha' al-Din spoke about national security as something new in the education sector, the Ministry of Interior had in fact been treating education as a part of the security apparatus for decades. Since the Nasser era, there had been conflicts between the state and opposition movements—particularly leftists and Islamists—who were active in schools and universities. The movement with the deepest presence in the Egyptian education system had been the Muslim Brotherhood (al-Ikhwan al-Muslimun).

The Brotherhood had tactically extended its reach into schools, kindergartens, education colleges, universities, after-school study centers, scout groups, youth camps, and mass media, all as a way to reach children, youth, and their families. By some estimates, over a fifth of their members worked as teachers in Egyptian schools (Youssef 2012, 176, 187). While it is far beyond the scope of this chapter to review the Brotherhood's long and tumultuous history with the Egyptian state and its institutions, a brief overview through the lens of education is merited. The Brotherhood's approach to education provides important context for understanding the heightened securitization of Egyptian education from the 1990s into the 2000s.

Education and the Muslim Brothers

> The Brotherhood is not a mere political force that seeks power; it is an identity-maker that aims to reshape societal norms and individualities as Islamic (Al-Anani 2016, 7).

The schoolteacher Hassan al-Banna (1906–1949) founded the Society of the Muslim Brotherhood (Jam'iyyat al-Ikhwan al-Muslimin) in Ismailiya in 1928. By day, al-Banna worked for the Ministry of Education as a teacher of Arabic and calligraphy at a government boys' primary school. By night, he gave lessons to students' parents and held discussions with workers, merchants, students, and others in coffee shops, cultivating his position as a local leader and community organizer. Al-Banna was supposedly inspired to found a society after a meeting with six disgruntled workers from the British-occupied Suez Canal Zone who labored under harsh conditions in an unjust *franji* (foreign/non-Muslim) environment. Although al-Banna had previously participated in Sufi groups, he did not want to set up a Sufi

5. Hassan al-Banna (seated, far right) at Taha Hussein School, Ismailiya. Circa 1930. (Photograph courtesy of the al-Aswad family).

order *(tariqa)*. He opted for a more contemporary structure that could unify Muslims through commerce, education, charitable services, and mass communication.

Prior to taking up his teaching post in Ismailiya, al-Banna was a student at Dar al-'Ulum. Established in 1873, it was the first modern teacher training institute in Egypt. Its purpose was to prepare teachers, many of whom came from al-Azhar, for the new national primary schools (see Aroian 1979). Al-Banna arrived in Cairo at the age of sixteen from the Nile Delta province of al-Beheira with the "eyes of a religious villager" (quoted in Mitchell 1993, 4). The atmosphere in Cairo, just four years after the end of World War One in 1918, three years after the 1919 Revolution in Egypt, and during the collapse of the Ottoman Empire in 1922, was electric and highly politicized. He vigorously condemned Kemal Atatürk's abolishing of the Ottoman Caliphate in 1924, and took up the cause of the reinstatement of the caliphate for the remainder of his life. Al-Banna formed strong opinions about the changing political and social order, and the place of education in it.[4]

As he advanced in his teacher training studies, al-Banna became increasingly weary of the spread of the new modernized schools, which were modeled to a large extent on educational institutions from Western and predominantly Christian Europe. He denounced these schools as being infused with "missionary and atheistic currents." Nonetheless, he would serve as a teacher in those very schools for several years. When he graduated from Dar al-'Ulum at the age of twenty-one, al-Banna wrote an essay that foreshadowed core aspects of the Brotherhood's ideology. He stated: "I believe . . . that my people . . . under the impact of western civilization . . . materialist philosophy, and *franji* [foreign] traditions, have departed from the goals of their faith . . . [R]ather than faith there is apostasy" (Mitchell 1993, 6). He expressed especial concern with young people who were straying from "the Islamic cause" (Mitchell 1993, 5). Through his work in the society and in schools, al-Banna strove to set youth onto what he viewed as the correct path and into the Brotherhood's fold.

The Brotherhood worked determinedly on two fronts when it came to reaching and exerting influence over Muslim children and youth. First, it took note of the new technologies of soft power, the tools of hegemony made possible by mass media and mass education, and created its own versions. The Brotherhood started its own media enterprise, initially by publishing books and magazines. It also opened its own schools, youth clubs, and scouts, all of which were modeled on already existing foreign or government models. The Brotherhood adapted these institutions to their goals, ideology, and internal structure. For example, the Rovers (al-Jawwala), was the Brotherhood's version of the Egyptian Boy Scouts. The Rovers resembled the Boy Scouts in appearance, with similar uniforms, youth camps, and sporting activities. However, in the 1940s, observers and critics remarked that the Rovers went beyond an organization for children's extracurricular sports and recreation. It was more akin to a paramilitary organization, and shared features found in other militant opposition groups (Mitchell 1993, 202).

Second, Brotherhood members infiltrated and exerted influence in already established organizations and institutions such as government schools, universities, and the Egyptian scouts.[5] For example, while establishing its own network of schools, the Brotherhood simultaneously instructed their male and female youth who were students in national schools to create an "Islamic atmosphere" (Mitchell 1993, 9, 172). Whereas al-Banna initially envisioned directing youthful Brotherhood members to the Rovers, which ran parallel to the national scout movement, he later saw the benefits of Brothers participating in and infiltrating the national scouting organization directly. In this way, they could exert influence inside the group and reach potential new recruits (Mitchell 1993, 202). The Brotherhood actively worked to populate the scouts with its members and take up leadership positions. Using the same strategy and tactics, the Brothers infiltrated trade unions and the armed forces (Ayubi et al. 1995), schools and universities (Herrera 2006a). This pattern of working on two fronts, establishing its own institutions and penetrating established networks and organizations, would become trademarks of the Society of the Muslim Brotherhood.

In less than two decades, the Brotherhood established itself as a force in Egyptian society. In 1948 it had some 200,000 branches throughout Egypt and about half a million active members of a population of about 18 million. It is hard to know the degree of support it had garnered from the general public, but with its influence in schools, mass media, scout groups, factories, hospitals, and companies, in addition to its presence in state and private institutions, its reach and influence were extensive. More than a mere Islamic society, it was becoming "a state within the State" (Ayubi et al. 1995).

Moving toward Militancy

In the post–World War Two period, the Muslim Brotherhood was growing as a powerhouse in Egypt, rivaled only by the liberal Wafd party. Though al-Banna publicly claimed he was not in favor of revolution and seizing state power, the Brotherhood established its own military wing called the Special Section. In the latter part of the 1940s, militants from the Special Section embarked on armed struggle against British and Jewish targets that resulted in killings and injuries. The government saw little choice but to dissolve the group. A series of armed confrontations ensued that escalated to political assassination. On December 28, 1948, a former Rover assassinated Prime Minister Nuqrashi Pasha. In retaliation, a government assassin killed Hassan al-Banna on February 12, 1949. The Brotherhood would take a more militant turn.

Sayyid Qutb emerged as the Brotherhood's next ideologue. Similar to al-Banna, Qutb was a graduate of Dar al-'Ulum and a primary school teacher. He joined the Brotherhood in 1950 on his return from the United States, where he had spent two years on a Ministry of Education sponsored trip to study instructional methods and curricula (1948–50). The experience had quite the reverse effect of what was intended. Instead of coming with ideas of how to apply education practices and techniques from the US context to Egypt, Qutb returned repelled by the materialism and hedonism of American society. As one author noted, Qutb believed "that history in general, and the Qur'an in particular, had stamped Egyptians and other Muslim peoples of the East with a 'spiritual' outlook on life. This differed appreciably from what he felt to be the abject materialism of Western and more particularly, American life" (Calvert 2001, 8; Calvert 2000). Qutb was alarmed by the growing influence of the United States on Egyptian political elites and Egyptian institutions. While he accepted that institutions needed to modernize, he was adamant that they should preserve fidelity to local customs and religious values.

Qutb moved the Brotherhood in a more radical direction. In brief, his key idea was that governments in Muslim majority societies such as Egypt were illegitimate because they failed to correctly follow the tenets of Islam as they instead blindly followed Western culture. He reached back to history in order to compare contemporary rulers to pre-Islamic pagan rulers in the time of "ignorance" and "cultural barbarism" known as *al-jahiliya*. Just as the early Muslims waged a holy struggle, or "jihad," against pagan rulers, so too, he argued, should contemporary Muslims embark on jihad against illegitimate rulers and governments, in order to be able to return to the "correct" path.

Qutb moved into a leadership role at a time when relations between the Brotherhood and the government of the Free Officers went from strained to catastrophic. On October 26, 1954, Brotherhood member Mahmud Abd al-Latif fired eight shots at Gamal Abd al-Nasser while he was delivering a live radio address in Alexandria about the British military withdrawal from Egypt. All the shots missed and Nasser survived, but the group would now experience the most brutal crackdown in Egypt's modern history. Nasser took the opportunity to neutralize the Communist and labor movements too, and eliminate dissent in the military.[6] He dismissed 140 army officers and had eight Muslim Brothers executed. Qutb's sentence was commuted to fifteen years in prison, though he was eventually executed by hanging on August 26, 1966.

While Qutb was in prison, he developed a counterproject to pan-Arabism which was exemplified through Nasserism in Egypt, Ba'thism in Iraq and Syria, and Bourguibism in Tunisia (Ayubi et al. 1995). In Qutb's alternative vision, pan-Islamism would lead to the return of the caliphate for the global Umma, and to the implementation of sharia law. One way of spreading the message of pan-Islam was through chants and slogans, similar to those of popular Arab nationalists. For instance, a common chant among nationalists during the 1940s and 1950s was "God is great and glory to Egypt." The Muslim Brotherhood deliberately left out reference to Egypt and chanted instead, "God is great and to Him be praise." They would sometimes continue the chant with the lines:

God is our Goal
The Prophet is our Leader
The Qur'an is our Constitution
Struggle is our Way
Death in the Service of God is the Loftiest of our Wishes
God is Great, God is Great[7]

These chants with no national reference traveled across communities and borders. They entered schools where Brotherhood presence was dominant and became part of students' daily rituals.

After Qutb's death, there would be enormous pendulum swings in the relationship between the Egyptian government and the Brotherhood. There were periods of immense crackdowns and waves of state repression and violence, which drove the Brotherhood underground and into more radical positions. There were also periods of truce, when the Brotherhood adapted a gradualist approach and publicly renounced violence.[8] Suffice it here to point out that during the Mubarak years, the Brotherhood and the government would engage in a checkered dance of truce and toleration. But the Islamist activism in schools and universities immensely challenged and strained attempts at rapprochement.

The Mubarak Years

In the 1980s and 1990s, there were growing numbers of criminal cases involving Islamists connected to universities, schools, and teacher training colleges. The director of the National Center for Educational Research (NCER), Dr. Abd al-Fattah Galal, prepared a report on extremism and education which he presented to the parliament in May 1993 (Rizq 1993). According to the report, ninety schools and three hundred teachers (listed by name) had links to violent Islamist organizations, notably al-Jama'a and al-Jihad. These teachers were concentrated in Upper Egypt, especially Qina and Asyut. For his part, Baha' al-Din asserted that the number of extremist teachers far exceeded these numbers and that his own intelligence reports revealed that extremism in education was not limited to specific geographic regions of the country, but was a nationwide phenomenon (Negus 1995).

An independent investigation by the weekly semiofficial magazine *Ruz al-Yusuf* found that the Muslim Brotherhood was buying up preschools and had a wide presence in elementary schools, while al-Jihad exerted control over teacher training institutes. For instance, al-Mushir Secondary School, located in a rural area of Asyut, was described as a "hideout" and "one of the most dangerous terrorist spots in Asyut" (Rizq 1993, 27). Its teachers reportedly preached to students that the Egyptian government was apostate, and played tapes of sermons by the dissident Sheikh Omar Abd al-Rahman (who would become the convicted mastermind of the 1993 World Trade Center bombing in the US).[9] The report also cited systematic discrimination against Christian students. Some teachers were known to ban Christians from their classes and forbid them from running for school elections. In a more bizarre report, an English teacher and spokesperson for al-Jama'a al-Islamiya instructed his students to write English from right to left since Arabic, the sacred language of the Qur'an, was written in this way. Another teacher used his Arabic classes to malign state television, calling it the "voice of Satan," and praised the achievements of Iranian leader Ayatollah Khomeini.

The Brotherhood and other Islamist groups were especially active in faculties of education. Baha' al-Din noted: "The extremists found that the best way to accomplish their goals was to concentrate on the faculties of education. . . . [If we don't do something about this] hundreds of teachers will graduate as believers in their ideas and it will be a catastrophe" (Baha' al-Din in *Akhbar al-Hawadith* 1993). In an attempt to rein in teachers and schools, the ministry changed acceptance criteria to education faculties. Instead of admitting students based solely on their grades in the nationwide college entrance examination, the Thanawiya 'Amma, the Higher Council for Universities set up committees to implement security checks.[10] The objective was to ensure applicants did not belong to any "misleading groups" with intentions to "demolish the educational process" (Baha' al-Din 1998, 56). Students who in normal times would have easily gained admission to an education faculty were being denied entry due to "security reasons" (*al-Usra al-Arabiya* 1993). Baha' al-Din and his counterpart at the newly formed Ministry of Higher Education, Mufid Shahab, instated new security and surveillance measures at student hostels that required all students to provide detailed data about themselves and their families. If a student lived outside of student housing, they had to supply a landlord's letter confirming where and with whom they were residing.

The Ministry of Education also invested more in teacher training missions abroad, invited foreign educational experts to Egypt, built more schools, and organized "counterextremist" seminars and citizenship training to help children develop "healthy characters" and stand up to terrorism.[11] The government similarly invested in the kind of student support that Islamist groups were offering, such as free tutoring, used books, subsidized housing, meals, and secondhand clothing. In 1992–93 for example, the Supreme Council for Education allocated LE 4.5 million toward social services for university students, from which roughly 150,000 students benefited. They also increased student housing capacity to 56,000. Approximately 7,500 university students partook in camps organized and subsidized by Egyptian universities in resorts south of Cairo in Helwan and on the Mediterranean coast in Alexandria (NCER 1994, 44). These youth camps incorporated symposia on social issues, and had an ideological as well as social and recreational function.

The Purge in K–12 Schools

> Those who try to tamper with the educational process must be sent away. (Baha' al-Din 1998, 55)

With Ministerial Decision Number 162 for 1992, the Ministry of Education started a campaign to purge extremist students, faculty, and materials from K–12 schools. District-level supervisors scoured school libraries for subversive print and audio materials, such as Islamist magazines, unauthorized religious books, political pamphlets, or cassette tapes of religious sermons. Tapes of the "Torture of the Grave" sermon *('adhab al-qabr)* were especially widespread *(Akhbar al-Hawadith* 1993). This sermon describes in terrifying detail the tortures that await wayward Muslims, with depictions of snakes in the grave, beatings, and a fiery underworld. The minister recounted how he was extremely upset after a mother complained that her daughter could not sleep after hearing one of these recordings, for fear that a snake would crawl over her at night.

Critics argued that this policy of censoring books and other materials was in contrast to Baha' al-Din's stated commitment to tolerance and liberalism. When asked in an interview (*Akhbar al-Hawadith* 1993) about censorship, he defended the state's role as protector of its children, saying,

> We [censor] books that support extremist ideas that are against the valid teachings of Islam. Psychologically speaking, a child does not have a formed character. . . . It's the state's responsibility to take care of the child and not leave him to face unhealthy situations. I don't approve of censorship, but I have the duty to protect the child physically, psychologically, and mentally. Until the child is formed, he has to be under the protection of the family and the state.

Purging materials was far easier than dismissing ministry employees, who were protected by socialist-era labor laws. As a workaround, the ministry transferred public school teachers and administrators to other government posts where they would not have contact with children. The minister had to deal with employee issues on a case-by-case basis through ministerial decisions. For example, Ministerial Decision 355 for 1994 ordered the teacher Mr. Lutfi Ibrahim be transferred to a post "far away from the schools." The archives hold scores of similar decisions. Between the summer of 1993 and March 1995, the ministry transferred roughly one thousand teachers out of schools and into other government posts. The minister declared that he was prepared to eliminate ten thousand teachers if necessary (*al-Hayat* 1995). Many teachers from Cairo were reappointed to jobs hundreds of kilometers away in Suhag, Qina, and Aswan, and effectively had to quit the ministry. In a well-publicized case in 1993, a female teacher near Cairo was transferred to an administrative job in Qina in Upper Egypt for playing the "Torture of the Grave" tape in her Arabic class. The minister pointed out that the class consisted of both Christian and Muslim students and that the teacher was supposed to be providing instruction in language and grammar, not religion. After officials from the educational district intervened on her behalf, she was given a "long vacation" instead of the transfer (*al-Ahram* 1993).

Lawsuits started to pile up, and in a number of cases, the courts ruled against the ministry. In a 1992 case that caught the attention of the press, the principal of The Mother of the Believers Secondary School for Girls (Umm al-Mu'minin al-Thanawiya li-l-Banat) was transferred to an administrative office for allegedly forcing a girl to wear the *hijab*. She filed a lawsuit claiming the charges against her were false. On February 18, 1993, the administrative court judge overturned the ministry's decision on the grounds that "inviting students to be conservative, respectable, and to wear the *hijab* is not in opposition to the constitution, which draws on the Sharia as the source of legislation" (*al-Sha'b* 1994). The Teachers' Syndicate remained silent throughout this period, causing one critic to accuse it of being "just a dead body of no use for teachers or for education" (*al-Usra al-Arabiya* 1993).

The curriculum also became part of the ministry's counter-Islamist strategy. In a speech before the Shura Council in 1993, Baha' al-Din put forward his plans for curricular reform by stating, "We should eliminate negative aspects of the syllabus which are in contradiction to science and technology." A development that especially brought some heat to the minister was the collaboration with the American Center for Curriculum Development (ACCD). The center had been formed to advise the ministry on how to make the curriculum more conducive to cultivating a more liberal, rights-centered, and technologically adept citizenry. On the advice of the ACCD, the minister considered consolidating the separate religion classes for Muslims and Christians into one single class, and replacing "religion" with a general "morals" class. Critics from across the political spectrum balked at the American involvement in Egypt's national curriculum, particularly in something as sensitive as the religion curriculum (Dunya 1993). The public outcry was so resounding that this idea had to be shelved (see chapter 9). In response, Baha' al-Din reassured the public that he would continue to consult the ulama of al-Azhar, the traditionally recognized guardians of Islam in Egypt, on matters pertaining to the religion curriculum for Islam. He had to walk this fine line between being a protector of religious values and education and purging what he viewed as extremist ideas and practices.

Private Islamic Schools Rise

Parallel with purging schools of Islamist influence, the Egyptian government was also actively supporting the liberalization and privatization of the education sector.[12] Many Egyptians who had been working in the oil rich countries of the Arab Gulf saw this economic opening as a tremendous opportunity (see Ismael 1986). Following the 1991 Gulf War, "Operation Desert Storm," scores of Egyptians returned home with substantial savings. As documented by Egyptian political scientist Amani Kandil (1998, 78), a high percentage of them were affiliated with the Muslim Brotherhood, and they invested in the new boom sectors of "construction, luxury housing, car dealerships, electronics, Islamic schools, media, and tourism (mostly pilgrimage—a multimillion-dollar business). A new breed of Brotherhood businessmen was born."

The Islamist business class saw the economic opening of the 1990s as a unique opportunity to combine business, education, and Islamism, a trend that began in fits and starts in the 1970s. But even as Arab governments supported policies to liberalize education, the media, and civil society, they never intended to relinquish control over their citizens' education, political activities, or communication behavior. At the end of the day, the government wanted to maintain control over official school knowledge and the upbringing of its citizens while pursuing a path of privatization. The new private Islamic schools would come to loggerheads with the government, the subject of chapter 7.[13]

7
Experiments in Counternationalism

Summary: The New Islamic schools coincided with the spread of Islamist currents in Egypt and throughout the MENAWA region. These schools, which can be viewed as microcosms of Islamist currents themselves, attempted to cultivate alternative ideas about citizenship and group belonging, and as such represented experiments in counternationalism. They depended on the technologies of state power to provide alternatives to it. This chapter reviews three private Islamic schools with different social class and political affiliations, and their contested to conciliatory relations to the state.

Private Islamic Schools

Sometime in the mid-to-late 1970s, private schools with an Islamic character were noticeably sprouting around Egypt. Their distinctly Islamic identity could initially be gleaned by their names: The Pulpit of Islam School, Salah al-Din, The Ring of the Holy Messengers, Return to the Caliphate, Modern Heavenly Journey, The Epitaph to Ibrahim, The Successors of the Prophet, Mother of the Believers, Science and Faith, Flower of Islam, and the list goes on. These were not Qur'anic schools or schools connected to the al-Azhar education network. Rather, this new category of private Islamic schools (*al-madaris al-islamiya al-khassa*) were registered primary, preparatory, and secondary schools that fell under the supervision of the Ministry of Education. They integrated additional religious elements into their programs by offering elective religion courses (in addition to the required religion course), and in their attempt to render the daily life of the school "Islamic." They also tended to market themselves as providing a more virtuous and pious atmosphere than government and foreign schools.[1]

New Islamic schools arrived on the education scene in two waves. From the 1970s to the 1980s they operated in the open, riding the tide of

Islamist identity politics, and the spike of investments, charities, and influence from the conservative oil rich Gulf countries, specifically Saudi Arabia. During this period there was a popular swell from below for the Islamization of society and its institutions. The governments of Anwar Sadat and Hosni Mubarak had been asserting their Islamic credentials through different channels including the constitution, public displays of piety, launching government-owned Islamic media, and supporting Islamic banking and other enterprises.[2] By the late 1980s the Ministry of Education had taken a conciliatory view of private Islamic schools (PIS) and undertook initial steps to regulate them.

In 1989, Minister of Education Fathi Sorour oversaw Draft Decree Number 1 for the Year 1989 Concerning the Private Islamic Schools. Article One dealt with defining this category of school: "The Private Islamic Schools, in addition to achieving the goals of pre-university education and following the official curriculum, aim at expanding studies of Islam and the Holy Qur'an." PIS were subject to all the standard inspections and oversight of other Egyptian private schools, but were to be distinctive in two main ways. In order for students to transfer from one year to the next, they needed a passing grade in Islamic Studies and the Holy Qur'an. Second, teachers in these schools, in addition to possessing standard credentials, had to "pass a religious test in the Holy Qur'an" (Article 27).

This decree never made it beyond draft form. The education minister was abruptly appointed to Speaker of the Parliament after a political assassination (as discussed in chapter 6). The new minister, Husayn Kamal Baha' al-Din, shifted course and took a firm position against the Islamization of education. The new Islamic schools continued to be established as part of the growing private school market, but tried to stay under the radar. From the early 1990s, they rarely carried "Islam" in their names, since being a self-identified Islamic school meant inviting extra government attention and oversight. From this point forward, the new Islamic schools adopted a stealth approach and attached more generic and "innocent" sounding names to their schools, such as "Green Gardens" and "Sunny Meadow."

To put these schools in numerical context, in 1995–96 there were a total of 1,130 private primary schools and 649 private preparatory schools in Egypt (National Center for Educational Research and Development 1996, 46). Of those, 197 at the primary level and 108 at the preparatory stage, or roughly 17 percent, were private Islamic schools. Tuition for PIS schools that operated entirely in Arabic started at LE 200 and were normally under LE 1,000 per year, not counting additional fees for extra activities and supplies.[3]

Private Islamic schools with English as the primary language represented a separate category, established after the 1990s: private Islamic English language schools (PIELS). These schools were mainly set up as investment companies (*sharikat istithmariya*) under the new administrative category of investment schools (*madaris istithmariya*) (see chapter 9). They catered to students of a higher socioeconomic status than the Arabic PIS and charged considerably higher tuition fees that could reach several thousand Egyptian pounds per year. By 1996, a total of twenty PIELS had been established in Egypt, in the urban centers of Cairo, Alexandria, Suez, and 6 October City.[4]

The new Islamic schools used the technologies of state power and tools of capitalism to grow their education businesses while cultivating alternative ideas about civic belonging and group identity. In this sense, they represented experiments in counternationalism. These schools veered into antiregime dogma and resistance culture, but to differing degrees. In order to glean the ways in which PIS and PIELS promoted rituals and practices for alternative citizenship and group belonging, the following section turns to three schools: a pioneer private Islamic school that catered to the urban professional classes and aspiring global elite at the end of the Sadat era; an unapologetically Muslim Brotherhood affiliated school located in an urban, poor, and more socially conservative part of Cairo; and an elite school that corresponded to the second wave of economic opening and privatization under Mubarak.[5]

School One: Evolution of a Pioneering School

The Open Door (*Infitah*) economic policies of President Sadat marked the first wave of educational privatization in Egypt. Dr. Zahira Abdin saw this opening as an opportunity and set out to establish private schools for Muslim children from the professional middle classes. At sixty-two years of age, she founded the first network of private Islamic English language schools in 1978. Dr. Abdin imagined that her schools would rival the prestigious private Christian missionary schools where she herself had been schooled. She wanted the future of the free economic life in Egypt "to be colored by Islam rather than by the materialistic rules of the modern capitalist economy."[6] Her goal was to "combine modern science with Islamic behavior," and instill in her students a deep faith and sense of morality, which she found lacking in the younger generations (Musallam 1992). She envisioned that graduates of her schools would work in international companies and serve as ambassadors for Islam abroad, particularly in the West.

Born into an elite family in 1917, Abdin had been a trailblazer on different fronts. She was one of the first women to graduate from the Cairo Medical College (later renamed Qasr al-'Ayni Faculty of Medicine), and in 1942 was the first woman to serve on its staff with a specialization in children's medicine. She established the Zahira Abdin Foundation to provide services for orphans, poor women, and those in need of surgery and medical care.[7] Dr. Abdin had strong networks in Europe and the Gulf. Through her contacts in the Muslim business community, she was able to raise funds for her new schools in a relatively short time. Her next goal was to recruit suitable teachers who could realize her vision.

As a Fellow of the Royal College of Physicians, Dr. Abdin made regular visits to London. There she often visited a Sufi Islamic center frequented by European, American, and other nationals who had embraced Islam. She approached members of the group about going to Egypt to teach in her new schools, which she described in highly idealistic terms. She painted her schools as spaces which carried the spirit of the first Muslim communities, where the practices of Prophet Muhammad were woven into everyday life. She told prospective teachers that they would contribute to the rebirth of Islam in the new global order. She inspired Mary, an American single mother in her mid-twenties with two young children, to venture to Egypt.

The Zahira Abdin Foundation sent Mary three one-way tickets and put them up temporarily in a room in the Rheumatism Hospital. Once in Egypt, Mary learned that her monthly salary would be the equivalent of $50, far lower than what she had expected. Recalling those initial days in Egypt fifteen years later, she reflected on her naiveté: "I hadn't even discussed my salary until I arrived in Egypt with my two kids. I was quite a gullible young lady." Nevertheless, she was enthusiastic about teaching in the new school and believed in its mission.

Mary recalled the school's first few years as "the golden years." The children learned about Islam in a relaxed, encouraging atmosphere, where teachers used positive reinforcement and activity-based learning. The style at their school was in stark contrast to government or Qur'anic schools that forced children to sit still and memorize lessons in a punitive environment. In the mornings, they sang a melody believed to have been sung by the people of Medina when the Prophet and his companions arrived there. They performed sketches dressed in miniature cloaks and turbans about how to properly perform their ablutions for the Muslim prayer. The Qur'an teacher gave little gifts to the girls and boys as a reward for every five verses of the Qur'an they committed to memory. One alumnus remembered getting a Matchbox car for his efforts, and talked about how that simple reward gave him a strong incentive to study and made him work hard in his Qur'an studies.

The school would undergo a shift in the 1980s following the assassination of President Sadat by Islamist militants in 1981. As a school with a known Islamic mission, it experienced enhanced state scrutiny and security checks. On several occasions governmental inspectors audited the school's financial records, made inquiries into the teachers' affiliations and political opinions, and searched the school grounds. It was during one of those visits that inspectors discovered the absence of an Egyptian flag in the courtyard. They further learned that the children did not sing the national anthem in the morning *tabur*. A teacher explained the school administration's reasoning for disregarding these national symbols and rituals: "We didn't think of saluting the flag as something very important. These children were not soldiers. But the governmental representative insisted that children must salute the flag first thing in the morning just like in a military camp. We did it, although we weren't convinced. It didn't mean anything to us."

Under pressure from government authorities, the school begrudgingly purchased a flag and incorporated the national anthem into the morning assembly, however with some alterations. It added its own declaration of allegiance prior to singing the anthem that combined Islam, nation, and internationalism, thereby broadening the oath beyond the Egyptian–Arab nation. With a teacher playing out the melody of the national anthem "Biladi, Biladi, Biladi" on the school's portable organ, the children proclaimed three phrases, which they repeated three times: "*La ilaha ila Allah, Muhammad Rasul Allah*" (There is no god but God and Muhammad is his Prophet); "*Tahya Gumhuriyat Masr al-'Arabiya*" (Long live the Arab Republic of Egypt); and "We are Muslims full of belief, love the Qur'an and live by the Qur'an" (spoken in English). Immediately following these pronouncements, they sang the national anthem.

The school experienced pressures from two directions: from the government to toe the national line, and from the newer teachers and school management who wanted the school to adhere to a more conservative version of Islam. These political/cultural contests between the state, the old guard, and the new guard, came to a head, as they often do, over the subject of women's dress. The new management instituted a dress code for female teachers that included a mandatory headscarf. Mary, the teacher who had been at the school from its inception and who did not wear a headscarf herself, recounted how the enforced veiling policy differed so fundamentally from the environment of the early years:

> The administration and a lot of the teachers were not veiled [though Dr. Abdin was]. These were very well-to-do friendly educated women. My best friend and fellow teacher had veiled after leaving the university, but she never once asked me to take it. Some other individual teachers tried to persuade me to put on the veil, but it wasn't required. I would just tell them, you know, "mind your own business." They would remain friendly, it was never a big issue. They probably felt it was their duty to counsel me, but it never became grounds for cutting me off socially.

Not only did the new school administrators require all female teachers to wear a headscarf, they also made it mandatory for girls from the first grade, when they were just six years old. The new crop of teachers also followed a more traditional pedagogic style, where punishment and passive learning were the norms. Compared to the early years, the atmosphere at the school became almost unrecognizable. Kamal, an alumnus of the school who had been there from its opening, recalled how the school lost its sense of community and became a much harsher and unforgiving place:

> Once when I was in first grade [under the old guard] I had to go to the principal because I didn't have a paper and pen. You know what she did? She gave me a paper and pen and sent me back to class. She didn't tell me, as the principal who took her place a few years later did, "Go stand outside the office and raise your arms in the air."

Another significant shift was that from 1984 teachers began enforcing segregation of the sexes. Kamal described the measures the school took to separate girls from boys:

It was as if suddenly it dawned on them that this was an Islamic school and boys should not be in classes with girls. This was a surprise to all of us. They installed doors to separate us, doors in the middle of the building with locks, and people standing with sticks guarding them. If girls looked out of the window onto the boys' playground they were punished.

The school eventually split into two separate buildings, one for boys and the other for girls. From that point on, children were segregated by sex from kindergarten through high school. Mary did not agree to take on the headscarf, was uncomfortable with the new regime, and eventually felt pressured to leave the school. She described the new teaching staff as "grim, Calvinist-type Muslims." For Kamal, these changes signified the decline of the school. He lamented, "In the beginning, the school was like a large colorful picture. Over time, the picture became darker and a lot smaller."

School Two: Schooling the Antination

Fatima Islamic School (used here as a pseudonym) was established in 1986 as a primary school in Dar al-Salam, one of the most densely populated areas in Cairo. Due to a shortage of schools, it was relatively easy for the owner and principal, Mr. Muhammad, to obtain the permit to build a private school on a plot of land he had inherited from his father. Mr. Muhammad, who grew up in the neighborhood, earned the financial capital to build the school after working for four years in Oman as a high school history teacher.[8]

A graduate of al-Azhar University's education section, Mr. Muhammad had long planned to open his own school. Not only did this make good business sense, but it provided a way to spread *al-da'wa*, or "the call" to true Islam. He was an active member of the Muslim Brotherhood and admired the writings of Sayyid Qutb (see chapter 6). He held the view that Egyptian society was in a pre-Islamic pagan state *(jahiliya)* and needed to be transformed according to the "righteous path." He strongly believed that children should be raised in an Islamic environment that adhered to the sharia, as opposed to a secular environment where people abided by the civil law of "corrupt politicians."

As a private primary school under the Ministry of Education, the school had to follow the mandated curricula and national examinations. However, the school found ways to transmit an Islamist ideology. For instance, instead of the required picture of President Hosni Mubarak on the wall in the principal's office, there were posters of gilded verses from the Qur'an and al-Aqsa Mosque in Jerusalem. Students greeted each other using Islamic salutations like "*al-salamu 'alaykum*" and were forbidden from using commonplace colloquialisms such as *izayyik* (how are you), *ahlan* (welcome), and bye-bye. Unlike in other national schools, there was no flagpole or flag in the courtyard, nor any pictures of the Egyptian flag next to President Mubarak, as one would find in other schools.

The owner applied his version of sharia law to school policy in extremely selective ways. For instance, the school institutionalized gender pay inequality on religious grounds. Women received two thirds of men's salaries. The principal justified this wage differential by claiming, "The Prophet himself said that in praying, women should be behind the men. In fact, women should be behind men in everything." This logic did not apply to the school fees, however, as girls paid the same fees as boys. Moreover, although Mr. Muhammad believed that segregation by sex was required in Islam, the school was mixed because it would not have been financially profitable to open a single-sex school, and there was not enough space to separate students into classes by sex. Instead, the classrooms themselves were separated with boys sitting on the right side and girls on the left. This kind of pragmatism, bending the "rules of Islam" in the interest of good business and profit, was woven into the fabric of the school.

Similar to other PIS, the school devised an alternative morning *tabur*. It began with a drum roll. Apart from the drum, there were no other musical instruments because of a commonly held conception that musical instruments are forbidden in Islam. The children performed exercises to the steady beat of the drum as they shouted in unison, "The glory of God. Thanks be to God. There is no God but God. God is Great." They repeated this sequence of praises four times. The rest of the *tabur* continued with announcements, recitation of Qur'an, and some other religious program that might include explaining a saying of the Prophet (hadith), or the singing of an Islamic song with the drum as accompaniment.

For the final portion of the *tabur* the school body sang an anthem entitled "Illahi, Illahi, Illahi" (My God, My God, My God). This anthem followed the same melody and cadence as "Biladi, Biladi, Biladi" (My Country, My Country, My Country), however with different lyrics and an alternative group message. For the purposes of comparison, the texts of both anthems are provided below:

"Illahi, Illahi, Illahi"	"Biladi, Biladi, Biladi"
My God, My God, My God,	My homeland, my homeland, my homeland,
You're my strength, you're my wealth.	You have my love and my heart.
Brothers! Let's establish	Egypt! O mother of all lands,
A state of the straight religious path.	You are my hope and my ambition,
My call is not and will not be mild,	How can one count
I rely upon God.	The blessings of the Nile for mankind?
My God, my God, my God,	My homeland, my homeland, my homeland,
You're my strength, you're my wealth.	You have my love and my heart.
My brothers who are the martyrs,	Egypt! Most precious gem,
Who want paradise,	Shining on the brow of eternity!
His way is very hard.	O my homeland, be forever free,
I rely upon God.	Safe from every enemy!
My God, my God, my God.	My homeland, my homeland, my homeland,
You're my strength, you're my wealth.	You have my love and my heart.
My brothers, let's reestablish	Egypt, noble are your children,
The state of glorious truth,	Loyal, and guardians of your soil.
A state of straight religion.	In war or peace
My call is not and will not be mild.	We will sacrifice ourselves for you.
My God, my God, my God,	My homeland, my homeland, my homeland,
You're my strength, you're my wealth.	You have my love and my heart.

And proclaim, "God is great!"

So it shocks the nonbelievers and they flee.

So proclaim "God is great!"

And glorify that God.

My God, my God, my God,

You're my strength, you're my wealth.

The anthem "Illahi, Illahi, Illahi" is interesting at the levels of both form and content. The melody is a composition from Sayyid Darwish (1892–1923), a legend of Egyptian popular music. The original lyrics of "Biladi, Biladi, Biladi" were adapted from a speech by the famous national-ist Mustafa Kamil Pasha (1874–1908). Even with its alternative lyrics, the Darwish tune is distinctly Egyptian and nationalistic. It would not neces-sarily carry evocative power for Muslims of other countries.

Looking at the two anthems side by side, it is striking how "My home-land" is calculatingly replaced with "My God," driving home the message that group loyalty should not be to a territory, namely Egypt, but rather to a deterritorialized God and by association, religious community. However, wrapping it in the form of the Egyptian national anthem confuses the alter-native message, because this anthem resonates specifically with Egyptians. Similarly, it is noteworthy that the word "Egypt" is consistently replaced with "Brothers" or "My brothers." Putting aside the patriarchal nature of this message, this wording signals that the Muslim Brothers are trying to create a society whereby they alone hold legitimate claims on the soci-ety. Another counternationalist message comes in the lines "And proclaim, 'God is great!' So it shocks the nonbelievers and they flee." This sentiment further reinforces a vision of a society that is the exclusive domain of the Brothers and their followers. Indeed non-Muslims—who in the Brother-hood conception are not only Christians and Jews for example, but also "pagan" Muslims who do not follow the Brotherhood's "correct" path—are the people who should "flee." This Islamist anthem uses the tools of nation building to subvert and deny Egyptian nationalism in favor of a Brother-hood nationalism.

*   *   *

Five years into opening the school, Mr. Muhammad needed a permit to expand and add a preparatory school wing, to make way for the new batch of primary school students. After submitting the necessary application, a team of inspectors from the Ministry of Education visited the school to make sure it was up to standards. Customarily, the school owner would receive such a delegation with deference and offer them refreshments. Mr. Muhammad did no such thing. He told his staff that like all government employees, these inspectors were corrupt and just wanted bribes. He was curt and rude with them. No one was surprised a few months later when the application for the second building was denied.

Having already started construction on the new wing, Mr. Muhammad changed tactics. He reapplied for the permit and prepared for the inspectors' visit. He strategically placed large portraits of President Hosni Mubarak in the entrance hall and on the wall behind his desk. He also purchased a large Egyptian flag and exhibited it prominently in the center of the courtyard. He led the inspectors to his office and offered them cold drinks and an assortment of cakes and maintained a congenial tone. The meeting seemed to go well, and the inspectors left with handshakes and smiles.

Not minutes after their departure, and with their car still pulling out of the dirt road outside the school gate, Mr. Muhammad's son, a student in the fourth grade, ran over to the entrance area and tore the portrait of Mubarak off the wall. He then kicked it into the corridor. His mathematics teacher laughed, picked up the picture, and carried it into their classroom. The teacher held the picture above his head with the full class of students watching, and slowly ripped it down the middle. With the picture now divided into two halves he asked, "What should we do with this now?" The class gathered around him, grabbing and ripping the picture. They stomped on it until it was reduced to shreds at their feet.[9] One month later, a certified letter arrived from the district education office. The request to add the preparatory stage to Fatima Islamic School had been approved.

School Three: Merchants of Elite Islamic Education

With the economic liberalization of the 1990s and markets in Egypt booming, a new genre of private Islamic school emerged, the five-star Islamic school. These more luxury brand schools catered to an aspiring and affluent "Muslim jet set" (Stenberg 1996, 20). In 1994 a new school opened in this space, al-Bashaer School. It projected an image of prestige for global Muslims and became an elite brand among Private Islamic English Language schools. The school was founded by an engineer and businessman, and was located in Maadi, a newer professional neighborhood catering to an affluent professional class. The school's management employed modern marketing and product branding techniques to advertise the school. Its logo was of two children, a girl and a boy, jumping up happily beneath a rainbow, wearing British elite school style navy blazers. In the marketing materials, which appeared in print and digital forms, the logo was on the left side and the school's two catchphrases, "Knowledge and Faith" (in English) and "In the Name of God" (in Arabic) on the right.

The school was sprawled across 2,850 square meters. Its facilities included two mosques, two swimming pools, large playgrounds, science laboratories, a library, a theater, a medical clinic, resource rooms, and a state-of-the-art computer lab. This was staffed with a full-time IT expert, a young bearded man who donned a white prayer cap and neatly ironed white thobe. He also managed the school's website. Families could expect the highest level of amenities, including custom air-conditioned school buses that picked up students at their door, and a state-of-the-art cafeteria.

The school projected a contemporary business savvy combined with the promise of providing a pious Islamic environment. The school integrated Qur'anic recitation *(tajwid)*, the noon prayer, Islamic salutations, religious images, and teachers with Muslim credentials, into the school. This school also found a way to map Islam onto a number of activities including sports. In keeping with the British system, every class had teams, or "houses" with a designated color and name. Being an Islamic school, the houses were named after the four successors of the Prophet Muhammad *(al-khulafa' al-rashidun)* as follows: the Green Team, Abu Bakr al-Siddiq; the Red Team, 'Umar ibn al-Khattab; the Yellow Team, 'Uthman ibn 'Affan, and the Blue Team, 'Ali ibn Abi Talib.

Like other PIELS, the management was quick to differentiate itself from other "non-Islamic" Western-oriented language schools. They were continually drawing a line between "Western" and "Islamic." Teachers counseled students against emulating Western fashion and hairstyles and consuming American and British films, television, music, and books. At the same time, the school prided itself on its high English language standards and ability to attract native English speakers (mainly female converts to Islam who were living in Egypt or were graduates of English language schools). From a pedagogic and practical point of view, it was not entirely clear how students were expected to attain a high level of English fluency without consuming English cultural products like film, television, and literature. One teacher noted that they preferred to teach children English through scientific texts and religious stories. English language literature was acceptable as long as it was "compatible with Islam." However, Western culture was selectively integrated in the school, which itself as a kind of Americanized Islamic school. For instance, the cafeteria offered lunch specials every Thursday from the (at that time) trendy American fast-food restaurants, McDonald's, Pizza Hut, and KFC. The school viewed the availability of American corporate fast food as a sign of prestige. There was no consciousness that American fast food and the corporate culture it represented might be incompatible with the school's core values.

Some critics raised ethical questions about the very business model of PIELS. The dean of the Faculty of Education in Alexandria, Shebl Badran, for instance, wrote disparagingly about how PIELS opportunistically used quotations from the Qur'an and hadith for their marketing. He contrasted the covers of their promotional brochures, which displayed Islamic signage, to the inside text, which described how the school's administration was in close cooperation with education experts in the United States and England. This critic asked, "Will the role of these schools be to bring up our children to colonize us by the next century? I think Islam is innocent of all this. Those new merchants in the market of child-rearing (tarbiya) are trying to profit from the Islamic sentiment which is prevailing in the society." He further raised the important issue of social class, and questioned whether a school purporting to be guided by Islamic values should only cater to the children of the rich. He asked, "Is it the objective of Islam to serve only the children of the very rich, the businesspeople, brokers, representatives of foreign companies, and drug dealers? Where are the children of the general public?" (Badran 1993, 19).

The school's charter paid lip service to "respect for other cultures, beliefs and nationalities," and from a legal point of view it could not discriminate based on religion. However, discrimination against non-Muslims was woven into the very DNA of the new private Islamic schools in implicit and explicit ways. In a meeting with the vice principal for instance, I asked if non-Muslim children were eligible to enroll in the school. She responded somewhat tentatively, "Yes, they can attend the school. But they might object to some of the things we are doing because we advocate an Islamic spirit and do things that non-Muslims may not want to participate in." At that time, only two Christian students had joined the school, and each stayed for just one year before transferring out.[10] A Christian woman hired to teach English was required to wear the headscarf, and she too left the school after a year. This school did not seem to create a welcoming environment for non-Muslims, or Muslims from different social classes for that matter. Its policies were exclusionary by design, and inimical to building community across lines of class, cultural, and religious difference.

Narrowing Nationalism

The new Islamic schools came onto Egypt's education landscape during two waves of economic openings, and the spread of the Islamist current in Egypt and the region. The new school owners, directors, and members of school boards often had backgrounds as doctors, engineers, and businesspeople, with little grounding in education and pedagogy. Where they did have backgrounds in education and pedagogy, it was more likely than not that they also had party affiliation to Islamist groups, particularly the Muslim Brotherhood. While these schools differed in terms of class affiliations, educational vision, and business models, they all shared to some degree a recognition of themselves as working toward a counternationalist project. This does not mean they rejected their Egyptian national identify. Rather, they were cultivating an exclusionary and narrow notion of citizenship that was not only based on being Muslim, but a particular kind of Muslim. In the Muslim Brotherhood school, being a citizen meant belonging to the Brotherhood itself; that was the basis for full group belonging. In the two language schools, citizenship was connected to a broader conception of global Islam, but that was also selectively anti-Western yet pro-capitalism, and came with a number of inconsistent rules and messages.

These schools were not operating in a vacuum, but with the oversight of government institutions, and the participation of Egyptian youth who had their own ideas of their place in their communities and society. Students often used their collective power to push schools in directions that were more compatible with their own ideas of citizenship and place in a changing world, as we will explore in chapter 8.

8

Downveiling

Summary: Downveiling refers to the shift by Muslim girls and women to less concealing and conservative forms of Islamic dress, or to changing embodied religious practices. This chapter reviews the phenomenon of downveiling through the lens of students at a private Islamic school in a middle-class neighborhood in Cairo. The phenomenon of downveiling illustrates how socioreligious change is dynamic, nonlinear, and codependent on several actors, including, in this case, the courts, security forces, teachers, principals, and adolescent girls.

Observing Downveiling

Sometime in the mid-1990s, I observed a number of acquaintances from diverse social and professional backgrounds shifting to lesser degrees of veiling, a phenomenon we can call "downveiling." Some of them even "unveiled" or removed their head covers altogether. A resident of Cairo since the mid-1980s, I had witnessed firsthand the wave of upveiling by university students and other women, a topic which was receiving scholarly attention (El Guindi 1999), so this behavior of "downveiling" piqued my curiosity. My understanding of this practice was anecdotal until I began conducting research in the new private Islamic schools. Schools are by no means the only, or even necessarily the most commonplace, arenas of downveiling. Nevertheless, they provided a compelling social context in which to trace the local dynamics that contributed to a practice which had become observable in segments of urban Egyptian society.

The Islamization of public spaces and social institutions such as schools became noticeable in the 1970s. One manifestation of this trend was the Islamization of the nation's schools. Numerous government and private schools institutionalized Islamic practices, such as enforcing an

Islamic uniform *(ziyy islami)*, primarily but not only for girls. Schools often required female students, staff, and sometimes even students' mothers, to don a head cover. Veiling has multiple gradations and ranges from the *hijab*, a scarf that covers the hair and is pinned under the chin, to a *khimar*, a substantially longer scarf that drapes the torso and arms, to the *niqab*, which covers the face, and is usually worn with an ankle-length dress.

The Ministry of Education had been trying to curb efforts by Islamists to create alternative social norms and practices in public and private preuniversity schools. Girls' school uniforms became a site of struggle in the culture wars between Islamists and factions of the government. In 1994, the Ministry issued its Ministerial Decision 113, titled "The Unification of the School Uniforms." It prohibited girls from wearing the *hijab* to school at the primary stage, and required that girls in the preparatory stage provide written permission from a guardian if they wanted to wear a head covering. Article 1, Clause 2 reads: "It is possible upon a written petition from the guardian that girls wear a head cover but not a face cover *(niqab)*, the color of which will be decided by the educational district." The order forbade teachers and students from wearing the *niqab*, on grounds that it presented a security risk by concealing the wearer's identity, and prevented teachers from effectively communicating in the classroom.

The new uniform regulation caused a public storm and was debated and strongly contested in the press and courts. After a number of rulings in lower courts against the ministry, it reached the Supreme Constitutional Court, where it was ultimately ruled constitutional and therefore enforceable. Ministry inspectors and state security forces were duly dispatched to schools throughout the country to ensure compliance with the new rules. The scenes and stories of uniformed men standing outside schools, harassing little girls with scarves and stopping them from entering their schools, did not play well with the public nor with school communities.

Initially, female members of these school communities were particularly outraged, and some unveiled students at the preparatory and secondary levels even adopted the *hijab* for the first time in protest. However, over the longer term, after the initial confrontation with security forces subsided, the new regulation served as a catalyst for many students and teachers who had been wanting to downveil, to finally have the chance to do so. This cycle of protest followed by downveiling will be illustrated by recounting events in a specific private Islamic school in a middle-class neighborhood in Cairo.

6. First grade girls in school uniform wearing headscarves at a private Islamic school, Cairo. 1993.

Since the school's establishment in 1981, the uniform for girls from first grade onwards had consisted of a long blue-gray smock, pants, and a mini-*khimar*. The school's founder and director, Sheikh Ahmad, had selected this uniform personally so that the female child would get used to comporting herself according to the teachings of her religion, as he saw them. This was because, as he proclaimed, "In Islam there is no gray. Everything is black or white. The *hijab* is a requirement, not a choice."

When a stamped letter with the new uniform regulations reached the school, Sheikh Ahmad initially refused to comply with them. He was convinced that he, and not the government, was religiously in the right. However, he faced the very real possibility of the ministry taking over his school's administration, which had happened in other private Islamic schools. Under pressure, the sheikh eventually agreed to eliminate the headscarf for girls at the primary level.

With the parents' universal cooperation—they all signed a release form—the headscarf remained mandatory for girls at the preparatory stage. Yet despite an unmistakable sense among staff, parents, and students that the government was unjustly interfering in the school's internal policy, an

7. The same girls, now in third grade, without headscarves, Cairo. 1995.

unexpected shift occurred among a number of them: they began modifying their own style of dress by downveiling.

The older students, aged eleven to fourteen, were the first to downveil. Backed by the protection of the law, the overwhelming majority of girls immediately substituted their drab uniform regulation khimar for a simple white headscarf. In another act of defiance against school policy, they decided among themselves to replace the gray smock, which they described as "ugly" and "unfashionable" *(baladi)*, for a more "normal" uniform of a tailored long gray skirt and white blouse. Soon thereafter, members of the school staff also began downveiling. Students were especially surprised when two senior administrators and feared school disciplinarians gradually substituted their dark ankle-length skirts of thick synthetic material for shorter (but still long and loose) shin-length cotton skirts. Step by step, they also replaced their thick nylon *khimar*, which extended down to their thighs, with shorter shoulder-length scarves. These women had adopted the *khimar* prior to being employed at the school in the early 1980s, in part to show their commitment to working in an Islamic environment, and also to comply with the school's dress codes. They could not wear a lesser degree of Islamic uniform than the children under their authority. When the primary school children ceased wearing a head covering entirely, and preparatory girls downveiled at their own initiative, the need to dress on a par with the students no longer existed. Over time, a number of teachers also modified their dress to less concealing and more functional forms of Islamic dress.

The general tendency among female staff toward downveiling had the effect of hindering others from upveiling or adapting "higher," more concealing, and more "virtuous" forms of Islamic dress. One senior teacher in her mid-forties had been expressing her desire to upveil, to make the transition from the *khimar* to the *niqab*. She said she had believed it was a religious obligation, but then reconsidered taking the step. With her peers substituting their *khimar*s for simpler and shorter headscarves, she did not feel encouraged to upveil. In fact, she eventually began to practice her own form of downveiling. She substituted the long skirt under her *khimar* for more comfortable loose-fitting pants, which she said she would have considered inconceivable and improper just a year before.

Many of the women with whom I spoke, both inside and outside the school, cited a number of largely mundane reasons for downveiling. Some women talked about how the tight nylon *khimar* caused their hair to thin and in some cases resulted in their getting bald patches. Others who routinely walked long distances to and from work complained of excessive sweating under the *khimar* and being uncomfortable throughout the day. Still others pointed out that their form of dress was too cumbersome and restricted them from moving about as their work required. Meanwhile, some unmarried *niqab*-wearers *(munaqqabat)* felt that their prospects of being approached for marriage were diminished when men had no chance of seeing their faces. The decision to downveil, in other words, was not explained in association with a crisis of faith or a retreat from religion. Neither did the women explain their decision as a matter of personal choice or a form of gender emancipation, a trope that was common in some feminist literature on gender and Islam.[1] Rather, downveiling appeared to be more of a relaxing of socioreligious practices, spurred largely by practical considerations. Following their decision to downveil, some women experienced degrees of social snubbing, in both subtle and overt ways. However, as more women engaged in downveiling, it became a more socially accepted practice with little fallout.

The trend of downveiling initially caused some scandal and a crisis of moral authority at the school. One seventh-grade student remarked, "Our school has changed a lot. In the beginning it was very strict and all our teachers wore the *khimar* or the *niqab*. Now a lot of our teachers who once wore the *khimar* wear very tight clothes with a little scarf," to which her friend added, "A very, very little scarf!" An eighth-grade girl complained that the vice principal scolded her for wearing a uniform skirt that fit too snugly around her hips and for not buttoning her blouse to the neck. She asked, "How can she comment on my appearance when she herself used to wear the *khimar*, took it off, and now only wears a scarf? She tells us not to wear tight clothing, but she sometimes wears very tight skirts with sandals."

Even as the students judged their teachers for double standards, they were largely supportive of each other in their peer groups. Students did not experience shaming or social pressure as a result of their own downveiling, since the original Islamic uniform had been imposed on them. Besides, there was pretty much unanimous consensus that the original uniform was unattractive and uncomfortable.

Downveiling is just one example of how schools served as vessels for political and cultural change. The process of downveiling was dynamic, nonlinear, and codependent on disparate actors, including the ministry, the courts, security forces, teachers, principals, and adolescent girls themselves. In a sense, the process of downveiling was illustrative of citizenship in action. It revealed how students experimented with pushing boundaries and reshaping norms in ways that made sense for how they viewed their place in their school community and the larger social order.

Part Three

Youth in a Changing Global Order

9

Education, Empire, and Global Citizenship

Summary: Global citizenship and related concepts such as human rights, participation, democratization, and gender empowerment, became international policy mantras of the post–Cold War era, or what many have labeled the neo-imperial order. These bedrock principles were supposed to filter through schools and civil society to shape youth subjectivities toward liberalism and globalism. Yet it was often not evident when these principles were being used to support neoliberal economic reforms, geopolitical goals, and the interests of the United States—which asserted itself as an imperial power in the region—or when they reflected more genuine progressive, universal, and emancipatory methodologies for change. By examining development interventions in Egypt between 1990 and 2010 around decentralization, privatization, and global citizenship education, this chapter interrogates the relationship between global power, state priorities, and education policy.

Education and Empire in the Post–Cold War Era

The fall of the Berlin Wall in 1989 provided the iconic imagery for a new era. Human rights would supposedly become the "official ideology of the new world order" and there would be transnational cooperation for an education for global citizenship (See Douzinas 2007, 32). The 1990s decade correspondingly signaled the neoliberal turn, when principles of the market—accountability, efficiency, and privatization to name a few— became more accepted as policy orthodoxies. These principles informed directions for educational restructuring around the world, including countries of the MENAWA region. National, bilateral, and multilateral developmental investment in basic education rose to record levels, especially after governments committed to the "Education for All" platform, as put forward at the World Conference on Education for All in Jomtien, Thailand, in March 1990.

As development interventions in education were moving at full speed, the global order was suddenly disrupted. The September 11, 2001, Islamist terrorist attacks on the United States caused a shift in orientation. The United States launched a "War on Terror" that contained both militaristic dimensions, as seen in the US-led wars on Afghanistan (2001) and Iraq (2003), and cultural and ideological ones, which took form in education and civil society interventions (Chhachhi and Herrera 2007).[1] With the world seemingly tilted towards unilateralism, and with a dominant United States, many analysts and scholars used the term "empire" and "neo-imperialism" to describe America's place in the global order. For a time, there was a mushrooming of empire literature and the concept seemed to be surpassing, or at least seriously competing with, "globalization" to denote the changing unipolar global order and global power.[2]

Education and its connection to empire was by no means a novel subject. Celebrated postcolonial scholars Frantz Fanon and Albert Memmi, among others, had long before argued with great eloquence that education constituted a form of cultural imperialism that led to a colonizing of the mind (Fanon 1963, Memmi 1965).[3] In invoking education and empire here, our objective is not to reproduce still relevant frames about how education systems reflect unequal structures of power and reinforce class, race, gender, national, and other hierarchies. The purpose, rather, is to interrogate the effects of the post–Cold War global order on education systems and the teaching profession, given its distinctive economic, geopolitical, and ideological underpinnings.

Through a focus on educational policy reform in Egypt, we will attempt to disentangle the language of global citizenship and democratization from realpolitik issues of global security, free trade, and war. This chapter focuses specifically on three policy interventions: educational decentralization; privatization and market reforms; and curricula reform for global citizenship, as exemplified in the course Values and Morals (al-Qiyam wa-l-Akhlaq). The questions guiding this inquiry are these: How was education being used as a device to support a particular kind of economic and political order in the post–Cold War and post–September 11 eras? Whose interests were the educational reforms serving, and what kind of educational regime was being promoted?

The 1990s: Egypt's Education Decade

Under Mubarak (1981–2011), the Egyptian government proclaimed the 1990s the "Education Decade" to demonstrate its commitment to the "Education for All" platform adopted at the Jomtien World Conference held in March 1990. The quantitative growth of Egypt's education sector from 1990 onward was immense and unprecedented. Egypt's state budget for education increased nineteen-fold from 1982 to 2002, from roughly LE 1.2 billion to LE 22.4 billion (approximately US $4.76 billion), with the greatest leap occurring in the 1990s. Between 1992 and 2002, more than twice the number of schools were built (a total of 12,350) than had been in the previous 110 years (Arab Republic of Egypt 2002). In 2005, Egypt's 37,000 schools absorbed 15.5 million students and 1.5 million teaching, administrative, and support staff on the Ministry of Education's payroll (UNESCO 2006, 9). Meanwhile, policies for the decentralization and privatization of education intensified. Children, and specifically girls, gained priority on international and national development agendas. This orientation came out of a larger developmental narrative promoting universal schooling, gender equity, and rights-based and global citizenship approaches to learning.

Despite impressive quantitative increases in school buildings, access, and enrollments, Egypt performed poorly, and sometimes abysmally, in developmental indices. In the 2005 World Economic Forum study of fifty-eight countries, Egypt was ranked last.[4] Whatever reservations one has about national rankings and development indexes, the copious resources and policy attention devoted to quality and to democratic and rights-based education were not yielding the desired results. To some degree, these reforms were a political strategy, and a ritualized one at that, in response to conditionalities attached to international aid. However, a deeper problem was that educational reforms were mired in conflicting visions for economic and social reform, and hardly took into consideration the position of youth themselves.

Decentralization

The three international agencies most involved in funding efforts for decentralization in Egypt were the World Bank, USAID, and the United Nations Millennium Development team, all of which were strongly associated with the United States. Phrases in their policy documents commonly referred to decentralization as leading to "local ownership," "democratic participation," and the "empowerment of citizens." For instance, the Egypt Human Development Report of 2005 stated:

> At the local level, decentralization enhances local and democratic participation, local institutional capacity building and better resource use. It leads to the rapid accomplishment of tasks, the empowerment of citizens, the appropriate response to local problems, accountability through local ownership, an improvement in basic services, and a decrease in transactions costs.[5]

Regarding education, advocates of decentralization argued that it would lead to more democratic governance of the sector and improve educational quality as measured by higher student performance. On the latter point, scant empirical research is available to support or refute such claims.[6] One empirical study found that the effect of decentralization on student outcomes was insignificant at best (Nasser-Ghodsi 2006). As for governance, decentralization of the education sector led to some decision-making, oversight, and budget allocations being decided at district levels. However, there was little expectation that these measures would transform the governance structure toward democratization. The educational bureaucracy in Egypt has been characterized by what educational sociologist Kamal Naguib has called a pyramidal hierarchical structure, in which an authoritarian and nonconsultative power structure was reproduced at every level (Naguib 2006). Decentralization in a system with these characteristics was more likely to create multiple pyramids, each with its own power structure, rather than open the way for a new culture of consultation and participation.

Another reason that decentralization was unlikely to pave the way for more democratization of education was that Egypt was and continues to be a security state. Since its independence following the Free Officers' coup in 1952, the head of state has routinely come from the highest ranks of the military. The security branches of police, intelligence, and military wield enormous power and use the coercive apparatuses at their disposal to wield control over the society. During times of political instability, such as clashes with Islamist militants, the connection between education and security has become even more apparent (Herrera 2006a) (see chapter 6). As one governmental report stated, "Education will continue to be the cornerstone of national security and a starting point for the promotion of the citizen and the nation" (Arab Republic of Egypt 2003, 9, 149). In other words, a good citizen, as conceptualized here, is one who conforms to the rules of a security state, irrespective of the degree of decentralization and local governance.

Privatization

Educational privatization allowed for a host of new players to enter the educational market and gave rise to a new category, investment schools *(madaris istithmariya)*. Unique in the history of Egyptian education, these schools were set up as investment companies *(sharikat istithmariya)*. Their governing boards often consisted primarily of businesspeople with little or no background in education. Some investment schools offered a menu of educational programs for different income groups. For instance, parents could choose from the more economical Arabic-language track, which led to the Egyptian Secondary Certificate, or opt for the much costlier international sections, which could include the British International General Certificate and the International Baccalaureate (IB). From the mid-1990s, the American high school diploma came into vogue and became part of the educational offerings for those who could afford it. American and British programs could cost anywhere from four to eight times more than Arabic programs at the same schools. At one private investment school in Cairo, fees for secondary students in the national Arabic program in 2003 were LE 4,200 per year, compared to LE 20,000 for the American section. Students who followed the Egyptian curriculum were relegated to an old building without air conditioning and had poorly paid teachers. In contrast, students following the foreign systems had exclusive use of a fully renovated air-conditioned building, a modern cafeteria, a new computer lab, and teachers who earned four times the salary as their colleagues across the courtyard. These schools institutionalized inequality through separate and unequal educational tracks and facilities.

In theory, opening up education markets could have stimulated some sort of educational pluralism or "school choice." However, privatization also ran the risk of further polarizing society into silos, with divisions along lines of social class, and political and religious affiliations. As reviewed in chapter 7, some private Islamic schools attempted to cultivate a tacitly counternationalist environment. In their policies and everyday practices, such schools supported the idea of a nation within a nation. Some of these schools also pursued discriminatory Muslim-only policies and treated female teachers as second-class professionals. These were just some of the unexpected manifestations of privatization.

When looking at education as a wider field, it becomes clear that the real expansion in education markets occurred in the unregulated and illegal market of private lessons. Families across the spectrum paid exorbitant sums of cash for private tuition, in the hope that their children would attain a high enough score on the National Secondary School Certificate, the Thanawiya 'Amma, to secure a place in a desirable faculty at the university.[7] In 2005, a nationwide survey of 6,006 households in Egypt found that children in 64 percent of urban households and 54 percent of rural homes attending public and private schools took private lessons (UNDP 2005, 55–56). Yet these figures likely did not even begin to measure the extent of private services offered in the education marketplace.

Illegal private lesson centers, which started mushrooming in the mid-1990s, catered to almost every socioeconomic group and were present in urban poor areas, high-end neighborhoods, and mid-sized towns. In Cairo, secondary school pupils who were already in expensive private schools customarily took private lessons in all major subjects, at a cost of LE 2,000 to 3,000 per subject, per year, at specialized lesson centers. Tutors with good track records—meaning those whose students scored especially high marks on the Thanawiya 'Amma—gained almost rock star status. One such tutor of chemistry, Ustaz Hani, broke away from a well-known lesson center in Cairo to start his own tutoring business when demand for him skyrocketed (many of his clients had secured high enough grades to enter medical and other high-demand faculties). He was known for his "millionaire" lifestyle. He drove a luxury German car and vacationed in a villa in the posh North Coast resort of Marina. His fashionable secretary handled his schedule, and the waiting list for his tutoring sessions grew by the day. However, markets are volatile, and the meteoric rise of a star tutor can be met with a crash when the examination results are published and another tutor's clients have superior results.[8]

With the deterioration of public schooling, educational markets were becoming successively more lucrative, but in ways that eroded trust between teachers and families. A language of criminality entered the public discourse around private lessons, with frequent references in the media made to lesson mafias, ringleaders, illegal centers, extortion, and profiteering (see Farag 1994, 2006 and chapter 5). Families, however begrudgingly, participated in the shadow education system, as they considered it necessary for their children to advance through the system. In markets where pupils were customers and teachers were competing with their peers in an unregulated private marketplace, the vocation of the teacher was inevitably eroded.

The Politics of Curriculum Reform

In the contemporary period, school systems worldwide share a remarkably similar curriculum structure, with a fairly standardized allocation of time for a common range of subjects, though with some regional variation (Meyer 1992). In the period from 1970 to 1986, the Middle East and North Africa (MENA) allocated a considerably larger amount of time to religion than other regions. Schools in the MENA region spent 11.8 percent of time on religion, compared to 3.8 percent in sub-Saharan Africa, 3.0 percent in Asia, 2.2 percent in Latin America, and 4.7 percent in North America and western Europe (Cha, Wong, and Meyer 1992).[9]

In the early 1990s, lessons dealing with human rights, democracy, ethics, world peace, environmental conservation, and the importance of international and regional bodies in promoting economic exchange and peaceful coexistence were incorporated into the preuniversity school curriculum.[10] By the end of the decade, a newer set of concepts were added across different subjects and included "fighting extremism, promoting human rights and women's issues, preventing discrimination against women, legal awareness, children's rights, traffic rules, and globalization" (National Center for Educational Research and Development 2001, 29).

In practice, much of the internationalization of the curriculum had been supported by USAID, which established the Center for Curriculum and Instructional Materials (CCIM) in 1989, popularly known as The American Center.[11] The minister of education at the time, Dr. Husayn Kamal Baha' al-Din, headed the center's board of directors, and USAID advisers provided technical assistance. From the earliest days of its establishment, the CCIM was controversial. Its initial interventions involved either changing or removing material from social studies, geography, and history books for all grades. For example, maps of Sinai were removed from textbooks, and the name "Palestine" was replaced with "Israel." Lessons pertaining to the Arab League, the Palestinian issue, and the Crusades—specifically the liberation of Palestine by Salah al-Din—were expunged from social studies and geography books. Part of the Islamic history curriculum was replaced by Pharaonic history (Ramy 1993).

Following a public outcry, the CCIM was closed by ministerial decree a few months after its opening. When the center reopened by another ministerial decree the following year, it stirred considerable debate in the Egyptian Parliament and opposition press. Public intellectuals of all political and ideological persuasions questioned the motives of the United States in tampering with subjects in the curriculum that deal with culture, religion, and history. The underlying argument was that this level of interference undermined Egypt's political sovereignty and assaulted its culture.

In the midst of these debates, the CCIM announced plans to introduce a new course called Values and Morals (al-Qiyam wa-l-Akhlaq). This course was supposed to substitute the required but separate religion classes for Muslims and Christians. The idea of eliminating religious classes was met with such overwhelming opposition that the minister had to quickly shelve the plan. The subject returned again following the World Education Forum (WEF) in Dakar, Senegal, in 2000. During the WEF much time was devoted to how the international decline of morals was causing terrorism and crime and how it was incumbent upon each nation to tackle the problem. Given its situation with militant Islamist groups, Egypt reasserted its commitment to develop the Values and Morals curriculum while keeping the religion courses intact. In the 2001–02 school year, the Values and Morals books were disseminated in first to third grades. By 2004–05, the course reached up to fifth grade. The Ministry of Education planned eventually to have the subject taught through the final year of secondary schooling, but never reached that goal. Fifteen years later, in 2020, the Ministry of Education announced a new book series, Values and Respect for the Other: Together We Build that harkens back to these early initiatives.[12]

The overarching goal of Values and Morals was to instill in children the values of global citizenship, which were taken to be affinity for science, global humanity, and international organizations. At the same time, the course reinforced fidelity to Egypt and God. The course books' authors, a team led by CCIM Director Dr. Kawthar Kojak, had to strike a delicate balance between internationalism, nationalism, and religion. The preface, included in each book, assured the reader that the subject dealt with "values and morals that are appropriate for our Egyptian society, our religious beliefs, and what we adhere to in terms of customs and traditions." The stated pedagogic methodology, echoing another priority of international education development, was "active learning," as opposed to "memorization and dictation." To ensure that the books harmonized with religion and

8. Cover of the first grade *Values and Morals* textbook, published by the Ministry of Education, Cairo. 2001.

nation, the authors concluded the preface with the words: "We ask God that both the teacher and student enjoy the content, in the framework of education, knowledge, fun and benefit, and that this brings good to our beloved Egypt. May God guide us to the right path."[13]

The study of curricula is best carried out through a multipronged process of analyzing the text, observing its reception in the classroom (see chapter 3 on home economics classes), discussing it with teachers and/or students, and deciphering the hidden curriculum. The books were colorful and—for the early grades—full of cartoons. They were organized around stories and activities "based on scientific and pedagogic guidelines" that were supposed to encourage the student to think independently, role-play, practice life skills, "imagine and create, search and experiment, and . . . express him/herself linguistically or artistically" (Arab Republic of Egypt 2001).

The course covered a series of themes that included cleanliness, honesty, freedom, the environment, peace, loyalty, and the economy. The books expanded on each theme as they progressed through the years. In first grade there were stories set in the home, the school, and the imaginary world of animals. Children were depicted interacting with peers and adults at the local level (home, school, community), the state level (schools, courts, police stations), and the international level (the United Nations). Interreligious understanding was an important theme, and different lessons showed how Muslim and Christian children realized their similarities.

Another recurring theme was the importance of obeying authority, represented as the parent, teacher, and government. For example, the final lesson in the third grade book, "Respect Is a Responsibility," was about obeying laws. It depicted a thief (a thin unshaven man in shabby clothing) being taken away in handcuffs by a frowning police officer. The second image was of the same man shaven in the caged area of an Egyptian courtroom, being tried in front of two judges as a stout lawyer pointed an accusing finger at him. The text read, "Men of law protect the rights of the individual" (Arab Republic of Egypt 2003, 25). The message was decidedly not about the conditions of the poor, downtrodden thief, but rather the role of the lawyer—well fed and well dressed—in prosecuting transgressions, which in this case appeared connected to poverty.

I observed two class sessions of Values and Morals in a primary government school in a working-class area. The subject was allotted one forty-minute period per week. In the first session, the teacher appeared in a hurry to get through the lesson. The first graders were fidgety in their wooden desks but took part in the class by way of repeating parts of the lesson in unison after the teacher's prompting. This particular lesson dealt with the subject of cooperation. The teacher held up a picture of a boy perspiring as he struggled to carry a heavy table on his own. A second picture showed him happily smiling as two children helped him carry the table. The teacher explained the scene: "This is an example of cooperation." She then asked the class, "What is this an example of?" and in semiunison, the students answered, "Cooperation." She repeated in a louder tone, "Huh, what is this an example of?" and with more gusto, they answered, "Cooperation" (ta'awun). A different session for second graders was on traffic rules and proceeded in much the same way, except that a boy received a whack on his palms for incorrectly answering a question about traffic lights. Even with limited classroom observation, it was evident that there was no difference in pedagogic style between this class and any other class, be it Arabic or mathematics. In other words, there was no sign of active or activities-based learning.

In focus group interviews I held with teachers about the course in two stages in 2006 and 2007, a common and frequent complaint was that the course was burdensome and a waste of time. Teachers worried about time management, and they were not convinced that this course provided any added value. Most participants felt that in an already overpacked curriculum, an extra subject simply detracted from the core subjects and added to their workload. A senior teacher summed up what can be called the benign response to the course:

> I'm not convinced by the Morals subject. I don't really think morals can be taught through classes and exams. I also think it's the job of parents and the religion curriculum, whether Islam or Christianity, to teach morals to students. In general, the Morals books aren't harmful, but they're not beneficial either.

By contrast, some teachers harbored genuine concerns that the course was tainted because of its association with the American Center. A number of them expressed directly, or implied, that it was part of an American conspiracy to control the minds of Egyptian children and lead them away from religion. This view received plenty of fuel in the opposition press. An editorial published in the opposition newspaper *al-Wafd*, represented a typical example of the conspiratorial critique:

> The morals curriculum is now being taught alongside religion in schools. We feel this is a step to eliminate religion classes in the future. First, the ministry will say that the morals curriculum is very similar to the religious curriculum. Then, it will say that the morals classes have an advantage over the religion classes as both Christians and Muslims attend them together. Thereafter, religion classes will eventually disappear. The question is, who is behind all of this? Is there a hidden power? It is worth noting that the 14th protocol in the secret Zionist protocols to control the world is "we should destroy all faiths." Their aim is to see future generations with no religion and no sense of patriotism (*al-Wafd* 2001).

In her book on Western influence in Egyptian educational reform in the 1990s, Fatma Sayed disparages the critical and sometimes conspiratorial positions taken by Egyptian public intellectuals and a range of political opposition when it comes to educational reform. She writes,

> Suspicion of a foreign plot behind every decision and opinion proposed by national education experts, inside or outside the [Ministry of Education], has jeopardized education reform efforts. As a result of public skepticism fueled by vigorous opinion campaigns, some projects have been terminated and several bilateral donors ([the Japanese] JICA, [the German] GTZ, [the Danish] Danida, and British aid) have decided to either reduce their direct involvement in basic education, in order to avoid provoking political and cultural sensitivities, or to direct their assistance to higher or technical education and subjects of study that are not related to the so-called identity-triangle [of national, religious, and cultural identity] (Sayed 2006, 147).

Sayed goes to great lengths to try to dispel conspiracy theories by citing examples of foreign-led initiatives and showing that donors have no ulterior motives but are simply supporting reforms for "Education for All" and better educational quality. She further argues that conspiracy theories would wane if domestic actors participated more fully in the reform process and if reform itself was carried out with more transparency. These points are extremely well taken. However, the problems that arise are not merely a matter of participation and transparency. Educational reforms, even ones which appear benign and benevolent such as global citizenship, stir up such public outcry precisely because of the public's inherent understanding of the connections between hard and soft power.

Soft Power, Hard Power, and Education Reform

If we consider the global context in which these changes toward decentralization, privatization, and global citizenship education take place, it is imperative to highlight two sides of influence: soft and hard power. Soft power, a term coined by Joseph Nye just at the end of the Cold War, refers to the ability of a powerful country to get other countries to do what it wants through persuasion and attraction, rather than by force or forms of monetary incentives (Nye 1990, 2004). The reason for invoking the concept of empire in this chapter has been precisely to position the United States in the nonneutral role it occupied while it was involved in curricula and other reforms. The United States was the strongest global military and economic power and exerted immense influence and muscle in the region. It pursued soft power through education, civil society, and general prodemocracy interventions. At the same time, it was involved in highly controversial and oftentimes illegal hard power maneuvers that included wars, other forms of military interventions, and massive arms sales.[14] In the aftermath of the September 11, 2001, attacks, soft and hard power engagements intensified. The wars in Iraq and Afghanistan were just two examples of hard power that caused mass trauma to the region. Moreover, these were happening at a time when the American-led curriculum center was calling for Egyptian children to show respect for the international order and live in peaceful and respectful ways. The irony, or hypocrisy, was not lost on teachers, nor on large swaths of the public. Sociologist of education André Mazawi cogently argues that in the post–September 11 period, the subtext of development discourses in education was informed by the need to "depoliticize" educational content, by highlighting its contribution to the students' acquisition of globally competitive skills and knowledge (Mazawi 2010). Courses on global citizenship and morals did not actually enable or encourage students to better understand and deliberate about actual critical issues pertaining to global power, inequality, and geopolitics, but rather served as a way to erase and mute these issues.

How did students, youths in high school and universities, think about their place in the world? How did they understand the global order and the meaning of public engagement, civic participation, and global citizenship? In the following three chapters (chapters 10, 11, and 12) we turn to youth themselves to redress knowledge gaps about the life conditions of young people, their ideas about education, livelihoods, national life and the global order, and their visions for the future.

10

Young Egyptians' Quest for Jobs and Justice

Summary: Youth in Egypt and throughout the region are the most schooled and globalized generation in history. Yet they are coming of age in an environment characterized by high rates of youth unemployment and underemployment, repressive political regimes, a youth bulge, post–September 11 moral panics about radicalization, and ongoing regional conflicts and wars. This chapter, first published in 2010,[1] uses the life history method to hear from young people directly about how they think about politics, the economy, education, and the meaning of citizenship. Their stories testify that youth are not so much preoccupied with religious politics, the focus of much analysis coming out of the global North, as with jobs and justice, arguably the issues that define this youthful generation.

Being Young, Arab, and Muslim

In media and in political and policy circles in the global North, especially the United States, there has been an undeniable preoccupation with Muslim youth. The concern was growing since the late 1980s but became more intense since the terrorist attacks on the US of September 11, 2001.[2] Within a climate of terrorist scares, rising rates of youth unemployment in the Muslim Middle East, a youth bulge, and an escalation of regional conflicts with no resolution in sight, questions and speculation about youth entered debates about education, democracy, security/radicalization, citizenship, and economic reform. Much attention was placed on two general areas: the challenges youth face in making the transition from school to work; and security and the spread of Islamist politics and radicalization (Roy 2004). Youth tend to be treated either as subjects to stimulate neoliberal development, or as religious and ideological actors with the potential for radicalization. Youth themselves are rarely consulted about their struggles,

149

about how they view their own status as citizens. They are allowed little scope in official narratives to question, reject, or offer alternative visions, demands, and arrangements for educational, societal, and economic futures.

Egypt and other middle-income and low-income countries in the region have held the inauspicious distinction of having the fastest growing labor force globally. In Egypt, unemployment is highest among the young (youth accounted for 80 percent of the country's total unemployed population), and proportionately higher among females and the educated (Assaad and Roudi-Fahimi 2007, 3, 19, World Bank 2004, 92).[3] Of youth who find employment, 69 percent of them labor in insecure circumstances with no formal contract, and nearly half are in temporary jobs not related to their desired careers (Silver 2007, 9).

A common theory in policy circles is that the youth bulge poses not only a development challenge, but potentially an opportunity, a "demographic dividend" or "demographic gift" (World Bank 2007, 4; Wolfensohn Center 2008). Having a high proportion of young people in a population is sometimes seen as an advantage, since their energies can be channeled in directions that lead to economic growth. There is evidence, for example, that the economic boom of the "Asian Tiger" countries from 1960 to 1990 was possible in part due to policies that capitalized on its youthful population and turned this human capital into an economic and social advantage (World Bank 2007, 4–5). The moral panic about having so many young people in society stems from the prospect that if their energies are not harnessed in productive activities, trouble will be in store. A lack of economic independence not only puts an undue burden on families and the state, but delays young people from marrying and forming families. Given high housing costs, it can take many years for a couple, often the man, to save enough to secure housing for a marital home. When the age of marriage rises, it often leads to youth frustration—sexual and otherwise—and manifests in ways that can cause further social problems (Singerman 2007).

Other anxieties stem from national and international security concerns relating to Islamic extremism and terrorism. As Esposito and Mogahed write in *Who Speaks for Islam? What a Billion Muslims Really Think*, "The conventional wisdom, based on old and deeply held stereotypes and presuppositions about extremists, has often fallen back on an intuitive sense that a combination of religious fanaticism, poverty, and unemployment drive extremism and terrorism" (Esposito and Mogahed 2007, 67–68). Their analysis of a Gallup World Poll, representing 90 percent of the world's Muslims (1.3 billion people) in thirty-five countries, calls these assumptions into question. They concur that unemployment and poverty are both major social problems but find that "neither unemployment nor job status differentiate radicals from moderates. No difference exists in the unemployment rate among the politically radicalized and moderates; both are approximately 20%" (Esposito and Mogahed 2007, 71). Clearly, there is a need to look for a different set of explanations to understand the trajectories and choices of young people. There is also an imperative to understand youth not just for their future potential as "human becomings," but as young social actors, as "beings" in the present, in their own right (Qvortrup et al. 1994).

To reach a better understanding of the lives, choices, and preoccupations of youth requires going to the source and talking to youth directly. As youth studies scholars Alcinda Honwana and Filip de Boeck note with reference to youth in Africa, "The voices, views and visions of young people themselves still wait to be heard and considered. We know remarkably little about them. Children and youth . . . have often remained our 'silent others,' our voiceless *enfants terribles*" (Honwana and de Boeck 2005, 2).

The methodological approach chosen for the inquiry discussed here is the life history method. Unlike a large-scale survey or multicountry poll, life histories cannot claim representativeness or provide the basis for statistical generalization. What the life history approach can offer, however, is the means to arrive at a deeper understanding of the life trajectories of individuals and, in so doing, gain insight into larger social collectivities and conditions, and suggest hypotheses for further inquiries. As Cole and Knowles elucidate in their work *Lives in Context:* "To understand some of the complexities, complications, and confusions within the life of just one member of a community is to gain insights into the collective. . . . [E]very in-depth exploration of an individual life-in-context brings us that much closer to understanding the complexities of lives in communities" (Cole and Knowles 2001, 11).

This chapter is organized around the life stories of two "twenty-something" urban youth from Alexandria, Egypt. They are both from the intermediate social classes (lower middle to middle class) that theoretically constituted the backbone of the modern Egyptian nation. They were born into the Mubarak regime (1981–2011) and came of age during a period of supposed economic and political liberalization. They harbored commonplace aspirations to be able to live their "youthhoods" while finding reasonable employment and achieving the financial means to marry and build a family. However, deficits of jobs and justice made these simple desires difficult to fulfill.

"Karim," a seasonal laborer aged twenty-two, is waiting for an opportunity to "begin" his life. He represents a "youth-in-waiting." "Dina," a university student aged twenty-one and still living at home, wants above all to live an ethical life and to be able to fulfill her desires for a career, love, marriage, and family. However, she is highly skeptical that she will be able to realize these everyday goals. Both of them are Muslim, but religion holds a different meaning to each of them in terms of their everyday practices and self-identity. Karim is inconsistent about religious practice, though at times he finds personal comfort in religion. Dina takes pride in her piety and wears her religion on her sleeve. Although the two differ in this respect, they converge in a markedly similar way in terms of the difficulties of being young in contemporary Egyptian society and their quest for an alternative order.

Karim: Waiting for Life to Begin

Karim spends his time in a combination of hanging out, worrying, sometimes working, indulging in drugs, and hoping. He lives his life in the present, taking pleasure when and where he can, and at the same time hopes for a better future. However he worries that he is not making the transition to adulthood, but rather a transition to nowhere. Following a long spate of unemployment and a recent breakup initiated by his girlfriend, he sees his chances at a "normal" life of love, marriage, and a family slipping out of reach. He spends much of his time in a coffee shop waiting to get picked up for short-term construction jobs. Wavering between desperation and hope, he says, "They are saying that there are opportunities. Where are these opportunities? Where is the starting point, the beginning? If only I could start, I could continue my life. But where is the starting point? Tell me: where can I begin?"

As a young boy, Karim never imagined he would be in such a rut. He is still trying to process his family's fall from relative prosperity to poverty in the space of just a decade. He remembers as a child when his family was enjoying mobility from the ranks of the urban poor to the middle classes. His father was a low-paid but resourceful construction worker in the 1970s. During the mid-1980s, when Karim was a small child, his father seized the opportunity to travel to Saudi Arabia to work in the country's booming construction sector. He made a good sum of money, much of which he invested in property and the education of his children, even though he himself had no formal schooling. His father built two houses—one for Karim's paternal grandmother, the other for his family—and enrolled his four sons and one daughter in private schools in Alexandria. He believed in the promise of education and that it would raise the social status of the family and prepare his children for middle class professions.

Karim's mother, who had completed her education to the preparatory stage, possessed knowledge of the school system and enjoyed a decent standard of literacy. Jealous of his wife's schooling and fearful that she would use it to try to assert superiority over him, Karim's father put a moratorium on the mother's involvement in their sons' studies. She was only allowed to assist their daughter with schoolwork, because he did not perceive her as posing a threat to his authority. When the mother so much as asked her sons about school, the father would berate and shout at her. As Karim recalls, "In our home the father was everything and everyone was expected to obey him."

The brothers attended an all-boys private school, Victoria College, that had been the bastion of the elite prior to the July 23 Revolution of 1952. It now caters to a social mix of students belonging to the financially strapped middle classes and upwardly mobile working or laboring classes. Teachers often insult the poorer students as being "uncultured" and the cause of the school's decline. Karim so internalized the class discrimination of the school that he himself, a victim of it, complains that the school's environment has deteriorated and become too "lower class" (*bi'a* in colloquial slang).

Karim displays a keen intelligence and interest in politics and social issues, yet he deeply dislikes school. His memories of it, and especially his teachers, are bitterly painful: "Teachers used to beat students badly and I got a good share of the beatings." He recalls the first day of class in ninth grade when his teacher began the lesson by warning him, "I've heard about you, so you'd better beware." This was "a really black day," he sighs. His school career was a series of failures and bare passes until finally, during a repeat year in secondary school, he left school for good. Nevertheless, his greatest regret is not having made it to university and the knowledge that he will go through life with the label of being an "uncultured" and "uneducated" man.

All three of Karim's brothers also dropped out of high school. Their inability to complete school could be attributed in part to a lack of parental support, and their father's policy of not hiring private tutors. Karim's sister is the only one of the five siblings who successfully completed her studies.

She went on to work in what the family considers a high-status job in a five-star hotel in Alexandria.

By the end of the 1990s, the family's savings were gone, drained from the expenses of school tuition and healthcare, the costs of raising five children, and free spending. Karim's family eventually fell into extreme poverty. All the children had to seek employment to support their basic needs. Without a high school degree and work experience, Karim initially relied on his father to help him find work in construction, specifically in tiling and painting. However, he has not been offered "good jobs" because of what he believes to be age discrimination. "Society doesn't give any chances to young people to prove themselves," he complains. "Young people *can* do some things adults can't do, but no one gives us responsibility. Even my parents still deal with me as a kid. They say youth is not the age of responsibility, but then what is?" Even though Karim lives at home, his family stopped providing him with financial or even moral support, as they are so preoccupied with their own problems and struggles for survival.

Karim measures his life as a series of failures, some of which he recognizes as his own fault, but others he considers the result of barriers and setbacks out of his control. He explains, "I'm not satisfied with myself at all. How can I be? I failed in everything: in education, in work, in building a family. I don't see my future in anything. I want to have a home and family, to succeed in my work. But what will happen? Only God can decide." He finds some solace in God, and prays when he is in the right frame of mind, but not on a regular basis.

He encounters indifference from his family, his government, and his society. His friends offer some solidarity, but no real help with how to move forward. His peer group is made up of other young unemployed men who, like him, are waiting for an opportunity, a change of fortune, a girl who would love them regardless of their financial situation. Even though some of his old school friends and neighbors call in on him, he avoids the ones who are faring better in the world—the ones with jobs, family support, and fiancées. His current circle of friends consists mainly of other young men who fill their time with a combination of drugs, prayer, surfing the internet for hours upon end, and waiting in coffee shops for a truck that might pick them up for a short-term construction job.

Feelings of despair mixed with boredom lead him in two directions. Sometimes he turns to the Qur'an and prays for solace, but more recently his preferred activity is to escape through hashish. He justifies his hashish use by explaining that it provides him with some moments of gratification and peace. For him, however fleeting, some good moments are better than none at all.

> I haven't managed to do a single thing in my life. I haven't achieved any of my goals, so I got into hash. The best thing about it is that it kills free time (al-faragh al-tam). I burn away six to seven hours in a state of happiness. It takes you away (biyi'zil) and I can find myself, achieve everything I ever wanted, without moving from my place. Do you understand what I'm saying? You find yourself having done so much when you haven't done anything. It's a way to escape from reality.[4]

When trying to understand and rationalize his situation, Karim returns repeatedly to the question of rights (haq or huquq [pl.])—the denial of rights, the importance of rights, and the devastating effect that the lack of rights and political corruption has on the ability of youth to earn a livelihood and enjoy a decent lifestyle. He views the twin elements of justice and jobs—or injustice and unemployment—as intricately interwoven. He stresses that opportunity and advancement result primarily from connections, bribes, and dishonesty, not from merit or hard work. Since he does not have the family connections to boost him, he figures his best option is to build a future abroad in the West, because, as he understands it, "abroad you can take your rights; here you cannot." But the path of legal emigration is closed to him. He cannot obtain a passport before completing his military service, something he is categorically opposed to doing due to his distrust and abhorrence of the Mubarak regime. He explains, "I can't serve in the military forces of this country. Why? Because it's just like Adel Imam says in the movie Terrorism and Kebab (al-Irhab wa-l-kabab), 'I do not serve the country. I serve the respectable pasha,' and this is very bad. I cannot do that."[5]

He describes the Mubarak regime as fundamentally corrupt, squandering the country's human and natural resources, and serving the interests of a small oligarchy. He also takes issue with Egypt's most important ally, the United States, whose military presence and development aid he views as highly dubious, divisive, and self-serving. He asks:

> Where is this US aid? No one sees or benefits from it and it divides us. Why can't Egypt undergo any real development without foreign

aid? The US takes its own opportunities. It had its dreams. But now it's going around starting wars and is driven more and more by greed and evil. I can't accept this way of doing things.

He sees tremendous potential in Egypt, if only it would follow some basic principles of fair play. He explains: "Imagine Egypt's potential if the ruling elite had real consciousness. We would see that in Egypt we have the Suez Canal. This is a great resource! This alone can let the people live like pashas. We have power through our workforce. We have agricultural land, and we have a massive desert. We have good things, very good things, but there is no mind!"

Despite his strong opposition to the Mubarak regime, Karim is skeptical about formal politics and has no interest in taking part in oppositional activities. He especially does not want to get involved with the Muslim Brotherhood, which he considers to be as authoritarian and corrupt as the government. He disapproves of militant Islam and terrorism, but explains that these are the offspring of oppression. While he is personally not pulled in this direction, he understands how others like him could be drawn in. He cautions that when young people are deprived of their rights and lack outlets to express their discontent, when their paths to gainful employment and autonomous adult life are closed, and when they face discrimination and observe injustices around them, they can resort to violence or terrorism.

I want to emphasize that the young person who becomes a terrorist sees his life as a closed path. It is closed in its past, its future, in its material and moral aspects. This person needs someone to help him. But he doesn't find anyone. He doesn't belong to a powerful family that can protect him from failed laws. The social and economic conditions don't provide him with any opportunities. He is angry that all the important things in his life, work and love, have failed. He doesn't believe in the social structure since it's neither just nor legitimate. He considers this system responsible for his own failures and problems of his society. This person can do nothing but escape.

Despite his glum reality, Karim lives in hope that a big change remains possible and that his life might take a turn for the better. He first has to find a way out of his current impasse, but is not sure how to move forward:

I see constraints everywhere: constraints from the ID card, the army, education, many things. But I feel like if I do something, I will do it in the right way. If I get interested in something, I will do it 100 percent. I need to succeed in something, but I can't find my way. I feel that something big will happen. What is it? When? Sometimes you find your heart secure. You think something will happen, but you don't know what it is. No one can say what will happen tomorrow. Life can turn upside down. I will wait.

When trying to understand and rationalize his situation, Karim, who suffered from occasional incapacitating feelings of "being stuck," returns repeatedly to the question of justice, of rights. Karim alludes to the fact that although he is alive, he does not feel like he is living. He does not possess what he considers a *life*. Living would require certain choices, conditions of freedom, opportunity based on fairness, and respect. He will wait.

Dina: Piety and Rights

Dina, a college student majoring in veterinarian science, lives at home in Alexandria with her parents and two sisters. Her father works as a lawyer and her mother, who earned a BA, is a stay-at-home mom. They maintain a modest but comfortable middle-class standard of living and enjoy close family relations. Religion plays an important part in the life of the family. They observe daily prayers and read the Qur'an together. Dina, who wears the *hijab* and has committed the Qur'an to memory, self-identifies as a pious Muslim youth. Like so many of her generation, she aspires to maintain "high moral standards," respecting her parents, her Islamic values and traditions, and following her ambitions. She is currently single but dreams of finding someone to love and with whom to build a family.

Dina combines a language of religious piety with a liberal discourse about freedom, rights, and justice. For instance, she depicts her home life as a setting in which "freedom and fairness" are the norms. She says, "Our parents give us a lot of freedom. They let us express our views freely and ask our opinions." When she speaks of restrictions she faces at home, such as the rule that she could not stay out past sunset, she does not frame this as a lack of freedom. She views her curfew, which she is unhappy about, as a judgment her parents make about safety and the reputation of girls. Freedom, on the other hand, relates more to human respect and dignity.

She juxtaposes her home life, which is built around relations of piety and fairness, to an external environment of corruption and decay. Her principal point of reference is the education system. From an early age, Dina performed at an extremely high level at school, but she does not mince words about the flaws of the education system. She describes it as "broken and sinking," and in dire need of reform, beginning with the need to change the "phantom of the examination system." She views school simply as a gateway to the university. She credits her mother, not her teacher, for her good grades and educational success. She scored highly on the Thanawiya 'Amma, but not high enough to enter the Faculty of Medicine. She settled for joining the School of Veterinary Medicine and at the time of the interview was a second-year student in this highly regarded faculty.

As a university student, her main grievances have to do with the lack of fair play in the education system and concerns about whether, after years of dedicated study, she will have the opportunity to apply her achievements and ambitions to a career. She is weary of the role of connections (wasta) in getting ahead. She had been dismayed at the degree of nepotism in higher education as she witnessed the children of professors and those with parents in position of power get the highest marks and job opportunities (apparently unwarranted), whereas those with no connections remained unnoticed, underrewarded, and underemployed. She laments, "Egyptian society is thoroughly based on connections which spread like wildfire." The root of the problem, she argues, emanates from a government that denies citizens even their most basic rights, as it promotes the interests of the rich and powerful. It uses the entire security apparatus to safeguard the few, as it neglects and persecutes the many. She explains:

> The police protect the wealthy and lock up the poor, who fill the state prisons. In the old days we had the saying, "The police are in the service of the people" (al-shurta fi khidmat al-sha'b). Now we say, "The police and the people are in the service of the nation" (al-shurta wa-l-sha'b fi khidmat al-watan). What I want to know is what, actually, is the meaning of the term nation (watan)? Isn't the nation supposed to be the people? Or does nation mean something else? Does it mean the president?

Mirroring Karim's sentiments about how Egypt has become synonymous with the president, she declares:

Egypt has become a kingdom of kings. But even in kingdoms the name of the president doesn't become a substitute for the name of the country. In England you don't have people saying "England is Elizabeth." But here we have the expression "Egypt is Mubarak" (*Misr Mubarak*). We need to change Egypt from the government of a king to a government of the people. Egypt is really going downhill.

The Mubarak regime's close association with the United States further reinforces Dina's judgment that the political elite look out for themselves at the cost of the interests and rights of an entire nation. She strongly criticizes the government's tacit acceptance and complicity in the policies of the "imperial United States," which she views as a "thug nation," especially vis-à-vis Iraq, Palestine, and Lebanon. She considers US interference in national economic policies through the International Monetary Fund and World Bank a central cause of the economic insecurity and unending hardships of the majority of Egyptian youth. Most upsetting to her is how the Egyptian government ignores the plight of its own people and punishes those citizens who agitate for political and economic reform. She stresses: "The government should start trying to listen to the problems of the people, and especially the youth, to give us our rights. We need our rights! Every citizen should have justice and the right to an honorable life." Despite her strong political views, Dina deems Egypt as "no place for political ambitions," because street activism carries heavy risks, such as torture and imprisonment.

Youth Cultural Politics and New Media

Given the deep distrust with which Karim, Dina, and presumably many more young Egyptians view politics and their government, how do they respond to their situation? During this period between 2006 and 2009, new information and communication technologies were changing the landscape of youth culture, youth sociability, and political engagement (See Bunt 2003, Etling et al. 2009; Maira and Soep 2004; United Nations Department of Economic and Social Affairs 2005). The rate of internet penetration in the Middle East in 2008 was 28.3 percent, higher than the world average of 25.5 percent. In the year 2000, there were a mere 300,000 internet users in Egypt, a number that increased to 6 million by 2006 and roughly 12.6 million by 2009.[6] The Egyptian blogosphere and social networking sites such as Facebook (launched in 2004 and available in Egypt in 2007), constituted a veritable cultural revolution, mainly as the result of the rapid increase and innovative engagement of youth internet users. The ways individual youth used new media differed considerably, but it would not be off the mark to suggest that most of them used it for some form or another of subversive activity.

Like growing cadres of youth in the region, Dina uses the internet as an alternative outlet for socializing, academic research, getting information about current affairs, and what might loosely be termed "political involvement." Since the time she started going online to support her academic work, which was three years prior, she had been a dedicated internet user. It did not take long after getting a computer "for her studies," which her parents bought on an installment plan, for her to discover that she could bypass the local media and access alternative news sources. She spends time reading political blogs and foreign newspapers about politics, the economy, and world affairs. She considers staying informed a moral duty and a political act, a way to resist being controlled by government propaganda and the establishment media. Yet she does not feel entirely at ease using the internet as a tool for direct political action, as some mainly youthful activists were starting to do.[7] She acknowledges its potential for civil disobedience, however. She herself exercises her own version of civil disobedience, though not by joining organized strikes or political movements, but rather by deliberately shunning official and semiofficial news outlets, and sharing information she deems valuable about national politics, regional politics, and economic development.

She acknowledges that the internet is a double-edged sword. On the one hand, she considers the virtual, uncensored space liberating. On the other hand, she worries that Egyptian and other youth would misuse the internet to imitate the "morally bankrupt" (munharif) aspects of Western youth culture. Many young people, she argues, use the internet in degenerate ways, accessing pornography and lowbrow entertainment, or flirting and forming immoral relations. Even after deriding the moral corruption of the West, she admits that if given the chance, she would go to the West to study and work, because these are "open societies" with strong economies where youth can "have their rights" and gain financial independence.

Dina grapples with ways of "doing the right thing" and of living a virtuous life, while also having her voice heard and her actions count toward some meaningful form of change. She tries in whatever ways she can to inform and influence others, to "transfer her [social and political] consciousness to family and friends" by circulating and forwarding news items and engaging in debates. She is especially keen on interacting with peers, in person and through social networking sites, because, as she explains, "Once they have consciousness of their rights and their ability to correct social wrongs, they have a duty to act for change."

The Big Struggles for Life's Simple Desires

When discussing the goals of her generation, Dina explains, "The ambitions of young people are modest. We want to live at a decent level (*'ala mustawa karim*), get a job, find love, and get married." Although seemingly simple desires, these goals appear hopelessly out of reach. Arguably the two greatest impediments facing youth are not the spread of Islamist movements or radicalism, but the scarcity of jobs and the absence of justice. Injustice—whether measured as a lack of fair treatment in schools, the role of connections in gaining employment, or the absence of accountability of the government and international actors in regard to economic and political policies—has a direct bearing on the current lives and future prospects of these young people.

Although the socioeconomic situations of Karim and Dina differ significantly, their stories provide a lens through which to understand the conditions of being young and Egyptian at a particular moment in time. Both identify the lack of jobs and justice as the preeminent problems youth face. Both experience the education system as unfair and corrupt, part of the larger societal problem. Finally, both draw on a language of rights in remarkably similar ways. Whether a new generational consciousness could lead to economic justice and livelihood opportunities is an open question. However, it certainly appears that rights, more than religion, embody the shared values of a generation and the basis upon which it would endeavor to change an unjust order. Little did Dina and Karim know that they were living on the precipice of a historic popular uprising, the January 25 Revolution of 2011, where many of their grievances and hopes for Egypt would be on full public display by millions of their fellow citizens.

11

Youth and Citizenship in the Digital Age: A View from Egypt

Summary: In the years leading up to the Arab uprisings of 2010–11, youth were learning, exercising citizenship, and forming a generational consciousness in fundamentally different ways than previous generations had done. The bulk of research and theorizing on generations in the digital age comes out of the global North. To fully understand the rise of an active generation, however, requires a more inclusive global lens. The Arab states and wider MENAWA region, with their surging youth populations and escalating rates of youth connectivity, combined with high degrees of unemployment and democracy deficits, provide an ideal vantage point from which to understand generations, power, and counterpower in the digital age. This study is informed theoretically by the sociology of generations and methodologically by biographical research with Egyptian youth.

Wired Generation

In late December 2011, education bureaus throughout Egypt dispatched all end-of-year examinations to schools in their districts. This was no business-as-usual year, however. The country had experienced the most momentous popular prodemocracy uprising in over half a century. The January 25 Revolution lasted eighteen days and led to the fall of President Hosni Mubarak on February 11, 2011. Mubarak had held office for thirty years, and many thought him invincible.

Students carried the spirit of revolution back to their schools and universities. They led sit-ins, demonstrations, and Facebook campaigns to expose corrupt teachers and administrators. They demanded reforms of the curriculum and examination system. They set up fundraising activities to help the families of the martyrs of the revolution. In the wake of these events, many students expected the government-administered annual examinations to provide an opportunity for them to write about some aspect of these participatory and collective acts stirring in the country. Instead, they found the Arabic questions for first-year high school students represented a conspicuously "prerevolution approach" to education. The one compulsory essay question from the examination administered from a local governate reads as follows: "Write a letter to the Supreme Council of the Armed Forces (SCAF) thanking them for supporting the revolution. Thank SCAF also for their steadfastness in protecting the nation from all agents, despite being opposed and insulted."[1]

SCAF was the temporary caretaker government composed of twenty-one high- ranking military officers. At the time, protests were continuing on a steady basis as people continued demanding a more democratic form of government and maintained their slogan for "Bread, Freedom, Social Justice." The examination question signaled that the temporary government continued to equate citizenship with obedience to authority, and treated education as a system that would ensure citizens fell in line, as if no revolution had ever taken place. But wired students had their own ideas about their place in the New Egypt. They had been experimenting with different ways of exercising citizenship, and agitating for a more inclusive system in which they, the young, were full participants. Pupils used the occasion of the examination to bite back at the system. Someone made a scan of the question and posted it on Facebook, where it circulated among different networks. This Facebook post spurred a lively debate about the performance of the SCAF and triggered vigorous debates and earnest deliberation about the pros and cons of further revolt. The incident illustrated in a small but telling way how the rifts between the pedagogic spaces of formal institutions and those of youth-driven communication spaces were in active competition. An underlying assumption guiding this research was that formal educational institutions had been losing their hold over the young and declining as sites of nation and citizenship building (Herrera 2010b). At the same time, and compared to previous generations, youth coming of age in the digital era were learning and exercising citizenship in fundamentally new ways.

Around the globe, a monumental generational rupture was taking place. It was being facilitated—not driven in some inevitable and teleological process—by new media and communication technologies. A body of literature on generations dating from the late 1990s to 2010 drew directly on communication and information technologies to name this generation, an affirmation of how generational and technological change were perceived as intertwined. In addition to Millennials and Gen Y, other terms for this generational cohort included the Net Generation (Tapscott 1998, 2009); the E-Generation (Krause 2007); the iGeneration (Rosen 2011); digital natives (Palfrey and Gasser 2008); Generation txt (Rafael 2003; Nielsen and Webb 2011); the Facebook, Twitter, and Google Generations (McDonald 2010; Rideout, Foehr, and Roberts 2010); and Generation 2.0 (Rigby 2008). I prefer the term "wired generation" as it captures how communication behavior led to a "rewiring" of cognitive processes (Herrera and Sakr 2014). As Egyptian youth activist and scholar Aly El-Raggal explains:

> Revolutions take place first of all in our minds. The new cognitive maps we develop lead to new outlooks on the world. It is no wonder that the new generation led the call for the revolution in Egypt because we were the only ones who succeeded in making an epistemological rupture with the system—and I mean the general system, not only the political one. (Herrera 2011)

Those wired members of this generation, born between the late 1970s and the early years of the millennium, functioned in ways that were more horizontal, interactive, participatory, open, collaborative, and mutually influential than cohorts from the analog, or predigital age (Edmunds and Turner 2005; Jenkins, Ito, and Boyd 2015).

Their tendency to be more collectivist led some to call them the "we" generation (Hewlett 2009; Jenkins 2008). The media and business writer Don Tapscott identified eight features of the wired generation related to their digital communications use: freedom, customization, scrutiny, integrity, collaboration, entertainment, speed, and innovation (Tapscott 2009). Another characteristic stemming from this generation's media behavior was what media theorist Clay Shirky (2010) called "symmetrical participation." Wired youth were not passive recipients of media and messages, as in the days when television and print media ruled, but played active roles in the production, alteration, consumption, and dissemination of content. Their relationship to the media was more proactive, participatory, and interactive.

For all the seeming advantages and virtues of the wired generation, a parallel body of work pointed to its limitations and harmful sides. For example, consider the following titles of some well-known critiques: *The*

Dumbest Generation: How the Digital Age Stupefies Young Americans and Jeopardizes Our Future (Bauerlein 2009), *The Narcissism Epidemic: Living in the Age of Entitlement* (Twenge and Campbell 2009), and *The Shallows: What the Internet Is Doing to Our Brains* (Carr 2010). These cautionary works raise valid concerns about how members of this generation exhibit signs of a short attention span, seek instant gratification, are unable or unwilling to read and think deeply, and lack the skills necessary for long-term vision and planning. This set of critical attributes does not cancel out the more positive qualities mentioned above, but brings to the table a more multifaceted picture, drawing attention to the challenges that digital natives would encounter over time. This combined literature about the virtues and vices of a wired generation raises questions about its ability to lead societies to a future social order that is more inclusive, sustainable, and just.

Sociology of Generations

The enduring question posed by sociologists of generations is why, or under what conditions, does one generation become conscious of its common situation and rise to steer the reins of history, while others follow the way paved by previous generations? Hungarian sociologist Karl Mannheim (1893–1947) grappled with this question in Germany in the period between the two World Wars (Mannheim 1952). Mannheim conceptualized generations as a "social phenomenon" rather than a biological or life-course category, since generations share a "common location in the historical dimension of the social process" (Mannheim 1952, 105; Pilcher 1994).

Members of a generation are not homogeneous, and differences among groups and individuals exist based on class, ideology, geography, and gender, to name a few axes of difference. However, members of a generation—like members of a social class—can achieve "actuality" when they develop a consciousness of their common interests and form group solidarity to harness their collective power. As Mannheim writes, "It is a matter for historical and sociological research to discover at what stage in its development, and under what conditions . . . individual members of a generation become conscious of their common situation and make this consciousness the basis of their group solidarity" (Mannheim 1952, 290).

He also notes that tectonic shifts along generational lines usually occur as the result of a social trauma and acceleration in the "tempo of social change" (1952, 309) through, for example, war, economic crisis (Wohl 1979), or a social, political, or technological revolution (Klatch 1999).

During such times, the young become less reliant on the "appropriated memories" of the older generations—those transmitted, for instance, through schools, mass media, and the family—and become more reliant on their own directly acquired experiences through a process of "fresh contact." During these periods and events, the young may cease to view the order of things as inevitable or desirable.

Mannheim takes a national approach to generations using the nation-state as the unit of analysis. However today, as youth around the globe develop common behaviors and attitudes stemming from their interactions with new media and communication technologies, we can speak at some level of global youth culture (Castells et al. 2007) and a global generation (Edmunds and Turner 2005). Sociologists Edmunds and Turner argue that global generations can rise and become active if they are able to access and exploit resources, innovate politically and culturally, and cultivate strategic leadership. They posit:

> Generations shift from being a passive cohort . . . into a politically active and self-conscious cohort . . . when they are able to exploit resources (political/ educational/economic) to innovate in cultural, intellectual or political spheres. . . . Resources, opportunity and strategic leadership combine to constitute active generations. (2005, 562)

In the early years of the spread of social media, the wired members of this global generation exhibited prolific innovation in cultural and intellectual spheres, and produced an explosion of ideas and creative content online. They pioneered networked forms of online to offline organizing, whether for the sake of fun and irony, as with flash mobs (Wasik 2006), or for more intentional political purposes, as with smart mobs (Rheingold 2003). Yet, even when a smart mob grew into a social movement—as happened with the Occupy Wall Street movement that started in New York City on the heels of the Egyptian revolution, Spain's Los Indignados movement, and the range of anti-austerity protests in Europe—it remains to be seen if this online-to-offline crowd-sourced organizing is leading to what Mannheim calls "actuality" (Estes 2011; Tharoor 2011; Toussaint 2012).

To fully understand the rise of an active generation requires moving outside North America and Europe, where the bulk of research and theorizing about generations has occurred. Egypt and the wider region provide an ideal vantage point from which to understand generations and power in the digital age.

Youth on the Rise

Throughout countries of the MENAWA region, sub-Saharan Africa, and other regions of the global South, people under thirty-five make up by far the largest percentage of all populations. Depending on the country, the youth bulge can range between 65 to over 80 percent of the population, with the twelve- to twenty-four-year age range especially high. In many of these countries, young people have grown up under militarized regimes ruled by autocrats and oligarchies that in most cases seized power decades ago (Herrera and Bayat 2010; Gebremariam and Herrera 2016). Youth also suffer from different forms of economic marginalization (Dhillon and Yousef 2009). The Arab states have the unwelcome distinction of some of the highest youth unemployment rates in the world.[2] For those with employment, the overwhelming majority labor in precarious circumstances with neither fixed contracts nor benefits, or else in jobs incommensurate with their education and training (Silver 2007) (see chapter 12). Indeed, youth unemployment rates are highest among high school and university graduates (Assaad and Roudi-Fahimi 2007). Neither schools nor universities seem capable of preparing their young people to deal effectively with securing livelihoods or participating in their societies in meaningful ways.

Citizens born in the 1980s and 1990s make up an exceedingly disaffected group. A female university student voiced a commonly expressed view when she said,

> The Egyptian political system governs people by steel and fire (al-hadid wa-l-nar). The government doesn't care about the demands of people and doesn't allow room for us to express our opinions or change the status quo. Security is the most important thing, but only wealthy people are protected by the police. The poor are always in state prisons.

Twenty-one-year-old Fatima reinforced this view when she said with indignation, "We all know that we live in a dictatorial society far removed from the democracy that we all want, all of us."

Young people had been developing awareness of their common grievances—the consciousness to which Mannheim refers—and forming bonds along generational lines using mobile and digital communication tools.[3] Still, digital inequality remains a reality, and large percentages of the population experience digital exclusion by virtue of poverty, location, or other factors.

Wired youth in Egypt were in the global vanguard when it came to using communication tools as a "weapon of opposition" (Eid 2004), building coalitions, and engaging in civil disobedience. The first widespread uses of the terms "Facebook Revolution" and "Twitter Revolution" in the Western media were in relation to Egypt in 2008 after two twenty-something Egyptian college students used the social networking sites to coordinate a strike in solidarity with textile workers in al-Mahalla al-Kubra, an industrial city in the Nile Delta region of Gharbiya.[4] These social networking terms were later applied to social movements in Moldova, Iran, and Tunisia in 2009, 2010, and 2011, respectively. The term "Facebook Revolution" resurfaced after it became known that the call for the January 25 Revolution originated from the Arabic Facebook fan page "We Are All Khaled Said" ("Kullina Khaled Said").

Many people justifiably objected to the term since it could be interpreted as ascribing agency to high-tech companies rather than to the people who used the technology (Aidi 2011; Herrera 2014). But it remains valid to argue that the groundswell of prodemocracy movements in Iran (2009), Tunisia (2010), Egypt (2011), and other countries of the region would probably not have been triggered at that historical moment without social media and the availability of new digital connection tools and technologies. How were Egyptian youth of the digital era—moving between schools, universities, and informal youth communication spaces—forming citizenship dispositions, and to what ends?

Methodology

The sociology of generations emphasizes the need for research that operates on three levels: the individual, the group, and the grounded historical context. The concept of "fresh contact," which is so pivotal to Mannheim's generational theory, refers historically to "an event in one individual biography" and the experience of a cohort of people "who are in the literal sense beginning a 'new life'" (Mannheim 1952, 293). It is therefore pertinent to come up with research strategies that allow for an understanding of autonomous individuals and age cohort collectivities at particular historical junctures. Biographical research offers just such an approach.

This inquiry uses an approach that combines "learning biographies" with "communication biographies." The objective is to learn how, in a period of advanced globalization, and with the incremental penetration of new digital communication tools in society, individuals are learning, gaining citizenship dispositions, and forming group affiliations. The idea is to look at how these processes intersect with schools and universities, the traditional media, and also leisure and consumer activities (Diepstraten, du Bois-Reymond, and Vinken 2006). As sociologist Henk Vinken (2005, 153, 155) elucidates, "The domains of leisure and consumption might well be the playing fields where young people and their closest associates exercise their generational consciousness," where they "build a new community identity . . . as well as alternative routes to establish solidarity, community life and involvement in the common good."

The data presented here comes from narrative interviews that took place in four stages between 2006 and 2011. I designed the interviews to understand how Egyptians in the age group of between sixteen and twenty-nine have been incorporating new media and communication tools into their everyday lives, and how this has changed over time. I adjusted interviews to keep in step with ever-changing communication tools and platforms. In 2006, for instance, conversations revolved more around texting and email behavior, whereas by 2010 the focus was more on social networking activities, and particularly on Facebook.

The participants for this study, born between 1981 and 1993, were part of a single generation insofar as they shared a common historical location, and were coming of age in a similar political-economic context and communications environment. Participants were selected through a process of snowball sampling combined with selective sampling, in order to ensure gender balance and the inclusion of individuals from diverse social, economic, and educational backgrounds. They hailed from urban poor to affluent middle-class areas in Alexandria and Cairo, with a small sample from towns on the outskirts of the cities. In total, this analysis draws on twenty-eight in-depth interviews and two focus group meetings with university students staggered in the years 2006, 2008, 2010, and 2011. Due to the wealth of data and given space limitations, I draw on biographical details of a small group of research participants—Mona, Fatin, Haitham, and Murad (all pseudonyms)—whose biographies contain some composite characteristics. The words of other youth are interspersed throughout the narrative to enrich the text and spotlight the multiplicity of voices informing this analysis.

Findings

In the post-2000 period, youth in Egypt and much of the region were learning culture, forming a generational consciousness, and actively engaging in public life away from schools and adult authority figures. These changes occurred in four phases and culminated in the January 25 Revolution of 2011. A fifth, post-revolution phase, is ongoing.

Phase I: Opening Frontiers

For many young Egyptians with access to the internet in the early years of the twenty-first century, their cultural frontiers opened in unexpected ways as they took part in online gaming and chat rooms. Take the case of Mona, a twenty-two-year-old agriculture student and amateur graphic artist from a semirural town. She described her family as culturally conservative and with allegiance to the Muslim Brotherhood. She recalled the excitement in 2006 when her parents bought a computer on installment for the household. She especially relished the time she spent in chat rooms, first ICQ and then Yahoo. Her English was limited, but that did not deter her. She was always curious about other cultures and dreamed about getting to know people from different parts of the world. Being from a religiously conservative family, she was not sure if she should chat with boys online. However, when a guy from New Zealand asked her questions about her religion, she started up an online friendship "to talk more about Islam." Having broken that first taboo of chatting with boys, she later sought out other "off-limits" groups. She chatted several times with Israelis because, as she explained, "we hear a lot about them in the news, and I wanted to know about them firsthand. It was normal. There was no big problem." Mona breached another national taboo in November 2009 during Egypt's "soccer war," when clashes between the Egyptian and rival Algerian team led to street violence and diplomatic tensions between the two countries. She sought out Algerians online to hear their side of the story. For Mona, chat rooms provided an opportunity to talk about and spread Islam, to broaden her social circles, and to seek out contrary positions to be able to form her own opinions about important issues of the day.

Murad, an architecture student at the University of Alexandria, was less inclined toward chat rooms and more drawn to "massively multiplayer online role-playing games" (MMORPGs). Murad grew up in Alexandria in the 1990s during the piety movement, when many of his classmates and peers were becoming more outwardly religious. He was uncomfortable with the conservative youth culture wave, which he found to be full of hypocrisy. He began to feel like an outcast. As he became more socially isolated, he slipped into depression. His lifeline at the time came from online gaming communities. At one point in high school, he spent up to eight hours a day online. His parents were concerned that he had a gaming addiction, and while that may have been true, these games were a kind of salvation for him. They provided a form of social acceptance that was lacking in his actual physical environment. His preferred game was the World of Warcraft (boasting 11.5 million subscribers worldwide in 2009), which he played on a European server. Murad recounted how these games helped him not only to learn better English, but also to "learn culture." For instance, during a game he taunted his opponent through the chat box with a homophobic slur. Other players immediately called him out. Their reactions took him by surprise and led to exchanges about discrimination around sexual orientation and other related issues. The community of players enforced its own codes of civility. Some of his online players became friends and even visited him in Egypt during their holidays. Though Murad later found work in an architecture firm and no longer has the time to play games, he was grateful for the many social, civil, and cognitive benefits they offered him at a crucial turning point in his life.[5]

Phase II: Cultural Revolution

If early contact with the internet opened up cultural frontiers, the second phase, which overlapped chronologically with the first, heralded a cultural revolution. With the arrival of torrent peer-to-peer file sharing in the early 2000s, a massive open library of the world's cultural and scientific outputs became accessible online. Twenty-four-year-old Haitham recalled that magical time when he had a gateway to art and music around the globe. He declared, "The computer changed my personality 180 degrees. It was the best thing that ever happened to me." Haitham, an Egyptian who had spent his childhood in Saudi Arabia, returned to Egypt with his family when he was thirteen. He loved mathematics and engineering but found that the Egyptian school system stifled rather than stimulated his avid mind. He searched outside of school for ways to feed his interests. Peer-to-peer file sharing supplied him with an endless and free, albeit illegal, supply of music, games, videos, films, and e-books. For Haitham, the computer became "like a gateway to heaven." For over a year he spent most of his waking hours downloading music and lyrics and meeting people with similar interests in online forums. He joined a group of Arabic music aficionados and worked on transferring 125 years of Arabic music recordings into digital format. If not for their labor, this music might have been lost.

Cinema was the next frontier. Haitham discovered the world of foreign films. He recalled, "I was totally immersed in consuming the internet. I wasn't working or studying, just consuming movies, songs, culture, and everything I didn't know before." Downloading a film was "painfully slow," but he had the tenacity to download the "100 Best Films of All Time" with Arabic subtitles. He took a liking to the Cohen brothers, Francis Ford Coppola, Woody Allen, Ingmar Bergman, Quentin Tarantino, and Danish Dogme cinema. After just two short years of using file-sharing programs, his cultural repertoire and English language fluency grew in ways that were unthinkable just a couple of years earlier. "Having this knowledge pumped into your head was like the Matrix," he observed. "Maybe someone who lived for seventy years wouldn't have had the chance to learn what we were able to in two years." Haitham, and scores of other young people, grew up online when the internet was largely unregulated and functioned as a global commons. Their exposure to, and interaction with, ideas, people, images, virtual spaces, and cultural products outside their everyday environments led to a sea change in their mentality and worldview.

In a society like Egypt's, where large segments of the population were culturally conservative and worried about negative foreign influences, not everyone was as enthusiastic as Haitham about the cultural opening provided by the online world. In the interviews that took place in 2006 and 2008, a number of respondents expressed concern that the internet could be a source of moral corruption. Speaking in 2006, Dina, a student in a teachers college, worried that young people used the internet in "morally wrong ways." Her views were shared by nineteen-year-old Samer, who argued that unlike individualistic Western youth, Egyptians valued marriage and family stability and were highly moralistic. He complained that the openness of the internet would tempt some users toward pornography or forming improper relationships. "We have our sexual mores from the prophetic traditions (al-sunna al-nabawiya), the Holy Book, and not [atheist books] which may lead to illnesses like AIDS," he said. For him, it was important that Arab youth benefitted from the knowledge available online, while understanding the limits dictated by religion and tradition.[6] In later interviews in 2010 and 2011, however, respondents expressed less concern that the internet would be a source of temptation and corruption and more alarm that this space would be closed through regulation and censorship. Anticipating that free access to online spaces would one day be restricted, Haitham developed an interest in open-source operating systems and began working toward keeping the internet free and open.

Phase III: Citizen Media

By the period 2006–2008, scores of "ordinary" Egyptian youth were using mobile phones and computers for familiar activities such as chatting, exchanging photographs, playing games, sharing jokes, and flirting. But one activity that especially stood out was how they were using these tools to circumvent official media and construct an alternative news universe.[7] High school and university students had come to understand the power inherent in selecting, circulating, and commenting on a news story that contradicted the official version of an event, or was absent altogether in mainstream news outlets. Moreover, studies had shown that this generation was thirsty for news. A 2008 survey on youth internet use in Egypt reported that 74 percent of respondents used the internet to stay current with the news, while 68 percent used it to download games, songs, movies, and programs (Rakha 2008). With communication tools at their disposal, youth who may not have otherwise been especially political were acquiring political sensibilities. Shayma from the College of Arts said, "Many youths are trying to change things through the internet. We are expressing our viewpoints through blogs and using the weapon of words to transform society."

Data on the Egyptian blogosphere—which was a dynamic form from 2005–2009, before social media disrupted the space—were imprecise. Estimates of the number of Arabic language bloggers ranged from 35,000 to 160,000. A leading study presented a picture of bloggers as being predominantly in the age range of twenty to thirty years old, and with the majority males, but with adolescent girls and young women of between eighteen and twenty-four years old a fast-growing group (Etling et al. 2009). There was much speculation about the ideological character of the Arabic blogosphere at the time, and whether it exhibited tendencies toward Islamism, democratic liberalism, secularism, or other frameworks. The Arab blogosphere in general did not appear to be oriented toward a certain political ideology, but there was evidence of "very little support for terrorism or violent jihad in the Arabic blogosphere and quite a lot of criticism [of it]" (Etling et al. 2009, 10). It was more fitting to think of the new communication space as an expansion of the public sphere (Lynch 2007).

Fatin, a young woman from Cairo University, explained how it was a natural transition to graduate from chat rooms to blogs. She began blogging with a group of friends, five boys and three girls, when she was twenty-one. They blogged anonymously so that they could explore taboo subjects. Their blog dealt with Islamic feminism and delved into questions about whether pious and practicing Muslim women could be feminists; about gender and psychology; and about cinema, culture, and a range of other topics. The act of writing to an unknown public gave Fatin great pleasure. She said, "I felt I wanted to open up, and I loved writing. Also, I wanted to see my words online. I don't know what difference it made, but I just loved it."

Haitham also experimented with blogging in 2005. He became close virtual friends with a tight-knit group of six to seven Arabic-writing male and female bloggers. They initially treated their blogs as private conversations with each other and a small circle of readers. However, when a Syrian blogger from their group disappeared—vanishing offline with no trace—they abruptly woke up to the risks of blogging in their respective police states.[8] For these pioneers, blogging had not started as a self-consciously political activity; rather, they were merely experimenting with a new kind of expressive art. Haitham had used his blog to share anything that caught his attention, such as music, films, current events, and rants about how much he hated school.

His blogging took a turn in 2005, however, during Egypt's parliamentary elections and first multicandidate presidential elections. At nineteen years old, Haitham walked the early steps of citizen journalism: "I was really interested in carrying out an experiment, of monitoring an election from inside a poll station. I went to a small village outside of Alexandria and started to observe what was happening. I saw how people would sell their votes and write 'yes' for Mubarak just for money. I took pictures and posted them on my blog."

He wasn't working for a particular political party or candidate, just acting as an independent citizen with an online voice. Throughout different parts of Egypt—in Aswan, Mansoura, and Cairo—other bloggers, some as young as fifteen and sixteen years old, undertook similar experiments.

Among the pioneers of Egyptian youth citizen journalism was Wael Abbas.[9] He was one of the first bloggers to effectively connect his blog to the new video-sharing site YouTube. In 2006 the Egyptian blogosphere was jolted after he posted a video clip of two police officers torturing and sodomizing a minibus driver, Emad al-Kabir. Not only did the horrifying and graphic video go viral, but al-Kabir came forward at the urging of human rights activists and pressed charges against the officers, leading to the unprecedented conviction of each police officer, and their sentencing to three years in prison.[10] This case emboldened many others to use social media to "name and shame" perpetrators of crimes and corruption. Young citizen journalists anonymously founded anticorruption blogs and websites across the country, from the south to the north. It was also during this period that the US Department of State and international civil society groups working in human rights took an interest in Egypt's cyber citizens. They spearheaded training and networking initiatives with young activists, who came to be known as "cyber-dissidents." It would not be off the mark to suggest that from this period on, the communication behavior of wired Egyptians was channeled toward political oppositional activities at least some of the time.

Phase IV: Becoming a Wired Generation

By the years 2007–2008, blogs were being surpassed by Facebook, the digital social media platform of choice for Egyptians, and memes were becoming a staple of online youth culture. In March 2008, there were some 822,560 Facebook users in Egypt, and by February 2011 that number had grown to more than 5.6 million (Burcher 2010 and Lim 2011). During the early months of the Arab uprisings alone (between January and April 2011), 2 million new Egyptian users joined Facebook. An overwhelming 75 percent of Egypt's Facebook users were between the ages of fifteen and twenty-nine, and 36 percent of those users were female (Mourtada and Salem 2011). In 2007, Fatin, like many other bloggers, transitioned from blogging to Facebooking. She explained: "For a while I was putting my posts both on my blog and on Facebook. Then I switched to Facebook only because you can filter the people you want to read your writings and tag people when you want to discuss an idea with them." A second reason for the shift had to do with security concerns. Fatin no longer felt comfortable transmitting her thoughts so openly in a blog to a public she did not know and could not control.

Murad also slowly phased out blogging in favor of being the administrator (admin) of a Facebook group. In 2008 his group about tolerance and art gained a modest but loyal following of about 350 members, who were mainly Egyptians in their teens and early twenties. Many of them got to know each other offline, and some of them started their own Facebook pages devoted to spinoff issues such as religious freedom, the headscarf, graffiti, and cinema.[11]

The movement-building potentials of Facebook became more evident in 2008, after a university student and part-time activist Isra' 'Abd al-Fattah received a text message from twenty-eight-year-old Ahmed Maher, an engineering student and fellow activist, suggesting they do something to support an April 6 strike planned by textile workers in the Nile Delta city of al-Mahalla al-Kubra. Isra' set up a Facebook event for a general strike, expecting to attract a small circle of activists. It was a surprise to her when the event went viral. The event then turned into a leading youth opposition group that operated online through a Facebook fan page, the April 6 Youth Movement (Harakat Shabab 6 Ibril) (Shapiro 2009). Yet for all the advantages and empowering features of Facebook organizing, it also carried heavy risks. The two creators of the April 6 event were both arrested. Maher was beaten for twelve hours by the state security police until he disclosed his Facebook password. His Facebook friend Wael Abbas posted images of Maher's bruised and beaten body on his blog.

By this time Facebook had become such an integral part of Egyptian youth culture that it went by the local vernacular "al-Face." This virtual space housed a cacophony of voices and innumerable groups, ranging from biology study groups, fans of Arabic singers, car racing aficionados, and volunteer associations, to hate pages against corrupt teachers, Muslim Brotherhood youth, Qur'anic memorization clubs, fashion watchers, and everything in between.

This period similarly gave rise to online creators who used Photoshop and other programs to generate memes that fused humor with biting political and social commentary. Take the example of the Middle East Peace Talks held at the Obama White House on September 1, 2010, and attended by the leaders of Egypt, Jordan, the Palestinian Authority, and Israel. A photograph from the talks showed President Obama leading the delegation. The semiofficial newspaper in Egypt, al-Ahram, had published a doctored image of the event with President Mubarak leading the group. Online bloggers and Facebook groups immediately seized on the crude misrepresentation and exposed the paper. The April 6 Youth movement accused Al-Ahram of representing "the corrupt regime's media" (see BBC 2010).[12]

Egyptian social media exploded in a carnival of memes with different takes on the original photograph. The online meme culture seemed to

9. Middle East Summit at the White House, Washington DC. From left to right: Hosni Mubarak (president of Egypt), Benjamin Netanyahu (prime minister of Israel), Barack Obama (president of the United States), Mahmoud Abbas (president of the Palestinian Authority) and King Abdullah II of Jordan. September 1, 2010. (Photograph from Google Images.)

be outmaneuvering analog news and—in tandem with other youth movements taking shape online—arguably contributed to a crisis of legitimacy for the Mubarak presidency.

At about the same time in 2010, diverse individuals and groups from among Egypt's Facebook youth *(shabab al-Face)* coalesced around the cause of Mohamed ElBaradei, former diplomat, director general of the International Atomic Energy Agency (IAEA), 2005 Nobel Peace Prize recipient, and Egyptian presidential hopeful. ElBaradei founded the National Association for Change in Egypt to advocate for electoral reform and pave the way for more representative democracy. Over a quarter of a million Egyptians from different religious, political, class, gender, and regional backgrounds joined the Mohamed ElBaradei Facebook page. As a critical mass of youth rallied behind ElBaradei, an incipient youth movement was forming. Using all the digital tools and online platforms at their disposal, members of this wired generation emboldened each other to challenge the status quo and encouraged each other to believe that Mubarak and the oligarchy ruling Egypt were not inevitable.

Mona, who by this time had joined a virtual community of female Arab graphic artists, made political cartoons that ridiculed President Mubarak. When asked if she was afraid of the possible consequences of her postings, she declared, "No! We're not afraid of them. What are they going to do, arrest millions of us? Because millions of us are doing this kind of thing." Fatin echoed this sentiment when she explained:

> There is something about being active on a social networking site that breaks all our concerns about anonymity. It's totally changing our attitude. No one can arrest thousands of people for what they're saying on Facebook and they can't control the millions of conversations taking place there.

Two of the admins involved in running the ElBaradei Facebook page, twenty- three-year-old Abdelrahman Mansour and thirty-year-old Wael Ghonim, went on to create an even bigger online sensation, the Arabic fan page and anti-torture campaign "We Are All Khaled Said" ("Kullina Khaled Said"). Naming their page after the well-known victim of police violence, the admins worked under the cover of anonymity partly for security reasons, but also to represent the faceless, unifying voice of the youth. They spoke from behind the mask of the airbrushed "every youth" portrait of the martyr Khaled Said, who in June 2010 was dragged from a cybercafe by two plainclothes policemen in Alexandria and beaten to his death on a public street in view of witnesses.

From its inception, the page operated on the principle of online to offline street action. The page housed a unique cultural space that was youthful, Arab, Egyptian, Muslim-oriented, educational, participatory, and subversive. Within hours of its launch, the admins called on members to get up from behind their computer screens and go out into the streets, initially to attend the public funeral of Khaled Said. The page continued to mobilize its members by organizing a series of anti-torture silent vigils, or civil disobedience style flash mobs (Herrera 2014).[13]

In the lead-up to the November 2010 presidential and parliamentary elections, the "ElBaradei" and "We Are All Khaled Said" Facebook pages were blocked. The temporary loss of Facebook caused its young users great anxiety. Twenty-one-year-old Ahmad talked about how he was genuinely distressed that Facebook might be permanently "turned off." He said that depriving him of Facebook would be like "blocking the air to my lungs." The social networking site had become an extension of his social, political, psychological, and even spiritual life.

Ahmad explained how he came to identify with the page and considered himself a part of the group that had coalesced there. Members of the "We Are All Khaled Said" page and movement abided by a set of crowdsourced codes for community participation: they should not use the space to insult each other's religion, to make fun of each other, for pornography or sexual harassment, for advertising, for spreading false rumors, or for spying. When someone crossed these lines, others would intervene by way of posting a corrective comment, starting a conversation on the post in question, or by asking the admin to remove that person from the group. Members of the group expressed pride in knowing that they had created what they believed to be a virtuous online society—one that stood in contrast to the corruption of institutions in Egyptian society.

The "We Are All Khaled Said" page surpassed even the "ElBaradei" page as Egypt's most active and consequential youth movement in over half a century. It had morphed into a unique community with its own identity, rebel culture, ethical codes, and politics, beyond the control of the admins. The true genius of the page was how it took the collective, generational "we" and branded it with a common identity, conviction, and purpose. The ElBaradei movement zeroed in on reform of the electoral process, whereas the We Are All Khaled Said cause targeted the state's menacing security apparatus and the corruption of the Mubarak government.

The "We Are All Khaled Said" page issued a call for a march on January 25, 2011—the national holiday observed yearly in honor of the police—in order to protest police corruption and torture. However, on the heels of the Tunisian revolution and the fleeing of Tunisian president Zine El Abidine Ben Ali from the country on January 14, the protest became a call for a revolution against "Torture, Corruption, Poverty and Unemployment." This event became the trigger for the eighteen-day revolution that brought down the thirty-year dictatorship of Hosni Mubarak. On the eve of the January 25 Revolution, the page had grown to 390,000 members and was receiving more than 9 million hits a day. The page was part of a network and alliance of youth groups organizing on Facebook,

10. A cartoon by Latuff depicting the martyr Khaled Said holding a diminutive President Mubarak. January 2011. (Image from the "We Are All Khaled Said" Facebook Page.)

including the April 6 Youth Movement and "Mohamed ElBaradei" page, among others.

The Facebook groups did not cause the January 25 Revolution, and the youth of the internet were not the only groups involved in it, but it is hard to imagine the popular uprising unfolding in the way that it did without the communication tools, online horizontal networking, and changing political and cultural behaviors of this wired generation.

Conclusions: Limitations of Civic Renewal in the Digital Age

Like their generational counterparts engaged in popular struggles in the Occupy Movements, the Indignados in Spain, and the Taksim Square protests in Turkey, to name a few, young Egyptians grappled with questions about how to move forward. Their hoped-for outcomes of the revolution, exemplified in the slogan "Bread, Freedom, and Social Justice," were far from inevitable. As it turned out, bringing down a dictator was the easy part. The hard work of deeper systemic change, of keeping alive the commitment to justice and unity, proved to be far greater challenges.

On a global level, Egyptian youth movements had been quick to experiment with social media. Groups had initially used it to build coalitions, create memes, forge more virtuous and experimental communities, get people onto the streets, and even trigger a revolution. The architecture of social media made it an effective tool for short-term, single-issue campaigns, and for scaling up movements with speed and energy. However, as users of social media soon learned, these platforms came with serious downsides and dark sides. The infiltration of bots, the spread of fake news, widespread cyberbullying, online sexual harassment, and the list goes on, represent just some of the features that carry often devastating consequences for young people and societies (Fuchs 2014).

The social media space does not manage complexity or long-term community building well. Due to the business model and political economy of tech companies, social media platforms are spaces that amplify rage over measured discourse (McChesney 2014). These same platforms that facilitated prodemocracy uprisings, were by 2013 and 2014 inundated with "bad actors" and the spread of misinformation. Famously, Islamic State recruiters effectively used online social media to target youth, some of whom only months before were involved in prodemocracy online campaigns. One seventeen-year-old Tunisian who had been the target of such a recruitment campaign cautioned, "Facebook is destroying the younger generation and the parents don't even know about it" (cited in Petré 2015). These platforms have proved to be full of peril for young people, and it comes from different directions.

In chapter 12, on the heels of the euphoria and visions of social renewal temporarily experienced by the youth of the uprisings, we try to understand why and how the political participation and livelihoods of young people did not noticeably improve, and in some cases deteriorated. To do this we conceptualize youth as a precarious class and explore what the late sociologist and philosopher Zygmunt Bauman meant when he observed, "Today's youth have been cast in a condition of liminal drift, with no way of knowing whether it is transitory or permanent" (Bauman 2004, 76).

12

It's Time to Talk about Youth in the Middle East as "The Precariat"

Summary: The Precariat refers to a new global class of people who labor in circumstances of extreme structural insecurity, whose lives are "fleeting and flexible, opportunistic rather than progressively constructed" (Standing 2011, 223). This concept describes conditions of life and labor among youth in the MENAWA region more lucidly and persuasively than the key policy literature on the region, as exemplified in *The Arab Human Development Report (AHDR) 2016: Youth and the Prospects for Human Development in a Changing Reality*. This chapter reviews three main policy priorities in the AHDR: security, education and markets, and youth entrepreneurship. It argues that any meaningful discussion of youth, education, and generations going forward should be mindful of the notion of the "precariat" and the condition of precariousness.

Who Are the Precariat?

In 2011, the year of the Arab uprisings, *The Precariat: The New Dangerous Class* by Guy Standing hit the bookstands. Standing, a labor economist and professorial research associate at the School of Oriental and African Studies (SOAS), gave a name and policy context to a new global class of people who labor in circumstances of extreme structural insecurity, and whose lives are "fleeting and flexible, opportunistic rather than progressively constructed" (2011, 223).

Drawing on decades of work at the International Labour Organization (ILO), Standing identifies the precariat as a growing global class who suffer from what he calls the four As: "anger, anomie, anxiety and alienation" (2011, 33). He recognizes that precarity is a condition that afflicts women and men across generations, but stresses its particular toll on youth. Standing's ideas particularly pertain to educated, credentialed, and to some degree, urbanized youth. The generational cohort born roughly between 1982 to 2002 with these features often gets subsumed under the title of "millennials," while those born later are often labeled "Gen Z." A large swath of these under-thirty-fives have played by the rules of supposed meritocratic systems of education, often at great cost and sacrifice to themselves and their families. Yet at the end of long, expensive, and laborious roads, they "are not offered a reasonable bargain" (2011, 12). While Standing's work is not informed by the context of the MENAWA region, he lucidly describes the condition of life and labor among educated, urbanized youth in the region.

Precarious—an Evolution

The word *precarious* has undergone many shifts in meaning and usage since it first entered the English lexicon in the seventeenth century (Gilliver 2016). Precarious derives from the Latin word *prex* or *prec*, meaning "prayer." In its early usage in the 1640s, precarius [*sic*] referred to something "obtained through prayer or supplication," such as the right to occupy land or hold a position. These favors were "given 'at the pleasure of' another person, who might simply choose to take it back at any time." People who were neither protected by laws, nor afforded rights of citizenship and due process, had to turn to God and the propertied and positioned class to secure some degree of security. By 1680 the word evolved to mean "dependent on the will of another." This element of dependency carried an inherent association with a "risky, dangerous, uncertain" situation.[1] From the twentieth century, the meaning of precarious shifted away from relations of dependency and whim, to insecurity resulting from physical danger. For instance, precarity would result from an "unsound, unsafe, rickety" structure (Oxford English Dictionary 2016). In the post–September 11, 2001, period in the United States, the term entered critical social theory with Judith Butler's work, *Precarious Life: The Powers of Mourning and Violence* (2004). Butler examined how the September 11 terrorist event unleashed a transnational chain of precarity for victims and perpetrators of violence. In 2011, Guy Standing brought the term into the realms of social policy, political economy, sociology, and labor economics.

Over the course of some three decades, Standing had been observing the gradual weakening of labor rights, citizenship rights, and due process in different regions of the world. He noted the steady closing of the commons, the decline of social safety nets, and the assault on unions and other forms of labor organizing. He also observed the changing nature of work, with the spectacular spread of digital technologies and automation that paved the way for app-based workers (such as Uber drivers) and a new form of freelance "independent contractors." Taking these interwoven changes into consideration, he merged the words "precarious," the overwhelming feature of work in the twenty-first century, with "proletariat," a class designation, into "the precariat." That term was evidently coined a decade earlier in Italian as "*il precariato*" following the 2001 anti-G8 protests in Genoa (Breman 2013), but Standing fleshed out the idea with the use of global labor data and his analysis of the changing nature of work.

Standing's critics have taken issue with his formulation of "precariat." They argue that he misunderstands the nature of "class" and that he is too Eurocentric, since he draws considerably—though not exclusively—on data from the global North (Breman 2013, Munck 2013). These criticisms hold some validity, but they also tend to miss the point. Standing is not talking about class in a traditional Marxian sense. Rather, he provides a language to see how disparate people on a mass global scale have been experiencing work and the struggle for livelihoods in a remarkably similar way. In other words, as more people recognize precarity as a common shared condition, and the more they understand the structures, policies, and organizations that perpetuate it, the more likely they are to stop seeing the problem as an individual one—that they simply cannot find the pathway to "success"—but as a structural one. Standing (2014) insists that the precariat, a class-in-the-making, "is the first mass class in history that has systematically been losing rights built up for citizens."

What Happened to the Active Youth of the Uprisings?

For a brief moment in 2011 and 2012, those in Western media, policy, and scholarly circles celebrated the role of youth in the Arab uprisings and branded young people in the region as "nonviolent champions of democracy." They were especially interested in the tech savvy "Facebook youth." However, as counterrevolution set in and several states, including Syria, Yemen, and Libya, spiraled into civil conflicts, wars, and refugee crises, the initial enthusiasm for the uprisings abated. The old paradigms for youth containment quickly made a comeback.

The international development community carried on as if the uprisings, the most momentous grassroots political and cultural events in the region in over a half century, had not even occurred. *The Arab Human*

Development Report (AHDR) 2016: Youth and the Prospects for Human Development in a Changing Reality, stands as a case in point. The United Nations Development Programme (UNDP) has produced *The Arab Human Development Reports* every five years since 2002. These reports, authored by groups of experts from and on the region, are meant to build partnerships with local stakeholders and serve as the "instruments for measuring human progress and triggering action for change."[2] They specifically provide guidelines for "region-specific approaches to human rights, poverty, education, economic reform, HIV/AIDS, and globalization."[3]

The 2016 AHDR on youth, released roughly six years after the start of the Arab uprisings, was an opportune moment for development scholars and policy experts to reflect on the seismic shifts occurring in societies across the region. The uprisings had been a clarion call from millions of people, and especially young people, that business as usual was no longer an option. Unfortunately, the opportunity was missed, and the AHDR 2016 instead put forward the old prescriptive model of development. The concepts participation, empowerment, and youth agency—all derived from human development and human capabilities approaches dating to the 1990s—framed the policy conversation on youth. A passage from the introductory chapter reads:

> Like its predecessors, this sixth AHDR is grounded in a concept of human development that embraces human freedom as a core value. . . . A central cross-cutting concept in the AHDR 2016 is youth empowerment. . . . Key to this concept is a sense of agency, whereby youth themselves become resolute actors in the process of change. The concept is embedded in self-reliance and based on the realization that young people can take charge of their own lives and become effective agents of change (UNDP 2016, 25).

Rather than acknowledge that young people were agents of change, and had been advocating for and realizing new forms of social, cultural, and political action, the report pushes for this narrative of "self-reliance." This is a way of placing the individual and a survival-of-the-fittest message at front and center (Giroux 2009), while relegating the collective, the social, and the commons, to the shadows. This ideological framing of empowerment advances a model of development in which young people are nudged to break their collective bonds of solidarity with each other in exchange for facing the future as competing individuals, a process that thrusts them into the ranks of the precariat.[4]

There are certain "big ideas" that underpin the AHDR's policy priorities around youth. The first pertains to security and translates to the idea that youth should be society's peacebuilders and peacemakers. The second relates to education and its connection to markets and economic growth. The third is about youth entrepreneurship, the seeming panacea for all forms of economic, social, and political reform. We take each one of these in turn.

Youth as "Peacemakers"

The 2016 youth report emerged out of the August 2015 United Nations Global Forum on Youth Peace and Security, held in Amman, Jordan. Following this event, the United Nations Security Council unanimously adopted Resolution 2250 of December 9, 2015, which urges "Member States to consider ways to give youth a greater voice in decision-making at the local, national, regional and international levels." The resolution highlights, "the threat to stability and development posed by the rise of radicalization among young people," and calls for more youth representation as peacebuilders. The problem with this formulation is that young people are called to be "empowered peacemakers" as if the security problems are of their making, or they have the power to influence massively powerful interests and actors. There is no recognition for instance, of the role of the arms industry in fueling insecurity, or of the hard power of North Atlantic Treaty Organization (NATO) allies in militarizing conflicts (see chapter 9). Rather, this formulation draws on the section of the Security Council Resolution 2250 that deals with prevention of youth violence, affirming "the importance of creating policies for youth that would positively contribute to peacebuilding efforts, including social and economic development, supporting projects designed to grow local economies, and provide youth employment opportunities and vocational training, fostering their education, and promoting youth entrepreneurship and constructive political engagement" (Article 11).

What, for instance, does "constructive political engagement" mean in states where young citizens lead exceedingly politically precarious lives? What does it mean in states where they get arrested, disappeared, and tortured for as little as retweeting a comment, standing in a public space to protest an injustice, posting a political joke on Facebook, or dancing in public?[5] On a different but related note, how can young people find a real place at the table of peace negotiations and peacebuilding during times of extreme destabilization and militarism, as in Syria, Palestine, Libya, Yemen, Iraq, Somalia, and Sudan, to name just some of the countries being decimated by warfare, conflict, the growth of militias, and extreme forms of repression? In the absence of any real recognition of hard power, invocations of youth empowerment and youth peacemaking ring hollow.

Education Is Not about Markets

The international policy community has been consigning education and formalized learning to the domain of the market for decades, focusing obsessively on educational outputs, testing, privatization, and related goals such as youth entrepreneurship and jobs. The AHDR 2016 follows the same pattern of unproblematically correlating education with jobs and the demands of the labor market. It states:

> Overcoming education system failure must be a priority for policymakers and educators, who should strive to achieve a good fit between the output of educational institutions and the demands of the labor market. This would involve a survey of the distribution of enrolments across subjects, skills and disciplines, upgrades in technical education and a review of curricula to promote problem-solving skills, entrepreneurial and management capacity and the value of self-employment (UNDP 2016, 184).

Putting aside the reductive understanding of education illustrated in this passage, we must begin by asking, "What are the demands of the labor market to which schools and universities must answer?" Currently, the market favors flexible, short-term, disposable, and cheap labor. In other words, corporations and global capital need an unlimited supply of young energetic people who are willing to intern, volunteer, work long hours, work remotely, work with weak or no contracts, continuously retrain, and not make demands for unions, benefits, or job security. This growing class, the precariat, are people who are "living through unstable and insecure labor, in and out of jobs, without an occupational identity, financially on the edge and losing rights" (Standing 2016, xiii).

Regrettably, the authors of the AHDR seem to have no problem doubling down on outputs, testing, and market-style approaches to education.

They disregard, indeed implicitly support, exploitative and unstable work conditions for young people that ultimately contribute to their personal insecurity. Educational institutions should certainly play roles in preparing young people for adult roles in work and society. However, the proponents of market-oriented education policies display a callous disregard for the ways in which schools and universities can strengthen citizenship by providing a space for nurturing social solidarity and a diverse array of human talents and abilities. They do not regard educational institutions as places for young people to develop such bonds and understanding across lines of difference, where they can think and work together to find creative solutions to the enormous challenges of contemporary life, and where they can revel in the joy of learning.

Entrepreneurship Is Not the Solution

The MENAWA is a region with a disproportionately high percentage of young people, a situation known as having a youth bulge. Within the Arab countries alone, there are over 100 million people in the age category of fifteen to twenty-nine. It is not clear, based on the literature, how many of them are expected to become self-employed entrepreneurs. However, this drive toward youth entrepreneurship is reminiscent of the late 1980s and 1990s, when United Nations agencies, global financial institutions, and nongovernmental organizations joined forces on a massive scale to promote microfinance as the path to alleviate poverty. After more than three decades of experimentation, the evidence points to that fact that microfinance, though beneficial to some, does not cure poverty, and has been a debt trap for many. Economists who have traced the adverse effects of microfinance have argued that it "constitutes a powerful institutional and political barrier to sustainable economic and social development, and so also to poverty reduction. . . . [C]ontinued support for microfinance in international development policy circles cannot be divorced from its supreme serviceability to the neoliberal/globalisation agenda" (Bateman and Chang 2012, 13).

Similarly, evidence is mounting that youth entrepreneurship, while it can certainly benefit some in the short term, is more likely to lead the young into debt, precarity, and a cycle of failures. The debt trap is already in clear evidence with the student loan epidemic in which growing numbers of students carry debilitating debt (Kamenetz 2006). While youthful drive and ambition are positive qualities to be nurtured and encouraged, it is disingenuous to propagate the myth that anyone with an idea, grit, and determination can be a successful entrepreneur. Economist Mariana Mazzucato (2013) has written extensively on how companies in the new economy, such as Apple and Google "that like to portray themselves as the heart of US 'entrepreneurship,' have very successfully surfed the wave of US government-funded investments." The internet, GPS, touchscreen displays, and Siri are among the startups that benefitted from steep US government funding. If Arab governments and businesses in the MENAWA region are serious about youth entrepreneurship, they should provide resources and aid to organizations to guide and support young talent, not lead them down a road of borrowing and crushing debt.

Youth and Precarity

Change is happening faster than the ideas and policies being designed to deal with it. As students and scholars, as members of international development and policy communities who sincerely want to advance security, dignity, livelihoods and democracy, we must acknowledge the ways in which some of the dominant development ideas and policies have contributed to the current unfavorable—and for many, dire—state of affairs. We collectively face the daunting task of forging an alternative future. If we listen to, respect, and take seriously the voices of youth that rang out during the 2011 uprisings, we will hear that ideas that have informed education, employment, and youth policies are not decontextualized from reality. Standing (2011, 113) posits that since youth "make up the core of the Precariat" they are the ones that "will have to take the lead in forging a viable future for it." A more rigorous and engaged scholarship can guide youth toward a road of opportunity, security and dignity, rather than push them further along a perilous path of precarity.

Part Four

Conclusions and Future Directions

13

Is the School as We Know It on Its Way to Extinction?

What is the future of education and the fate of the school? These questions rose to the fore during the Covid-19 pandemic in 2020. At that time, school closures worldwide effectively threw the education of 1.5 billion students and youth into turmoil.[1] In crisis mode, many school systems transitioned to distance learning. Later, when the pandemic was better understood and more under control, they opted for "hybrid" or "blended" learning models.

In Egypt, the pandemic also created a crisis, but in some respects, the country was better equipped than others to deal with it, especially at the preparatory and secondary stages. On the one hand, the government had been investing heavily in the digital transformation of the education sector as part of the Education 2.0 reforms to build a "New Education System." But of even more relevance was the fact that for several years, over decades really, formal education had been becoming a shadow of its former self. The unregulated and pervasive system of out-of-school private lessons had been totally upending traditional schooling. Large proportions of families and students had effectively been navigating the unruly and constantly evolving market of education. A vignette from the field provides the context for when I started to ask the questions, "Is the school on its way to extinction?" And if so, "What is on the horizon to replace it?"

It was a Tuesday in March of 2007. I had an appointment to conduct focus group interviews with teachers about some changes in the curriculum in a boys' public secondary school (tenth to twelfth grade) in a medium-sized city in the Nile Delta.[2] I arrived at 11 a.m. and the principal, Abla Ibtisam, and her three deputies, were at the gate to greet me. We exchanged pleasantries and headed upstairs to the library where a group of teachers were waiting for our scheduled discussion. I had visited many Egyptian public schools, and on the surface, things looked familiar.

My first impression was that the school was in exceptionally good condition, extremely clean and well maintained. This was, after all, a newer school built to absorb the city's growing population. But there was something amiss. Apart from the sounds coming from the din of car horns and vendors outside the school walls, the atmosphere was quiet, calm. Tranquility is hardly a feature of a boys' public high school at full enrollment capacity. It suddenly dawned on me that there were no students in the school, not a single one. Except for the porter, cleaners, and clusters of teachers and other school staff sitting together reading newspapers, chatting, or sipping tea in the corridors on each floor, the school was empty.

I asked Abla Ibtisam about the whereabouts of the students, thinking that maybe they were on a fieldtrip or off at a special facility to do sports, even though the courtyard was large and well equipped. She and her colleagues looked at each other and chuckled. She replied somewhat sheepishly that they were at home studying for the secondary school examination, the Thanawiya 'Amma, which was over three months away. Her male colleague interjected, "You know, these exams are very important. The students can't afford to waste time at school." I thought about the words "waste time at school." The students, their parents, the teachers, the principals, and probably the education authorities in the local district who frequently visited schools, all agreed and accepted that being present at school months before a consequential Ministry of Education examination was a waste of time. The examination at that time was staggered over two years, meaning that students in tenth and eleventh grades would be sitting for it. When I gently inquired why the ninth-grade students were also absent from school, the principal explained that they too needed to start preparing for the Thanawiya 'Amma from now.

The situation took an even more bizarre turn when I learned that the entire teaching and administrative staff were obliged to remain at school for the entire work day. The staff arrived at 8 a.m. and signed their names in the school's log, a condition for receiving their salary and remaining a ministry employee. At 8:10 a.m. with the full register of staff inside, the porter bolted the gate shut, literally locking them all inside. At 2 p.m. when the final class bell rang, teachers rushed from different directions toward the gate while the porter slowly opened it. They jostled to exit through the narrow opening and seemed in a terrible hurry. Many of them were dashing off to the homes of the very pupils who were absent from school to give them private lessons. I recounted this vignette to several people in Egypt in the following months, and not a single person was the slightest bit surprised. "This is completely normal," a student assured me. "No one learns in school anymore. We all learn in the private lessons."[3]

The ritualized performance around schooling continued, with the government and multilateral organizations allocating huge sums to build new schools, update the curricula, engage in teacher training, administer examinations, and increase national enrollments. However, the "schools of the nation," as described in Part One in this volume, were becoming empty shells, literally, of their former selves. Instead of being sites of learning and citizenship formation, of managing difference and social belonging, of human struggles and dramas, schools seemed to be morphing into places for disciplining teachers. And because of the dysfunction of the overall system, many teachers had gone rogue. They created their own parallel system for teaching.[4] In the process, numerous teachers of core subjects proved to be exceedingly innovative educational entrepreneurs. Many teachers transitioned from the time-honored practice of going from home to home to give small group lessons, to the much more efficient and profitable practice of giving lessons in one-stop-shop private lesson centers. These centers could be anything from a couple of rooms to a stand-alone six-storey building. They have sprouted in high-end urban districts, popular urban areas, villages, and mid-size towns up and down the country, and cater to a diverse socioeconomic cross section of the population. Like restaurants, lesson centers provide menus with the costs of teachers and services by subject. Since these centers are formally "illegal," their owners have to dole out kickbacks and bribes to a long chain of enablers.

The star teachers often branch off on their own. Some of them launch their own centers (see chapter 9) while others become veritable one-man shows (the star private teachers are usually, but not always, men). In 2016 the media reported stories about how teachers, through their agents and/or business managers, were renting entire public-school buildings, theaters, and stadiums, to hold their lessons after school hours, even though it was formally illegal to do so according to Ministry of Education Decree No. 592 of 1998. For instance, a celebrated high school teacher of philosophy and psychology, Mr. Sayed al-Iraqi, rented a sports stadium to hold a revision lesson the day before the Thanawiya 'Amma examination. He allegedly charged LE 60 per student (or LE 15 depending on the source) and had a turnout of somewhere between one thousand and five thousand students.[5]

11. Teacher giving a mass revision lesson in a stadium, Cairo. 2016. (Image from *al-Masry al-Youm*, January 19, 2016.)

Though an impressive turnout, the number of students who can fit in a stadium pale in comparison to the next trend, online lessons by educational "influencers." With potential customers and viewers in the millions (there are 23 million students in Egyptian public schools, not to mention many millions of Arabic-speaking students outside Egypt), educational entrepreneurs of the digital age are taking learning and private lessons to new levels.

Digital Transformation, the Next Frontier

Fast-forward to 2020 with Egypt and the world in the throes of the Covid-19 pandemic. The virus proved to be a great accelerant of already existing trends, and perhaps nowhere more so than in education. Egypt's Ministry of Education and Technical Education had rolled out an ambitious project of educational reform in 2018. The minister of education, Dr. Tarek Shawki (2017–present) has been leading the charge to update the education system and align it with the realities and demands of the Fourth Industrial Revolution or 4IR.[6] In the words of Klaus Schwab (2016) of the World Economic Forum, the 4IR is "characterized by a range of new technologies that are fusing the physical, digital and biological worlds, impacting all disciplines, economies and industries, and even challenging ideas about what it means to be human."

The ideas and debates about how to retool education for the twenty-first century are taking place in a global context characterized by the rise of a new generation, "Generation Alpha" who started being born in 2010. They are expected to be the largest generation in history. Some features of this generation are shorter attention spans and expectations for the gamification of education (McCrindle and Fell 2020). This generation is being schooled at a time of uncertainty about what the world of work and professional life will look like when they reach adulthood. In his commentary, "The Fourth Industrial Revolution and Education," John Butler-Adam posits, "It no longer makes sense to ask children what they would like to 'do' when they grow up. By the time they enter the world of work, a large portion of current job types will have disappeared, and as many (if not more) jobs, presently not defined, will have become both every day and essential" (2018).

In Egypt, uncertainty about the future is combined with population pressure in the present. In 2021, the population of Egypt reached 104 million, with 61 percent under thirty.[7] Added to the demographic situation are the high rates of youth underemployment and unemployment (up to 33 percent according to the ILO), in a society just a few years on from mass uprisings where youth frustrations and discontent were on full display (2011–2013). Under the government of Abd al-Fattah al-Sisi (2014–present), future-oriented development goals, which include mega urban development and educational transformation (see Introduction) are proceeding at enormous financial cost, at an uncommonly fast pace, and with very little consultation nor toleration for dissent.[8]

In "normal times," the digital transformation of aspects of preuniversity education, which are costly and controversial, might have taken years for public buy-in, if at all. However, as a result of the pandemic, the robust investment in digital content and platforms allowed Egypt to transition to distance education with relative ease after the first wave of school closures in March 2020. Out of necessity, large swaths of the society participated in digital learning environments at breakneck speed.[9] Minister Shawki rolled out an ambitious scenario for blended learning or the "hybrid model" in fall 2020. The plan included building an ecosystem of eight platforms and services; most were free, but some were to charge nominal fees (see table 3 by grade).[10]

Perhaps the most controversial announcement regarding Egypt's blended learning model was that secondary school students would go to school two days per week, but only for "non-core" activities like sports, extracurricular programs, and homework. Since all secondary students were given government-issued tablets, they would receive their core instruction online or via television and do all assessments on the tablets. As provocative as it was that secondary students would not receive instructions in schools,

Table 3. Digital learning platforms in Egypt, September 2020, as presented by Dr. Tarek Shawki, minister of education and technical education[11]

Grade	TV channels	EKB* LMS**	Study. EKB	Virtual streaming classes	Eduflix: E-lessons library	Edmodo	E-books library	Ask the teacher
4	✓		✓	✓		✓		
5	✓		✓	✓		✓		
6	✓		✓	✓		✓		
7	✓		✓	✓		✓		
8	✓		✓	✓		✓		
9	✓		✓	✓	✓ + $	✓	✓ + $	✓
10	✓	✓	✓	✓	✓ + $	✓	✓ + $	✓
11	✓	✓	✓	✓	✓ + $	✓	✓ + $	✓
12	✓	✓	✓	✓	✓ + $	✓	✓ + $	✓

*EKB refers to the Egyptian Knowledge Bank
**LMS refers to Learning Management System
$ refers to services for fees

it was perhaps the first time the policy about school attendance was actually in step with the reality.[12]

"Disruption" is a term regularly used to refer to innovation in the high-tech world. A "disruptive technology" displaces an established technology and in the process creates a completely new industry (see Christensen 1997). Disruption by definition denotes a radical transformation of some sort but does not carry an inherently positive or negative value. The act of upending the older education system and replacing it with a different one does not necessarily "fix the old problems" or lead to improved outcomes for the majority of the population. And invariably, any educational experiments will need to be adjusted and corrected along the way.

Blended learning, and the digital transformation of the education sector more broadly, offer solutions to some critical problems. But they are invariably creating a host of new problems and challenges. When considering the digital transformation of education, concerns abound about surveillance and online monitoring of children and youth, cyberbullying, digital inequality, and environmental strains, to name just a few issues. Some preliminary questions that come to mind are these: In this knowledge economy, will the free and publicly accessible knowledge of today end up behind paywalls tomorrow? If so, what will be the implications be for educational access, equity, and opportunity? Will the digital footprints children leave using government-issued tablets, and accessing their platforms and applications, come back to haunt them later in life? What will the effects of digital tracking and surveillance be on the ability of future generations to participate in civic life? And from an environmental point of view, given that participation in online or remote learning requires high rates of consumption of energy and electronic devices—and eventual disposal of those devices—what are the environmental impacts? These are all questions that need intense investigation and scrutiny.

The thing about educational research is that you can never know where it will take you. One needs to be nimble enough to follow where it leads, and humble enough to know that you can only ever scratch the surface. In our roles as chroniclers of education practice, and as critical and humanist educators who believe in inclusive education and values of social solidarity, fairness, and the endless possibilities of human learning and creativity to confront and solve the immense challenges of our times, we endeavor to recognize the people whose labor, aspirations, and struggles keep the education sector worth fighting for. As we march further into a twenty-first century laden with perils and unknown consequences, but also abounding in opportunities, we try to take stock of the past and envision a future. In the throes of overwhelming structural and resource challenges, contentious politics, and spectacular technological advances and disruptions, we strive to build knowledge and engage in dialogue about how education can best serve and support the common good, the global good.

Notes

Notes to Introduction

1   Different acronyms are used to describe the region, the most common being MENA, the Middle East and North Africa. To encompass a broader territory with a common historical and geopolitical location, I use MENAWA, the Middle East, North Africa, and West Asia.

2   The roots of Arabic words and definitions are taken from Hans Wehr, 1980. *A Dictionary of Modern Written Arabic*. Librairie du Liban (Third Printing).

3   As historian Barbara Metcalf (1984, 3) defines, "*Adab* means discipline and training. It also denotes the good breeding and refinement that results from training, so that a person who behaves badly is 'without *adab*.'"

4   St. Augustine cogently articulated this distinction: "Wisdom is properly called the knowledge of things divine, whereas the term 'knowledge' is properly applied to the knowledge of things human." St. Augustine, *De trinitate*, in Migne, *Patrologia* Latina, 42, 1037 (Book 14, ch. I, 3) as cited in Rosenthal 1970, 36.

5   In Egypt in 2015, the Ministry of Vocational Education was merged with the Ministry of Education and Upbringing. The Ministry's new name became the Ministry of Education and Technical Education.

6   See Sedra 2011 on the relation between the rise of the modern state and education in nineteenth century Egypt, and Yousef 2013 and 2017 for the ways in which the provision of education changed the Egyptian public's relationship with the state.

7   The official name of the Egyptian Constitution of 1923 is "Royal Decree No. 42 of 1923 on Building a Constitutional System for the Egyptian State."

8   The British occupation of Egypt dates to 1882. Following World War I, the British gained protectorate status over Egypt, giving them sweeping governing powers.

9   For the place of cinema in Nasser's Egypt, see Gordon 2002, and on the music of Umm Kulthum, see Danielson 1998.

10 The United Arab Republic was initially a sovereign state and political union between Syria and Egypt, with its capital in Cairo. Syria seceded from this union in 1961.

11 In his autobiography, *Out of Egypt*, André Aciman (1994) describes how this process of the decosmopolitanization of Alexandria took place.

12 Azhari schools followed the same curricula as general education schools, with the addition of an intensive program in religious studies including Qur'anic recitation, Qur'anic exegesis *(tafsir)* and Islamic jurisprudence *(fiqh)*. A key difference between Azhari and general schools was that, for the most part, the two systems followed different university tracks: the former prepared its students for al-Azhar University, and the latter for the national state universities. Under certain conditions, graduates of Azhari secondary schools could join national universities, and students of general secondary schools could join certain faculties of al-Azhar University (see NCERD 1994, 33). In terms of the ratio of Azhari schools to general schools in the Basic Education phase, in 1993, Azhari institutes constituted roughly 12 percent of the primary schools and 16 percent of the preparatory schools in the country (CAPMAS 1994, 202–205).

13 The full text of Article 18 reads: "Education is a right guaranteed by the State. It is obligatory in the primary stage. The State shall work to extend this obligation to other stages. The State shall supervise all branches of education and guarantee the independence of universities and scientific research centers, with a view to linking all this with the requirements of society and production." Article 12 states, "Society shall be committed to safeguarding and protecting morals, promoting genuine Egyptian traditions and abiding by the high standards of religious education, moral and national values, the historical heritage of the people, scientific facts, socialist conduct and public manners within the limits of the law."

14 Anwar Sadat shared the Nobel Peace Prize in 1978 with US president Jimmy Carter and Israeli prime minister Menachem Begin for their participation in the Camp David Peace Accords.

15 For more on the politics of education in Egypt, see Amin 2001 and Mirshak 2020b.

16 See the classic work of Gellner 1983 and the critique that his perspective represented "methodological nationalism" (Siebers 2019). For a review of nationalism in state curricula, see Attalah and Makar 2014.

17 The term "hidden curriculum" was first coined by Philip W. Jackson (1968) in his *Life in Classrooms*, but the concept was earlier described in the work of sociologist Emile Durkheim (1961). "Hidden Curriculum" has since been a foundational concept in a number of important works in critical theory that deal with ideology and class (see Apple 1982, Bowles and Gintis 1976, Giroux 1983, Willis 1977), gender (Hernández, González, and Sánchez 2013), and higher education (Margolis 2001), to name just a few key works and orientations.

18 The author has elaborated on forms of "wired citizenship" (Herrera and Sakr 2014). For a treatment of citizenship education in formal and nonformal educational spaces after the January 25 Revolution, see Dorio, Abdou and Moheyeldine 2019.

19 In July 2020, Minister of Planning and Economic Development Hala al-Said stated that Egypt had started construction on thirty-four new

4G cities. See *Egypt Today*, September 13, 2020. The New Administrative Capital is the main project. It sprawls across 714 square kilometers and will include twenty residential neighborhoods, intended to accommodate up to 6.5 million people. The Government of Egypt explains the "national mega projects" as a means by which to "enhance the competitiveness of the economy, create employment opportunities and attract foreign and domestic private investments. With work underway by more than 1,000 companies and nearly two million Egyptian workers, these national mega projects are contributing to a new chapter in Egypt's economic progress." See http://www .egyptembassy.net/media/Egypt-Megaprojects-Factsheet-Sept.-2018.pdf. Others refer to these as "vanity projects" that "deepen the military's hold over the economy and provide no tangible broad economic benefit" (Mandour 2019).

20 In the interest of full disclosure, since 2019 I have been serving as the director of the Education 2.0 Research and Documentation Project (RDP). Minister of Education Dr. Tarek Shawki recruited me for this role; however the RDP operates independently without interference from the ministry. The project was initially funded by the British Foreign and Commonwealth Office; however following the Covid-19 pandemic, the funds were cut. The project continued on a voluntary basis. At the time of writing, it is pursuing other options for research funding.

21 For more information on the new education system in Egypt, see the policy videos on the Education 2.0 Research and Documentation (RDP) YouTube channel at https://bit.ly/3mbn68c

22 Prior to becoming minister of education, Shawki held other key positions as the dean of the School of Sciences and Engineering at the American University in Cairo (2012–2016) and a researcher and professor of theoretical and applied mechanics at the University of Illinois at Urbana-Champaign (1986–1998). Concurrent with his position as minister, Shawki serves as secretary general of presidential specialized councils in Egypt (2015–present, as of 2021).

23 At the time of writing, the author was compiling an oral history record of the reforms in connection to the work of the Education 2.0 Research and Documentation Project (RDP) (see note 20 above). In interviews with key advisers and partners to the minister of education, the concept of "a blank page" came up repeatedly. The minister's team began conceptualizing a new system unencumbered by the past. However, they would have to adjust their vision and plans when confronted with the political and material realities on the ground.

Notes to Chapter One

1 I originally conducted this study for a master's thesis in anthropology and sociology at the American University in Cairo. Many thanks to my thesis adviser, the late great Dr. Cynthia Nelson, and the community at Falaki School, especially Abla Adalat, Ustaz Ali, Ustaz Mahmud, Ustaz Emad, Abla Siham, and Abla Amira.

2 In 1990, the exchange rate was 3.3 Egyptian pounds to 1 US dollar.

Notes to Chapter Two

1   The preparatory stage is divided into three years: year one, which corresponds to seventh grade; year two, which is eighth grade; and year three, or ninth grade.

Notes to Chapter Three

1   For accounts of gender, women's issues, and girls' education in nineteenth- and early twentieth-century Egypt, see Abu-Lughod 1998, M. Badran 1995, and Baron 1994.

2   An in-school survey conducted by the author revealed that 60 percent of the students' mothers had no formal schooling, compared to only 15 percent of fathers.

3   It is interesting to note that at this point in time, only a small minority, roughly 10 percent of girls, wore the headscarf. When I visited the school six years later, some 80 percent of the students donned a headscarf, an indication of the rapid spread of the Islamist piety culture throughout Egyptian schools and society.

Notes to Chapter Four

1   The exchange rate in 1990 was LE 3.3 (Egyptian pounds) to US $1. By 2018, with an exchange rate of LE 17.8 to US $1, the salary range was roughly LE 1,100 for an assistant teacher, LE 5,000 for a senior teacher, and up to LE 10,000 for the most senior administrator (see Arab Republic of Egypt, Civil Service Law No. 81 of 2016).

2   On the topic of the correlation between women's employment and marital violence, for example, Bhattacharya, Bedi, and Chhachhi (2011, 1676) argue, "women's engagement in paid work and ownership of property, are associated with sharp reductions in marital violence."

Notes to Chapter Five

1   On the shadow education system, see Bray 1999, 2003, and 2006.

2   See Fergany 1994 and Hua 1996 (cited in Bray 1999, 24).

Notes to Chapter Six

1   For analysis of education policy and influences during the Mubarak years, see Ginsburg and colleagues 2010, and for a treatment of the inconsistent political education reforms at that time, see Korany 2011.

2   From Baha' al-Din 1997, 84, 58, translated from the Arabic by the author.

3   During the entirety of Baha' al-Din's tenure as minister of education, Egypt was operating under emergency law. At the time, human rights groups reported regular abuses and Egypt was a partner with the United States in the extraordinary rendition program (see Huq 2006).

4   Al-Banna had a number of intellectual influences, among them the Muslim reformers Rashid Rida and Muhammad Abduh.

5   As early as 1945, the Egyptian national university was a hotbed of political activity in which the Muslim Brothers and their supporters occupied one side, with the Wafd, communists, and their supporters in the opposing camp.

6   As historian Khaled Fahmy (2021, 108) writes, "the regime used the incident to try to completely destroy the Brotherhood: the group's assets were confiscated, and thousands of members were rounded up and subjected to indescribable torture in police dungeons. With the Brotherhood decimated, the last source of opposition was silenced. In a little over two years Nasser's regime had managed to consolidate its hold over the country and had succeeded in putting a lid over the spirited popular movement of the previous decade that had threatened to take Egypt along the path of a radical social revolution."

7   The Arabic transliteration of this is "*Allahu ghayatuna. Al-Rasul za'imuna. Al-Qur'an dusturuna. Al-Jihad sabiluna. Al-Mawt fi sabil Allah asma amanina. Allahu akbar, Allahu akbar*" (Mitchell 1993, 193–4). By the 1980s, the Brotherhood had simplified its slogan to "Islam is the solution."

8   Numerous authors have analyzed the record of the relationship between the Brothers and the state in great detail. See Kandil 2015; Wickham 2013; Tadros 2014; Pargeter 2013; Mitchell 1993; Mellor 2017; Ayubi et al. 1995.

9   Another report revealed how in a small village in Upper Egypt militant Islamic groups were controlling the schools, which they used to deal in weapons and ammunitions (Maughith 1998, 2–3).

10 The government also started cracking down on Islamist students in the national universities, particularly in faculties of engineering, medicine, and pharmacy, where they were most active (Bollag 1994). As noted by Hazem Kandil (2015, 10 and 22), the Muslim Brothers showed "an aversion towards those with a background in the social sciences" and were known for their "anti-intellectualism."

11 See Baraka (2008) who reviews how the ruling National Democratic Party in Egypt initiated a number of citizenship programs to counter violence and extremism. He argues that revising the social studies curriculum could be a means for resolving some of the contentious citizenship issues. This is a proposition I take issue with, since citizenship training needs to cut across disciplines and be embedded in everyday practices, rather than be reduced to a discrete subject.

12 These free market–oriented policies were part of the structural adjustment measures imposed by the International Monetary Fund and other multilateral donors. They constituted a continuation and acceleration of an earlier Open Door *(Infitah)* phase of economic reforms implemented under Sadat in the 1970s. In a post-1989, post–Cold War, global order that saw the United States as the global hegemon, aid money was tied to "democratization," namely political liberalization and the opening up of civil society. The growth in the nongovernmental organization (NGO) sector, including Islamic educational and youth centered NGOs, would be prodigious. In 1976 there were a total of 7,593 nonprofit associations. By 1993 that number had

doubled to 15,000, and the numbers would continue to mushroom. Islamic associations accounted for 25 percent of the total number of associations registered with the Ministry of Social Affairs in 1980, and 34 percent in 1993 (see Kandil 1998, 139 and 145).

13 This combination of economic liberalization without political liberalization has been named the "dictator's dilemma" (see Howard et al. 2011).

Notes to Chapter Seven

1 See, for example, Roy (2004) on the "virtuous" society.

2 See Bayat's *Making Islam Democratic* (2007) about the relation between the Mubarak regime and the Muslim Brotherhood during this period. The Brotherhood claimed publicly that it was taking a more reformist stand and denounced of militant Islam. What it was advocating privately and internally among its closed leadership circle was not entirely clear.

3 The author compiled statistics on private Islamic schools with the help of a dedicated research assistant, Fatma, who was a fourth-year sociology student at an Egyptian university. We located the names and phone numbers of all the private schools through a directory of private schools in Egypt and through a series of questions, ascertained if their school was one of the new Islamic schools, or a PIS.

4 The majority of private Islamic language schools (PIELS) in Cairo are located in the professional neighborhoods of Maadi, Mohandessin, Nasr City, Heliopolis, and the Pyramids area. Two schools are located in Imbaba, a densely populated informal neighborhood with some one million inhabitants, located on the western bank of Giza. The PIELS in Alexandria are located in Sidi Gaber, Sidi Bishr, and Moharram Bek. Suez City and 6 October City each had one school.

5 Some of the material on the following three schools has appeared in previous publications (Herrera 2000, 2001, and 2003).

6 Interview with the author, cited in Herrera 2000, 168.

7 Abdin was a pioneer in community and preventative health. In 1956 she established the Centre of Rheumatic Heart Diseases in Children, which grew into several branches. In the 1970s she established the Child's Health Institute and later became chairperson of the NGO, Friends of Children's Heart Disease. By the 1990s the Zahira Abdin Foundation also included two orphanages, a retirement home for women, and a department for low-cost surgery (Herrera 2000, 166–167).

8 This case study was compiled through a series of interviews with "Tareq," a teacher from the school and a security guard in a building I frequented. We met several times over a six-month period to talk in both a systematic and informal way about his life and experiences at the school. Tareq tried to arrange a meeting for me with the school owner, but he refused, saying he did not have anything to say to "an American." Unlike the school owner, Tareq said he was able to distinguish between the American people and the American government.

9 It is worth noting here that when I was watching via social media and satellite television the early scenes of the January 25 Revolution in Cairo, where protestors tore down portraits of Hosni Mubarak, ripped, burned, and stomped on them, I recalled this scene from Fatima Islamic School. I wondered how many protestors had rehearsed these sorts of performances in their schools, where antinational and antiregime messaging was par for the course.

10 This information is based on interviews by the author with the vice principal and with a schoolteacher. I did not have access to school records to confirm this information.

Notes to Chapter Eight

1 See Mahmood (2005) for a critique of feminist liberal approaches to women's agency in Egypt and Muslim societies more broadly.

Notes to Chapter Nine

1 Some scholars use the frame of "empire" to examine the rapacious effects of militarism on education systems in Palestine and Iraq (Ahmad and Vulliamy 2009; Saltman 2007a and 2007b).

2 The prolific empire literature can be broken down into three general categories. The influential work *Empire* by Michael Hardt and Antonio Negri (2000) belongs to a category of its own. The authors used empire to capture a postnational, decentered, and deterritorializing world with expanding frontiers, where multitudes, rather than members of discrete nation-states, forge alliances around issues of labor, rights, and global democracy. The second and more conservative view from the global North invokes empire's "civilizing mission" to spread democracy (see for example Ferguson 2003 and 2004; Ignatieff 2003; Kaplan 2006). The third critical approach locates empire within an inequitable economic system rooted in predatory geopolitics, with the United States, the nation-state empire, at the center of power (see for example Arrighi 2005; Bhatt 2007; Giroux 2005; Harvey 2003; Hoganson 2016; Khalidi 2004; Kiely 2005; Lacher 2006; Mann 2003; Stoler and Bond 2006; Žižek 2004).

3 See also French philosopher Michel Foucault (1978; 1980) on schooling the body and mind and the knowledge/power nexus, and Martin Carnoy (1974), who in the tradition of critical social theory and education, cogently lays out in his *Education as Cultural Imperialism* that modern education is intricately tied to a context of colonialism and capitalism. Numerous critical education scholars have since produced further work along these lines.

4 In 2011–12, the year of the January 25 Revolution uprisings, Egypt fell from 94th to 118th place. The 2013–14 report put the quality of Egypt's primary education in last place (Schwab 2013).

5 See Sakr, as quoted in United Nations Development Programme 2005, 48.

6 See Hammad 2013 for an analysis of the rhetoric versus the reality of decentralization in Egypt.

7   According to a 2002 World Bank report, nearly 9 percent of the total Gross Domestic Product went toward education (60 percent in the public sector and 40 percent in the private sector). The World Bank (2002, 26) applauded Egypt for the "commendable commitment by both the government and household to education."

8   From a socioeconomic point of view, there are different ways of analyzing deregulation and privatization in education. As suggested by Hartmann (2007 and 2013), first is the free market approach, which maintains that competition between educational entrepreneurs can lead to more choice and better-quality services. Second, the moral economy approach holds that when trust in social institutions is lost, venality and corruption can take over.

9   As Starrett (1998, 10) elaborates in *Putting Islam to Work*, "Muslim states have followed a different course to modernity, insisting explicitly that progress requires a centrally administered emphasis upon moral as well as economic development."

10   These concepts were embedded in international conventions and frameworks, including the Convention on the Rights of the Child, the Dakar Framework for Action, and the Millennium Declaration (see the National Center for Educational Research 1994, 76).

11   For a cogent analysis of USAID and power in Egypt, see Mitchell 1995.

12   In a press conference on September 8, 2020, Minister of Education Dr. Tarek Shawki announced that upon the president's orders, the ministry was adding a book series to the curriculum for first to third grades with the title Values and Respect for the Other, Together We Build. The book was initially introduced in third grade and was to be made available later for first and second grade. Along similar lines, the ministry launched a new book for the secondary stage, in cooperation with the Ministry of Endowments, called Building the National Character (Shawki 2020d).

13   Arab Republic of Egypt 2001, i–ii (translation from Arabic by author).

14   There is an extensive literature on US militarization, the use of drones, illegal rendition programs, and arms sales in the MENAWA region (See Gendzier 2005; Marshall 2020). The ACLU fact sheet on extraordinary rendition states: "the extraordinary rendition program is illegal. It is clearly prohibited by the United Nations Convention Against Torture and Other Forms of Cruel, Inhuman, or Degrading Treatment, ratified by the United States in 1992" (American Civil Liberties Union 2005).

Notes to Chapter Ten

1   This chapter has been adapted from a chapter previously published by the author (Herrera, 2010b) in the volume *Being Young and Muslim: New Cultural Politics in the Global South* (Herrera and Bayat 2010). The life history research on which this chapter is based was initially undertaken as part of a larger comparative study at the International Institute of Social Studies, coordinated by Ben White, with funding from Plan Netherlands. I coordinated the Egypt component of the research in collaboration with Professor Kamal Naguib of

Alexandria University, who trained a small team of graduate student assistants from the Faculty of Education to carry out and transcribe the interviews. For other published accounts drawing on that data, see Herrera 2006b and Naguib 2008. Many thanks are due to the participants of the study who so generously gave of their time, and to Sanaa Makhlouf who assisted with Arabic-to-English translations.

2   For an excellent analysis of the post–Cold War context in which this was occurring, see Mamdani 2004.

3   According to Assaad and Barsoum (2007, 19), from the British mandate period to the present, unemployment has been "primarily a problem of educated youth." However, the problem has become more pronounced during the past decade. They note: "Youth with a secondary education or above made up 95 percent of youth unemployment in 2006, up from 87 percent in 1998 . . . In fact, university graduates are the only educational group whose unemployment rates increased since 1998." See also World Bank 2009.

4   In his work on middle-class Indian men, Nisbett (2007) calls this phenomenon of young men's use of escapism to pass their time as "timepass."

5   Adel Imam is a celebrated Egyptian comedian who starred in the enormously popular comedy *Terrorism and Kebab*, directed by Sherif Arafa in 1993. The film is a hilarious satire of the frustrations of an everyday Egyptian man who takes hostage employees and visitors at the Mugamma' administrative building in downtown Cairo, the symbol of state bureaucracy, only to demand a meal of kebab for everyone.

6   For detailed country-specific and regionwide statistics on internet users worldwide, see the internet World Stats website. The internet penetration rate had doubled by 2020 to 54 percent.

7   The Egyptian Movement for Change, more popularly referred to as Kifaya (Enough), formed in 2004 with a prodemocracy, antiregime platform. It carried out rare and daring anti-Mubarak demonstrations during which slogans such as "No to the extension [of Mubarak's presidency]; No to hereditary succession" were chanted.

Notes to Chapter Eleven

1   The question comes from the first-year Arabic examination administered in December 2011 at a high school for boys located in an educational district in the Governorate of Gharbiya.

2   In 2008 the figures were roughly 25 percent in Egypt, 31 percent in Tunisia, and a staggering 77 percent in Syria (Chaaban 2008).

3   Internet use in Egypt—the most populous Arab country with 82 million people in 2011, and 104 million in 2021—was spreading exponentially. In 2000 there were a mere 300,000 users, a number that increased to 6 million in 2006, 10.5 million in 2008, 17 million in 2010, and 21 million in March 2011. People under thirty-five use the internet at far higher rates than other age cohorts. According to one study in 2008, 58 percent of Egyptians

between the ages of eighteen and thirty-five had access to computers, and among them 52 percent were internet literate. At that time, 36 percent of youth had their own home computer, and the numbers were growing (Rakha 2008).

4   Isra' 'Abd al-Fattah, who was dubbed the president of the "Facebook Republic," and Ahmed Maher used their Facebook networks to coordinate support for the striking workers. They were both arrested and detained as a result of their activism.

5   Murad's experiences echoed studies of online gaming, which found that they often served as much more than a way to pass time. Rather, they epitomized "the ways in which contemporary identities, expectations, and understandings about the world may be shaped and influenced" (Beavis 2007, 52).

6   These attitudes were mirrored in a government survey on the internet use of 1,338 Egyptians between the ages of eighteen and thirty-five. It found that 72 percent of youth surveyed considered the internet "a bad influence on themselves"; 71 percent thought "the internet is dangerous for children"; 43 percent believed "that the internet has negatively impacted family ties"; and 89 percent agreed to "having a law in place that monitors/censors internet content" (Rakha 2008). Even accounting for the biases of a governmental survey, it is highly plausible that in 2007–2008 young people were not entirely comfortable using a medium so free of adult supervision. However, those attitudes appear to have changed significantly in the succeeding years.

7   Within ten years, the amount of misinformation and conspiracy theories would also spread exponentially through informal news circuits. See Herrera 2015 about the darker sides of internet use in Egypt.

8   Howard's (2010, 113–116) table "Blogger Arrests in the Muslim World, 2003–2010" is a very good source for understanding the risks of blogging in the region. See also Gasser, Maclay and Palfrey 2010 on digital safety in developing countries.

9   Abbas' blog can be found at http://misrdigital.blogspirit.com/. See also a 2007 CNN story about how YouTube shut down and then restored Abbas's account and torture videos at http://www.cnn.com/2007/WORLD/meast/11/29/youtube.activist/.

10 The popular blog *The Arabist* played an important role in disseminating news about the case (see El-Amrani 2007).

11 I personally got to know "Murad" by private messaging him on his Facebook page and asking for a meeting with him in Egypt in 2008. I appreciate his willingness to talk with me about his path from video game addict to graffiti artist to Facebook admin. I kept in touch with Murad up until the time he deactivated all his social media accounts in 2011, as the space was becoming more surveilled and putting other users at risk.

12 To view the doctored image of Hosni Mubarak leading the delegation at the Summit, see the article, "Hosni Mubarak Left Red Faced Over Doctored Red Carpet Photo" in The Guardian, September 16, 2020 https://bit.ly/3pCyCM6.

13   The "We Are All Khaled Said" Facebook page and the people behind
      it turned out to be more complicated than a mere spontaneous youth
      movement and anti-torture campaign. The author delves deeper into the
      page and larger questions of power in the digital age in the book *Revolution in
      the Age of Social Media* (Herrera 2014).

Notes to Chapter Twelve

1   Online Etymology Dictionary, 2017.
2   To get a better sense of how these ideas were being perpetuated and
      reproduced, we should consider the authors of the report. In total, seventy-
      four people are listed as having contributed or advised on the report in
      some capacity, broken down as follows: fourteen members of the core team;
      eighteen background paper authors; eight members of a readers' group;
      thirteen UNDP regional bureau representatives; and twenty-one members
      of a youth consultative group. This collection of people reflects a diversity
      of opinions, ideological positions, and disciplinary differences and priorities.
      After the report was released, three of the authors of its Chapter 4, "The
      New Dynamics in the Inclusion and Empowerment of Young Women,"
      wrote an essay expressing their misgivings about the editorial process.
      They had become concerned after long passages of their chapter on young
      women—which they had been commissioned to write—were removed from
      the report without explanation. The meaning and spirit of the chapter were
      subsequently altered. They explain: "Large sections of our text had been
      excised, including one in which we gave examples of ways in which young
      women transgress norms surrounding marriage and heteronormativity;
      another dedicated to young women as producers of culture; and a further
      section about online activism. . . . [O]ur chapter ended up in an obscure
      editorial process that lacked any proper consultation or transparency. . . . It is
      our understanding that several Arab ambassadors were involved in the pro-
      cess of reviewing the report" (Al-Ali, Ali and Marler 2016).
3   See the United Nations Development Programme statement on its website.
4   This pattern of the development community insisting on certain narratives
      that favor existing power structures is taken up in literature on colonial and
      decolonial studies in relation to international development. See, for instance,
      Bhambra 2007 and Kothari 2006.
5   See the Middle East and North Africa section of the online platform Global
      Voices for reporting on a wide range of issues pertaining to censorship,
      arrests, and intimidation of youth activists and social media users.

Notes to Chapter Thirteen

1   These numbers of out-of-school students come from UNESCO.
      See the website of UNESCO's Global Education Coalition (https://
      globaleducationcoalition.unesco.org/members), "a platform for collaboration
      and exchange to protect the right to education during this unprecedented
      disruption and beyond. It brings together more than 175 members from

the UN family, civil society, academia and the private sector to ensure that #LearningNeverStops."

2   This vignette comes from the author's field notes, made during four research visits to Egypt in 2007 and 2008, some of which appear in Herrera 2008b.

3   See Sarah Hartmann (2008), who made a similar observation. Also see the work of Assaad and Krafft (2015) who ask, "Is free basic education in Egypt a reality or a myth?"

4   In education literature this parallel system has been called the "shadow education system" (see chapter 5).

5   See *al-Masry al-Youm* 2016 and *al-Wafd*, June 19, 2016. In another article, some students defended their teacher, claiming the cost for the revision was LE 15 per student, not LE 60 as reported by some news outlets. Mohammed Morsi, a third-year high school student who attended the session at the stadium, said that his teacher Mr. al-Iraqi did not usually give lectures at the stadium and only did so because of increased demand. He added that all students loved him and wanted to benefit from the revision session before the final examination (El-Fagr 2016). See also Mr. al-Iraqi's Facebook fan page: https://www.facebook.com/sayed.3rakii.5aat.a7mar/ and his YouTube page, where he offers free lessons: https://www.youtube.com/watch?v =R2gpl8GpEIE. Many thanks to Asmaa Al-Sayed for assisting with research on this topic.

6   The sector changes for a multidisciplinary curriculum, and activity-based learning in years K–3, went by the name "Education 2.0."

7   In the previous six years, 2014–2020, the ministry built more than 75,000 classrooms at a cost of LE 24 billion, but the system still had a deficit of 73,000 classrooms. Demographers project that Egypt's population could reach 119 million by 2030 (Egyptian Streets 2020; Shawki 2020a; 2020c).

8   In its World Report 2020, Human Rights Watch documented a number of abuses under the government of al-Sisi, including lack of due process, violence against women and girls, arbitrary arrests, and a host of other actions.

9   For example, after the school closures on March 15, 2020, the ministry introduced the online platform Edmodo to allow all students to access their classes remotely and submit their end-of-year assessment, a research project, which was novel in itself. In a matter of weeks, huge numbers of students (11.5 million), teachers (1.16 million) and parents (750,000) had subscribed to Edmodo and successfully uploaded their end-of-year projects (see World Bank, Harvard University, OECD 2020).

10 In fourth to eighth grade, individual schools would decide if students would be at school two or three days per week. On off days, they would pursue their "schooling" from home in a scenario where parents were to play roles of "critical partners" and "mentors." Additionally, in an effort to replace and control private lessons, a program called Strengthening Groups (Majmu'at Taqwiya) was initiated. Here teachers would conduct extra paid lessons and students would be able to pick whomever they wanted to study with, even if they were from a different school. The teachers would receive 85 percent of

the revenue, with the remainder going to the school and possibly the district. The minister announced an additional ambitious project called Every Child Connected to enable all presecondary students to access online curricula through their own device. The state would not cover this cost, but subsidized it, by way, for instance, of interest-free installment plans.

11 Thanks to Hany Zayed for compiling this table, with data taken from a presentation slide by Dr. Tarek Shawki (2020b).

12 See Shawki (2020b, 2020c).

References

Abdallah, Ahmed. 1985. *The Student Movement and National Politics in Egypt*. London: Saqi Books.

Abu-Lughod, Lila, ed. 1998. *Remaking Women: Feminism and Modernity in the Middle East*. Princeton: Princeton University Press.

Abu-Lughod, Lila. 2008. *Writing Women's Worlds: Bedouin Stories*, 15th anniversary edition. Berkeley: University of California Press.

Achcar, Gilbert. 2006. *The Clash of Barbarisms: September 11 and the Making of the New World Disorder*. 2nd edition. Boulder, Colorado: Paradigm.

Aciman, André. 1994. *Out of Egypt: A Memoir*. New York: Farrar Straus and Giroux.

Ahmad, Ameera, and Ed Vulliamy. 2009. "In Gaza, the Schools are Dying Too." *The Guardian*, January 10.

al-Ahram. 1993. "al-Raqs 'ala angham al-mutatarrifin." April 22, 1993, 3.

Aidi, Hisham. 2011. "Leveraging Hip Hop in US Foreign Policy." In *Middle East Report*, 260: 25–39.

Akhbar al-Hawadith. 1993. "al-Khitat al-kamila li-muwagahat shabakat al-mutatarrifin fi qita' al-ta'lim." May 13, 1993.

Al-Ali, Nadje, Zahra Ali, and Isabel Marler. 2016. "Reflections on Authoring the Chapter on Young Women for the 2016 Arab Human Development Report." *Jadaliyya*, December 9, 2016.

El-Amrani, Issandr. 2007. "Three Years in Prison for Emad al-Kabir Torturers." *The Arabist* November 5, 2007. https://arabist.net/blog/2007/11/5/three-years-in -prison-for-emad-al-kabir-torturers.html

Al-Anani, Khalil. 2016. *Inside the Muslim Brotherhood: Religion, Identity, and Politics*. Oxford: Oxford University Press.

al-Arabiya Arab TV. 2009. "Obama Al-Arabiya Interview: Full Text." Interview by Hisham Melham. January 26, 2009. https://www.huffpost.com/entry/obama -al-arabiya-intervie_n_161127.

American Civil Liberties Union. 2005. Fact Sheet: Extraordinary Rendition.

Amin, Galal. 2001. *Whatever Happened to the Egyptians? Changes in Egyptian Society from 1950 to the Present*. Cairo: American University in Cairo Press.

Apffel-Marglin, Frédérique, and Stephen Marglin, eds. 1996. *Decolonizing Knowledge: From Development to Dialogue*. Oxford: Clarendon Press.

Apple, Michael W. 1982. *Education and Power*. Boston: Routledge and Kegan Paul.

Apple, Michael W. 2000. *Official Knowledge: Democratic Education in a Conservative Age*, 2nd edition. New York: Routledge.

Arab Republic of Egypt. 2001. *al-Qiyam wa-l-akhlaq: al-sana al-ula al-ibtida'iya*, part 1: 2001–2002. Cairo: Ministry of Education.

Arab Republic of Egypt. 2002. *Mubarak and Education: Qualitative Development in the National Project of Education, Application of Principles of Total Quality*. Cairo: Ministry of Education.

Arab Republic of Egypt. 2003. *al-Qiyam wa-l-akhlaq: al-sana al-thalitha al-ibtida'iya*, part 2: 2003–2004. Cairo: Ministry of Education.

Arab Republic of Egypt. 2016. Civil Service Law No. 81 of 2016.

Aroian, Lois A. 1979. "Education and Employment: The Graduates of Dār al-'Ulūm 1873–1923." *Journal of the American Research Center in Egypt* 16: 163–174.

Aroian, Lois A. 1983. "The Nationalization of Arabic and Islamic Education in Egypt: Dar al-Ulum and al-Azhar." *The Cairo Papers in Social Science*. Cairo: American University in Cairo.

Arrighi, Giovanni. 2005. "Hegemony Unravelling." *New Left Review* 20: 5–71.

Assaad, Ragui, and Ghada Barsoum. 2007. "Youth Exclusion in Egypt: In Search of 'Second Chances'." *Middle East Youth Initiative Working Paper*, 2. Wolfensohn Center for Development and Dubai School of Government.

Assaad, Ragui, and Farzaneh Roudi-Fahimi. 2007. *Youth in the Middle East and North Africa: Demographic Opportunity of Challenge?* Washington, DC: Population Reference Bureau.

Assaad, Ragui, and Caroline Krafft. 2015. "Is Free Basic Education in Egypt a Reality or a Myth?" *International Journal of Educational Development* 45: 16–30.

Attalah, Motaz, and Farida Makar. 2014. "Nationalism and Homogeneity in Contemporary Curricula." Cairo: Egyptian Initiative for Personal Rights, The Social and Economic Rights Unit.

Ayubi, Nazih, Denis J. Sullivan, Philip S. Khoury, Beverley Milton-Edwards, and Gabriel R. Warburg. 1995. "Muslim Brotherhood." In *The Oxford Encyclopedia of the Modern Islamic World*, edited by John L. Esposito. Oxford: Oxford Islamic Studies Online.

Badran, Shebl. 1993. "al-Tujjar al-judud li-tarbiyat al-atfal." *al-Sha'b*.

Badran, Margot. 1995. *Feminists, Islam and Nation: Gender and the Making of Modern Egypt*. Princeton: Princeton University Press.

Baha' al-Din, Husayn Kamal. 1997. *al-Ta'lim wa-l-mustaqbal*. Cairo: Dar al-Ma'arif.

Baha' al-Din, Husayn Kamal. 1998. *Patriotism in a World without Identity: The Challenges of Globalization*. Kualyoub, Egypt: Al-Ahram Commercial Press.

Baldor, Lolita. 2009. "Under Obama 'War on Terror' Catchphrase Fading." *Yahoo News*, January 31, 2009.

Baraka, Pakinaz. 2008. "Citizenship Education in Egyptian Public Schools: What Values to Teach and in Which Administrative and Political Contexts?" *Journal of Education for International Development* 3.

Baron, Beth. 1994. *The Women's Awakening in Egypt: Culture, Society and the Press*. New Haven: Yale University Press.

Bateman, Milford, and Ha-joon Chang. 2012. "Microfinance and the Illusion of Development: From Hubris to Nemesis in Thirty Years." *World Economic Review* 1: 13–36.

Bauerlein, Mark. 2009. *The Dumbest Generation: How the Digital Age Stupefies Young Americans and Jeopardizes Our Future.* New York: Penguin.

Bauman, Zygmunt. 2004. *Wasted Lives: Modernity and Its Outcasts.* Oxford: Wiley.

Bayat, Asef. 2007. *Making Islam Democratic.* Stanford: Stanford University Press.

BBC News. 2010. "Egyptian Newspaper under Fire over Altered Photo." September 15, 2010.

Beavis, Catherine. 2007. "New Textual Worlds: Young People and Computer Games." In *Youth Moves: Identities and Education in Global Perspective*, edited by Nadine Dolby and Fazal Rizvi, 53–66. New York: Routledge.

Bhambra, Gurminder K. 2007. *Rethinking Modernity: Postcolonialism and the Sociological Imagination.* Palgrave Macmillan UK.

Bhatt, Chetan. 2007. "Frontlines and Interstices in the Global War on Terror." *Development and Change* 38 (6): 1073–1094.

Bhattacharya, Manasi, Arjun S. Bedi, and Amrita Chhachhi. 2011. "Marital Violence and Women's Employment and Property Status: Evidence from North Indian Villages." *World Development* 39: 1676–1689.

Bollag, Burton. 1994. "Battling Fundamentalism: Crackdown on 'Islamists' at Egypt's Universities." *The Chronicle of Higher Education* 40: 40–42.

Borg, Carmel, and Peter Mayo. 2002. "Towards an Anti-Racist Agenda in Education. The Case of Malta." *World Studies in Education* 2 (2): 47–64.

Bowles, Herbert, and Samuel Gintis. 1976. *Schooling in Capitalist America: Educational Reform and the Contradictions of Economic Life.* New York: Basic Books.

Bray, Mark. 1999. *The Shadow Education System: Private Tutoring and Its Implications for Planners. Fundamentals of Educational Planning 61.* Paris: United Nations Education, Scientific and Cultural Organization, International Institute for Educational Planning.

Bray, Mark. 2003. *Adverse Effects of Private Supplementary Tutoring: Dimensions, Implications and Government Responses.* Paris: United Nations Education, Scientific and Cultural Organization, International Institute for Educational Planning.

Bray, Mark. 2006. "Private Supplementary Tutoring: Comparative Perspectives on Patterns and Implications." *Compare* 36 (4): 515–30.

Breman, Jan. 2013. "A Bogus Concept?" *New Left Review* 84, November–December, 2013.

Bunt, Gary R. 2003. *Islam in the Digital Age: E-Jihad, Online Fatwas and Cyber Islamic Environments* (Critical Studies on Islam). London: Pluto Press.

Burcher, Nick. 2010. "Facebook Usage Statistics by Country: July 2010 Compared to July 2009 and July 2008." July 2, 2010. https://www.nickburcher.com/2010/07/facebook-usage-statistics-by-country.html

Butler, Judith. 2004. *Precarious Life: The Powers of Mourning and Violence.* New York and London: Verso.

Butler-Adam, John. 2018. "The Fourth Industrial Revolution and Education." *South African Journal of Science* 114, No 5/6.

Calvert, John. 2000. "'The World Is an Undutiful Boy!' Sayyid Qutb's American Experience." *Islam and Christian-Muslim Relations*. Vol. 11: 1, 87–103.

Calvert, John. March 2001. "Sayyid Qutb in America." *Newsletter of the International Institute of the Study of Islam in the Modern World* (ISIM), 8.

Carnoy, Martin. 1974. *Education as Cultural Imperialism*. New York: McKay.

Carr, Nicholas. 2010. *The Shallows: What the Internet Is Doing to Our Brains*. New York: W. W. Norton.

Castells, Manuel, Mireia Fernández-Ardèvol, Jack Linchuan Qui, and Araba Sey. 2007. *Mobile Communication and Society: A Global Perspective*. Cambridge, MA: Massachusetts Institute of Technology Press.

Central Agency for Public Mobilization and Statistics. 1994. "Report for 1994." Cairo: Government of Egypt.

Cha, Yun-Kyung, Suk-Ying Wong, and John W. Meyer. 1992. "Values Education in the Curriculum: Some Comparative Empirical Data." In *School Knowledge for the Masses: World Models and National Primary Curricular Categories in the Twentieth Century*, edited by Aaron Benavot, David Kamens, and John W. Meyer. 139–151. Washington, DC: Falmer Press.

Chaaban, Jad. 2008. "The Costs of Youth Exclusion in the Middle East." *Middle East Youth Initiative Working Paper* 7. Wolfensohn Center for Development and Dubai School of Government.

Chhachhi, Amrita, and Linda Herrera. 2007. "Empire, Geopolitics and Development." *Development and Change* 38 (6): 1021–1040.

Christensen, Clayton. 1997. *The Innovator's Dilemma: When New Technologies Cause Great Firms to Fall*. Boston: Harvard Business Review Press.

Cole, Ardra L., and Gary Knowles, eds. 2001. *Lives in Context: The Art of Life History Research*. Walnut Creek: Altamira Press.

Constitution of Egypt. 1923. Unofficial translation prepared by Joy Ghali on behalf of International IDEA.

Constitution of the Arab Republic of Egypt. 1956. https://www.sis.gov.eg/newvr/theconistitution.pdf.

Constitution of the Arab Republic of Egypt, 1971. http://www.refworld.org/docid/3ae6b5368.html.

Constitution of the Arab Republic of Egypt. 1971. (Amended in 2007). Constitution.net.org.

Constitution of the Arab Republic of Egypt. 2014. https://www.constituteproject.org/constitution/Egypt_2014.pdf

Cote, James E. 1995. *Generation on Hold: Coming of Age in the Late Twentieth Century*. New York: New York University Press.

Danielson, Virginia. 1998. *"The Voice of Egypt": Umm Kulthum, Arabic Song, and Egyptian Society in the Twentieth Century*. Chicago: University of Chicago Press.

Dhillon, Navtej, and Tarek M. Yousef. 2009. *Generation in Waiting: The Unfulfilled Promise of Young People in the Middle East*. Washington, DC: Brookings Institution Press.

Diepstraten, Isabelle, Manuela du Bois-Reymond, and Henk Vinken. 2006. "Trendsetting Learning Biographies: Concepts of Navigating through Late-Modern Life and Learning." *Journal of Youth Studies* 9 (2): 175–193.

Dorio, Jason, Ehaab Abdou, and Nadine Moheyeldine, eds. 2019. *The Struggle for Citizenship Education in Egypt: (Re)Imagining Subjects and Citizens*. New York: Routledge.

Douzinas, Costas. 2007. *Human Rights and Empire: The Political Philosophy of Cosmopolitanism*. New York: Routledge-Cavendish.

Dunya, Hoda. 1993. "Wazir al-tarbiya wa-l-ta'lim yarud 'ala al-mutatarifin." *October*, May 2, 1993.

Durkheim, Emile. 1961. *Moral Education*. New York: Free Press.

Dziuban, Charles, Charles R. Graham, Patsy D. Moskal, Anders Norberg, and Nicole Sicilia. 2008. "Blended Learning: The New Normal and Emerging Technologies." *International Journal of Educational Technologies in Higher Education* 15 (3): 1–16.

Eccel, A. Chris. 1984. *Egypt, Islam and Social Change: Al-Azhar in Conflict and Accommodation*. Berlin: Klaus Schwarz Verlag.

Edmunds, June, and Bryan Turner. 2005. "Global Generations: Social Change in the Twentieth Century." *British Journal of Sociology* 56 (4): 559–577.

Egyptian Streets. 2020. "Egypt's Population Increases by 1 Million in 8 Months: Population Council." *Egyptian Streets*. October 8, 2020. https://egyptianstreets .com/2020/10/08/egypts-population-increases-by-1-million-in-8-months -population-council/

Eid, Gamal. 2004. "The Internet in the Arab World: A New Space of Repression?" Arab Network for Human Rights Information Report.

Esposito, John, and Dalia Mogahed. 2007. *Who Speaks for Islam? What a Billion Muslims Really Think*. New York: Gallup Press.

Estes, Adam Clark. 2011. "The Arab Spring's Advice for Occupy Wall Street." *The Atlantic*. November 1, 2011.

Etling, Bruce, John Kelly, Robert Faris, and John Palfrey. 2009. *Mapping the Arabic Blogosphere: Politics, Culture, and Dissent* (Berkman Center Research Publication No. 2009–06). Cambridge, MA: Berkman Center for Internet and Society at Harvard University.

el-Fagr. 2016. "Talabat al-dars al-khususi bi-l-istad yudafi'un 'an 'al-Iraqi': 'al-hissa bi-15 geneih wi-l-mudarris mastaghallish had.'" June 19, 2016. https://www .elfagr.com/2178807

Fahmy, Khaled. 2021. "Gamal Abdel Nasser." In *Global Middle East: Into the Twenty-First Century*, edited by Asef Bayat and Linda Herrera, 103–116. Berkeley: University of California Press.

Fanon, Frantz. 1963. *The Wretched of the Earth*. Translated by Constance Farrington. New York: Grove Press.

Farag, Iman. 1994. "L'enseignement en question: enjeux d'un debat." *Égypte/Monde Arabe* 18/19: 241–330.

Farag, Iman. 1996. "L'enseignement en Égypte: économie politique d'une libéralisation annoncée." In *Âge libéral et néo-libéralisme*, edited by Mustapha Kamel Al-Sayyid, 247–273. Paris: CEDEJ.

Farag, Iman. 2006. "A Great Vocation, a Modest Profession: Teachers' Paths and Practices." In *Cultures of Arab Schooling: Critical Ethnographies from Egypt*, edited by Linda Herrera and Carlos Alberto Torres, 109–134. New York: State University of New York Press.

Fergany, Nader. 1994. *Survey of Access to Primary Education and Acquisition of Basic Literacy Skills in Three Governorates in Egypt.* Cairo: UNICEF; Almishkat Centre for Research and Training.

Ferguson, Niall. 2003. *Empire: The Rise and Demise of the British World Order and the Lessons for Global Power.* New York: Basic Books.

Ferguson, Niall. 2004. *Colossus: The Rise and Fall of the American Empire.* New York: Penguin Press.

Ferguson, Susanna. 2018. "'A Fever for an Education': Pedagogical Thought and Social Transformation in Beirut and Mount Lebanon, 1861–1914." *Arab Studies Journal.* 16 (1): 58–83.

Foucault, Michel. 1978. *Discipline and Punish: The Birth of the Prison.* New York: Pantheon Books.

Foucault, Michel. 1980. *Power/Knowledge: Selected Interviews and Other Writings 1972–1977.* Edited by Colin Gordon, translated by Colin Gordon, Leo Marshall, John Mepham, and Kate Soper. New York: Pantheon Books.

Freire, Paulo. 1970. *Pedagogy of the Oppressed.* New York: Continuum.

Fuchs, Christian. 2014. *Social Media: A Critical Introduction.* Thousand Oaks, California: SAGE.

Gasser, Urs, Colin Maclay, and John G. Palfrey. 2010. *Working Towards a Deeper Understanding of Digital Safety for Children and Young People in Developing Nations.* The Berkman Center for Internet and Society at Harvard University.

Gebremariam, Eyob B., and Linda Herrera. 2016. "On Silencing the Next Generation: Legacies of the 1974 Ethiopian Revolution on Youth Political Engagement." In *Northeast African Studies* 16 (1): 141–166.

Gellner, Ernest. 1983. *Nations and Nationalism.* Ithaca, New York: Cornell University Press.

Gendzier, Irene. 2005. "Democracy, Deception and the Arms Trade." In *MERIP.* 234: Spring.

Gilliver, Peter. 2016. *Precarious.* Oxford English Dictionary. Oxford: Oxford University Press.

Ginsburg, Mark, Nagwa Megahed, Mohammed Elmeski, and Nobuyuki Tanaka. 2010. "Reforming Educational Governance and Management in Egypt: National and International Actors And Dynamics." *Education Policy Analysis Archives* 18 (5).

Giroux, Henry A. 1983. *Theory and Resistance in Education: Towards a Pedagogy for the Opposition.* New York: Bergin & Garvey.

Giroux, Henry. 2001. *Theory and Resistance in Education.* Westport, CT: Bergin and Garvey.

Giroux, Henry. 2005. *Against the New Authoritarianism: Politics after Abu Ghraib.* Winnipeg, Manitoba, Canada: Arbeiter Ring.

Giroux, Henry. 2009. *Youth in a Suspect Society: Democracy or Disposability?* New York: Palgrave Macmillan.

Gordon, Joel. 2002. *Revolutionary Melodrama: Popular Film and Civic Identity in Nasser's Egypt.* Chicago: Middle East Documentation Center.

El Guindi, Fadwa. 1999. *Veil: Modesty, Privacy and Resistance.* Oxford: Berg Publishers.

Hammad, Waheed. 2013. "The Rhetoric and Reality of Decentralisation Reforms: The Case of School-Based Management in Egypt." *International Studies in Educational Administration (Commonwealth Council for Educational Administration & Management)* 41 (2): 33–47.

Harding, Sandra. 1991. *Whose Science? Whose Knowledge? Thinking from Women's Lives*. Ithaca, New York: Cornell University Press.

Hardt, Michael, and Antonio Negri. 2000. *Empire*. Cambridge, MA: Harvard University Press.

Hartmann, Sarah. 2007. "The Informal Market of Education in Egypt—Private Tutoring and Its Implications." In *Youth, Gender and the City*, edited by Thomas Hüsken, 91–124. Cairo: Goethe Institute.

Hartmann, Sarah. 2008. "'At School We Don't Pay Attention Anyway'—The Informal Market of Education in Egypt and Its Implications." *Sociologus* 58 (1): 27–48.

Hartmann, Sarah. 2013. "Education 'Home Delivery' in Egypt: Private Tutoring and Social Stratification." In *Private Tutoring across the Mediterranean: Power Dynamics and Implications for Learning and Equity*, edited by Mark Bray, André E. Mazawi, and Ronald G. Sultana, 57–75. Rotterdam: Sense.

Harvey, David. 2003. *The New Imperialism*. Oxford, United Kingdom: Oxford University Press.

al-Hayat. 1995. "Husayn Kamal Baha' al-Din: ba'd istib'ad al-mu'allimin al-mutatarrifin ijra' ajilan wa-lakin al-hal al-haqiqi huwa tatwir al-manahij al-dirasiya." p. 17.

Hernández, Ma, Prisca González, and Salvador Sánchez. 2013. Gender and Constructs from the Hidden Curriculum. *Creative Education*, 4, 89–92.

Herrera, Linda. 1992. "Scenes of Schooling: Inside a Girls' School in Cairo." *Cairo Papers in Social Science* 15 (1): 1–89.

Herrera, Linda. 2000. "The Sanctity of the School: New Islamic Education and Modern Egypt." PhD Diss., Graduate School of Arts and Science, Columbia University, New York.

Herrera, Linda. 2001. "Downveiling: Gender and the Contest over Culture in Egypt." *Middle East Report*, 219, 16–19.

Herrera, Linda. 2002. "'The Soul of a Nation': Abdallah Nadim and Educational Reform in Egypt (1845–1896)." *Mediterranean Journal of Educational Studies* 7 (1), 1–24.

Herrera, Linda. 2003. "Islamization and Education: Between Politics, Culture and the Market." In *Modernizing Islam: Religion and the Public Sphere in the Middle East and Europe*, edited by John Esposito and François Burgat, 167–189. London: Hurst & Company.

Herrera, Linda. 2004. "Education, Islam, and Modernity: Beyond Westernization and Centralization." *Comparative Education Review* 48 (3): 318–326.

Herrera, Linda. 2006a. "Islamization and Education: Between Politics, Profit, and Pluralism." In *Cultures of Arab Schooling: Critical Ethnographies from Egypt*, edited by Linda Herrera and Carlos. A. Torres, 25–52. New York: State University of New York Press.

Herrera, Linda. 2006b. "When Does Life Begin? Youth Perspectives from Egypt." *DevISSues* 8 (2): 7–9.

Herrera, Linda. 2008a. "Education and Empire: Democratic Reform in the Arab World?" *International Journal of Educational Reform*, 17(4), 355–574.

Herrera, Linda. 2008b. "New Developments in Educational Policy in the Arab World: Privatization, Rights and Educational Markets in Egypt." *Forum 21, European Journal on Child and Youth Research* 2 (12): 68–76.

Herrera, L. 2010a. "Education and Ethnography: Insiders, Outsiders, and Gate-keepers." In *World Yearbook of Education 2010: Education and the Arab World: Political Projects, Struggles, and Geometries of Power*, edited by André Mazawi and Ronald Sultana, 117–131. New York: Routledge.

Herrera, Linda. 2010b. "Egyptian Youths' Quest for Jobs and Justice." In *Being Young and Muslim: New Cultural Politics in the Global South and North*, edited by Linda Herrera and Asef Bayat, 127–143. New York: Oxford University Press.

Herrera, Linda. 2011. "Generation Rev and the Struggle for Democracy: Interview with Aly El-Raggal." *Jadaliyya*. October 14, 2011.

Herrera, Linda. 2012. "Youth and Citizenship in the Digital Age: A View from Egypt." *Harvard Educational Review*, 82 (3), 333–353.

Herrera, Linda. 2014. *Revolution in the Age of Social Media: The Egyptian Popular Insurrection and the Internet*. New York and London: Verso.

Herrera, Linda. 2015. "Citizenship under Surveillance: Dealing with the Digital Age." *International Journal of Middle East Studies* 47 (2): 354–356.

Herrera, Linda. 2017. "It's Time to Talk about Youth in the Middle East as 'the Precariat.'" In *META (Middle East—Topics & Arguments)*. Volume 9: 35–44.

Herrera, Linda. 2018. "Media and the Arab Family." In *Arab Family Studies: Critical Reviews*, edited by Suad Joseph, 437–448. Syracuse, NY: Syracuse University Press.

Herrera, Linda. 2020. "Blended Learning is Coming to a School Near You: Research Reflections from Egypt during Covid-19." *Education 2.0 Research and Documentation Project (RDP)*.

Herrera, Linda, and Asef Bayat. 2010. Being Young and Muslim in Neoliberal Times. In *Being Young and Muslim: New Cultural Politics in the Global South and North*, edited by Linda Herrera and Asef Bayat, 3–24. New York: Oxford University Press.

Herrera, Linda, with Rehab Sakr, eds. 2014. *Wired Citizenship: Youth Learning and Activism in the Middle East* (Critical Youth Studies Series). New York: Routledge.

Herrera, Linda, and Rehab Sakr, 2014. "Introduction: Wired and Revolutionary in the Middle East and North Africa." In *Wired Citizenship: Youth Learning and Activism in the Middle East*, edited by Linda Herrera and Rehab Sakr, 1–16. New York: Routledge.

Herrera, Linda, and Carlos A. Torres, eds. 2006a. *Cultures of Arab Schooling: Critical Ethnographies from Egypt*. New York: State University of New York Press.

Herrera, Linda, and Carlos A. Torres. 2006b. "Introduction: Possibilities for Critical Education in the Arab World." In *Cultures of Arab Schooling: Critical Ethnographies from Egypt*, edited by Herrera and Torres: 1–24. New York: State University of New York Press.

Hewlett, Sylvia. 2009. "'Me' Generation Becomes the 'We' Generation." *Financial Times*, June 18, 2009.

Hoganson, Kristin L. 2016. *American Empire at the Turn of the Twentieth Century: A Brief History with Documents.* Boston and New York: Bedford/ St. Martin's.

Honwana, Alcinda, and Filip de Boeck, eds. 2005. *Makers and Breakers, Made and Broken: Children and Youngsters as Emerging Categories in Postcolonial Africa.* London: James Currey.

Howard, Philip N. 2010. *The Digital Origins of Dictatorship and Democracy: Information Technology and Political Islam.* New York: Oxford University Press.

Howard, Philip N., Sheetal Agarwal, and Muzammil M. Hussain. 2011. "The Dictators' Digital Dilemma: When Do States Disconnect Their Digital Networks?" *Issues in Technology Innovation, Center for Technology Innovation at Brooking* 13: 1–11.

Hua, Haiyan. 1994. "Which Students Are Likely to Participate in Private Lessons or School Tutoring in Egypt? (A Multivariate Discriminant Analysis)" Ed.D. Thesis, Harvard Graduate School of Education, Harvard University.

Human Rights Watch. 1993. *Human Rights Watch World Report*, Egypt.

Human Rights Watch. 2020. "Egypt: Events of 2019". In *World Report 2020*, edited by Human Rights Watch.

Huq, Aziz. Z. 2006. "Extraordinary Rendition and the Wages of Hypocrisy." *World Policy Journal* 23 (1): 25–35.

Ignatieff, Michael. 2003. *Empire Lite: National Building in Bosnia, Kosovo, Afghanistan.* New York: Vintage.

Ille, Sebastian, and Mike W. Peacey. 2019. "Forced Private Tutoring in Egypt: Moving Away from a Corrupt Social Norm." *International Journal of Educational Development* 66: 105–118.

Ismael, Jacqueline S. 1986. "Conditions of Egyptian Labor in the Gulf: A Profile on Kuwait." *Arab Studies Quarterly* 8: 390–403.

Jackson, Philip W. 1968. *Life in Classrooms.* New York: Holt, Rinehart and Winston.

Jenkins, Henry. 2006. *Fans, Bloggers, and Gamers: Exploring Participatory Culture.* New York: New York University Press.

Jenkins, Henry. 2008. "Obama and the 'We' Generation. *Aca-Fan*, February 18, 2008.

Jenkins, Henry, Mizuko Ito, and Danah Boyd. 2015. *Participatory Culture in a Networked Era: A Conversation on Youth, Learning, Commerce and Politics.* New York: Wiley.

Kamenetz, Anya. 2006. *Generation Debt: Why Now Is a Terrible Time to Be Young.* New York: Riverhead Books.

Kandil, Amani. 1998. "The Nonprofit Sector in Egypt." In *The Nonprofit Sector in the Developing World*, edited by Helmut K. Anheier and Lester M. Salamon, 122–157. Manchester: Manchester University Press.

Kandil, Hazem. 2015. *Inside the Brotherhood.* Cambridge: Polity Press.

Kaplan, Robert D. 2006. *Imperial Grunts: On the Ground with the American Military, from Mongolia to the Philippines to Iraq and Beyond.* New York: Vintage.

Kellner, Douglas. 2003. "Toward a Critical Theory of Education." *Democracy and Nature*, 9:1, 51–64.

Khalidi, Rashid. 2004. *Resurrecting Empire.* Boston: Beacon Press.

Kiely, Ray. 2005. *Empire in the Age of Globalisation: US Hegemony and Neo-liberal Disorder.* London: Pluto Press.

Klatch, Rebecca E. 1999. *A Generation Divided: The New Left, the New Right and the 1960s*. Berkeley: University of California Press.

Korany, Osama. 2011. "Reformative Changes in Educational Leadership in Post-revolutionary Egypt: A Critical Appraisal." *Educational Research* 2 (10): 1553–1564.

Kothari, Uma. 2006. "From Colonialism to Development: Reflections of Former Colonial Officers. *Commonwealth & Comparative Politics*, 44:1, 118–136.

Krause, Kerri-Lee. 2007. "Who Is the E-generation and How Are They Faring in Higher Education?" In *Brave New Classrooms: Educational Democracy and the Internet*, edited by Joe Lockard and Mark Pegrum, 125–140. New York: Peter Lang.

Lacher, Hannes. 2006. *Beyond Globalization: Capitalism, Territoriality, and the International Relations of Modernity*. New York: Routledge.

Leonardo, Zeus. 2020. *Edward Said and Education*. New York: Routledge.

Lim Yung-Hui. 2011. Which Countries Have Over 1 Million Facebook Users? *GreyReview*, February 27. https://bit.ly/3xkgUxX

Lynch, Marc. 2007. "Blogging the New Arab Public." *Arab Media and Society* 1. https://www.arabmediasociety.com/blogging-the-new-arab-public/

Mahmood, Saba. 2005. *Politics of Piety: The Islamic Revival and the Feminist Subject*. Princeton: Princeton University Press.

Maira, Sunaina, and Elisabeth Soep. 2004. *Youthscapes: The Popular, the National, the Global*. Philadelphia: University of Pennsylvania Press.

Mamdani, Mahmood. 2004. *Good Muslim, Bad Muslim: America, the Cold War, and the Roots of Terror*. New York: Pantheon Books.

Mandour, Maged. 2019. "Sisi's Vanity Projects." *Sada*. Washington DC: Carnegie Endowment for International Peace, August 6.

Mann, Michael. 2003. *Incoherent Empire*. London: Verso.

Mannheim, Karl. 1952. "The Problem of Generations." In *Essays on the Sociology of Knowledge*, edited by Paul Kecskemeti (originally published 1928). London: Routledge and Kegan Paul.

Margolis, Eric, ed. 2001. *The Hidden Curriculum in Higher Education*. New York and London: Routledge.

Marshall, Shana. 2020. "The Defense Industry's Role in Militarizing US Foreign Policy." *MERIP* 294.

al-Masry al-Youm. 2016. "Shahid: muraja'at laylat al-imtihan fi 'al-istad': al-mudarris bi-yakhud 'ala al-ras 60 geneih." June 19, 2016.

Maughith, Kamal. 1998. "al-Ta' lim al-dini bayna al-tasamuh wa al-'unf." Paper presented at Association for the Development of Democracy, Conference on "Political Violence and Religion in Egypt." Cairo, May 19–20, 1998.

Mayo, Peter. 2012. *Echoes from Freire for a Critically Engaged Pedagogy*. London: Bloomsbury Academic.

Mazawi, André E. 1999. "The Contested Terrains of Education in the Arab States: An Appraisal of Major Research Trends." *Comparative Education Review* 43 (3): 332–352.

Mazawi, André E. 2010. "'Naming the Imaginary': Building an Arab Knowledge Society and the Contested Terrain of Educational Reforms for Development."

In *Trajectories of Education in the Arab world: Legacies and Challenges*, edited by Osama Abi-Mershed, 201–25. London: Routledge.

Mazzucato, Mariana. 2013. "Taxpayers Helped Apple, but Apple Won't Help Them." *Harvard Business Review*, March 8.

Mbembe, Achille. 2001. *On the Postcolony*. Oakland: University of California Press.

McChesney, Robert W. 2014. *The Digital Disconnect: How Capitalism Is Transforming the Internet against Democracy*. New York: The New Press.

McCrindle, Mark, and Ashley Fell. 2020. *Understanding Generation Alpha*. Northwest, Australia: McCrindle Research Pty Ltd.

McDonald, D. 2010. *The Twitter Generation Encounters the Classroom*. Southern Association for Information Systems (SAIS) 2010 Proceedings online.

McLaren, Peter. 2005. "Critical Pedagogy in the Age of Global Empire: Dispatches from Headquarters." In *Discourses of Education in the Age of New Imperialism*, edited by Jerome Satterthwaite and Elizabeth Atkinson, 3–24. Stoke on Trent, United Kingdom: Trentham Books.

McLaren, Peter, and Nathalia Jaramillo. 2007. *Pedagogy and Praxis in the Age of Empire: Toward a New Humanism*. Rotterdam, The Netherlands: Sense.

Mead, Margaret. 1928. *Coming of Age in Samoa*. New York: William Morrow and Co.

Mead, Margaret. 1930. *Growing Up in New Guinea*. New York: Doubleday.

Mellor, Noha. 2017. *Voice of the Muslim Brotherhood: Da'wa, Discourse, and Political Communication*. London: Routledge.

Memmi, Albert. 1965. *The Colonizer and the Colonized*, translated by H. Greenfeld. New York: Orion Press.

Metcalf, Barbara D. ed. 1984. *Moral Conduct and Authority. The Place of Adab in South Asian Islam*. Berkeley: University of California Press.

Meyer, John W. 1992. Introduction. In John W. Meyer, David H. Kamens, and Aaron Benavot, *School Knowledge for the Masses: World Models and National Primary Curricular Categories in the Twentieth Century*. Washington, DC: Falmer Press.

Mirshak, Nadim. 2020a. "Authoritarianism, Education and the Limits of Political Socialisation in Egypt." *Power and Education* 12 (1): 39–54.

Mirshak, Nadim. 2020b. "The Politics of Education." In *Oxford Handbook of the Sociology of the Middle East*, edited by Armando Salvatore, Sari Hanafi, and Kieko Obuse. Oxford: Oxford University Press.

Mitchell, Richard P. 1993. *The Society of the Muslim Brothers*. Oxford: Oxford University Press.

Mitchell, Timothy. 1995. "The Object of Development: America's Egypt." In *Power of Development*, edited by Jonathan Crush, 129–157. New York: Routledge.

Morrow, Raymond A., and Carlos A. Torres. 2000. "The State, Globalization and Educational Policy." In *Globalization and Education: Critical Perspectives*, edited by Nicholas Burbules and Carlos Torres, 27–56. New York: Falmer Press.

Mourtada, Racha, and Fadi Salem. 2011. "Arab Social Media Report: Civil Movements: The Impact of Facebook and Twitter." *Dubai School of Government* 1 (2): 1–30.

Munck, Ronaldo. 2013. "The Precariat: A View from the South." *Third World Quarterly* 34 (5): 747–762.

Musallam, J.E. 1992. "Professor Zahira Abdin: Sacrifice and Struggle." *Al-Ahram Weekly*, October 1992: 8–14.

Naguib, Kamal. 2006. "The Production and Reproduction of Culture in Egyptian Schools." In *Cultures of Arab Schooling: Critical Ethnographies from Egypt*, edited by Linda Herrera and Carlos Alberto Torres, 53–82. New York: State University of New York Press.

Naguib, Kamal. 2008. *Thaqafat al-shabab al-misri: al-ihbatat wa-l-tattalu'at wa-ab'ad al-muqawama*. Cairo: Mahrousa Press.

Nasser-Ghodsi, Nadia. 2006. "What Is the Effect of Educational Decentralization on Student Outcomes in Egypt? An Analysis of Egypt's Education Reform Program" Master's thesis, Palo Alto, CA: Stanford University.

NCER (National Center for Educational Research). 1986. *Development of Education in the Arab Republic of Egypt: 1984/85–1985/86*. Cairo, Egypt.

NCER (National Center for Educational Research). 1991. *al-Durus al-khususiya: dalil wa-ta'rif*. Cairo, Egypt.

NCERD (National Center for Educational Research and Development). 1994. *Education Development: National Report of Arab Republic of Egypt from 1992–1994*. Cairo, Egypt.

NCERD (National Center for Educational Research and Development). 1996. *Education Development: National Report of Arab Republic of Egypt from 1995–1996*. Cairo, Egypt.

Negus, Steve. 1995. "Militants Expelled from Schools." *Middle East Times*, 1, 16.

Nielsen, Lisa, and Willyn Webb. 2011. *Teaching Generation Text: Using Cell Phones to Enhance Learning*. San Francisco: Jossey-Bass.

Nisbett, Nicholas. 2007. "Friendship, Consumption, Morality: Practicing Identity, Negotiating Hierarchy in Middle-Class Bangalore." *Journal of the Royal Anthropological Institute* 13, 935–950.

Nye, Joseph S. 1990. "Soft Power." *Foreign Policy* 80: 153–171.

Nye, Joseph S. 2004. *Soft Power: The Means to Success in World Politics*. New York: Public Affairs.

Organization for Economic Co-operation and Development. 1996. *Employment and Growth in the Knowledge-based Economy*. Paris.

Online Etymology Dictionary. 2017. "Precarious."

Osava, Mario. 2009. "World Social Forum: Crisis as Opportunity for 'Another World'." *Inter Press Service*, February 1, 2009.

Palfrey, John, and Urs Gasser. 2008. *Born Digital: Understanding the First Generation of Digital Natives*. New York: Basic Books.

Pargeter, Alison. 2013. *The Muslim Brotherhood: From Opposition to Power*. London: Saqi Books.

Passavant, Paul A., and Jodi Dean, eds. 2004. *Empire's New Clothes: Reading Hardt and Negri*. New York: Routledge.

Petré, Christine. 2015. "The Jihadi Factory: Why a Suburb of Tunis Has Become a Breeding Ground for Islamic State Foot Soldiers." *Foreign Policy*, March 20, 2015.

Pilcher, Jane. 1994. "Mannheim's Sociology of Generations: An Undervalued Legacy." *British Journal of Sociology* 45 (30): 481–495.

Powell, Walter W., and Kaisa Snellman. 2004. "The Knowledge Economy." *Annual Review of Sociology* 30: 199–220.

Qvortrup, Jens, Marjatta Bardy, Giovanni Sgritta, and Helmut Wintersberger, eds. 1994. *Childhood Matters: Social Theory, Practice and Politics*. Vienna: Avebury.

Rafael, Vicente. 2003. "The Cell Phone and the Crowd: Messianic Politics in the Contemporary Philippines." *Public Culture* 15 (3): 399–425.

Rakha, Marwa. 2008. "Egypt: 89% of Youth Support Internet Censorship Law." *Global Voices Online*, November 26.

Ramy, S. 1993. "Impact of US Assistance on Educational Policy in Egypt: A Case Study on the Center of Curriculum and Instructional Materials Development 1989–1992." Master's thesis, American University in Cairo, Egypt.

Reid, Donald. M. 1991. *Cairo University and the Making of Modern Egypt*. Cairo: American University in Cairo Press.

Rheingold, Howard. 2003. *Smart Mobs: The Next Social Revolution*. Cambridge, MA: Basic Books.

Rideout, Victoria, Ulla Foehr, and Donald Roberts. 2010. *Generation M2: Media in the Lives of 8-to-18-Year-Olds. A Kaiser Family Foundation Study*. Menlo Park, CA: Henry J. Kaiser Family Foundation.

Rigby, Ben. 2008. *Mobilizing Generation 2.0: A Practical Guide to Using Web 2.0 Technologies to Recruit, Organize, and Engage Youth*. San Francisco: Jossey-Bass.

Rizq, Hamed. 1993. "Matlub mudarrisin li-l-'iqab al-badani." *Ruz al-Yusuf*. May 10, pp. 26–28.

Roberts, Brian. 2002. *Biographical Research*. Glasgow: Open University Press.

Rosen, Larry. 2010. *Rewired: Understanding the iGeneration and the Way They Learn*. New York: Palgrave Macmillan.

Rosen, Larry. 2011. "Teaching the iGeneration." *Educational Leadership* 68 (5): 10–15.

Rosenthal, Franz. 1970. *Knowledge Triumphant: The Concept of Knowledge in Medieval Islam*. Leiden: E.J. Brill.

Roy, Olivier. 2004. *Globalized Islam: The Search for a New Ummah*. New York: Columbia University Press.

Rushkoff, Douglas. 2019. *Team Human*. New York: W.W. Norton & Company.

Saltman, Kenneth. 2007a. *Capitalizing on Disaster: Taking and Breaking Public Schools*. Boulder, CO: Paradigm.

Saltman, Kenneth. 2007b. *Schooling and the Politics of Disaster*. New York: Routledge.

Satterthwaite, Jerome, and Elizabeth Atkinson, eds. 2005. *Discourses of Education in the Age of New Imperialism*. Stoke on Trent: Trentham Books.

Sayed, Fatma H. 2006. *Transforming Education in Egypt: Western Influence and Domestic Policy Reform*. Cairo: American University in Cairo Press.

Schwab, Klaus, ed. 2013. *The Global Competitiveness Report 2013–2014*. Geneva: World Economic Forum.

Schwab, Klaus. 2016. "The Fourth Industrial Revolution: What it Means, How to Respond." World Economic Forum, January 14. https://www.weforum.org/agenda/2016/01/the-fourth-industrial-revolution-what-it-means-and-how-to-respond/

Sedra, Paul. 2011. *From Mission to Modernity: Evangelicals, Reformers, and Education in Nineteenth-Century Egypt.* London: I.B. Tauris.

al-Sha'b. 1994. "al-Ta'n fi qarar wazir al-tarbiya wa-l-ta'lim bi-tahrim al-hijab ka-wajib." Cairo.

Shapiro, Samantha M. 2009. "Revolution, Facebook Style." *New York Times,* January 22, 2009.

Shawki, Tarek. 2020a. "Challenges: Details of the New Academic Year 2020–2021." Excerpt from September 8, 2020 Minister of Education and Technical Education Press Conference. Video by the Education 2.0 Research and Documentation Project. https://www.youtube.com/watch?v=1ezq03VinSA

Shawki, Tarek. 2020b. Digital Learning Tools: Details of the New Academic Year 2020/21. Excerpt from September 8, 2020 Minister of Education and Technical Education Press Conference. Video by the Education 2.0 Research and Documentation Project. https://www.youtube.com/watch?v=NsV9i4S-LJU

Shawki, Tarek. 2020c. "Egypt's Education Strategy Beyond the Crisis." Video Interview with the American Chamber of Commerce. September 22, 2020. https://www.amcham.org.eg/events-activities/events/1301/egypts-education -strategy-beyond-the-crisis

Shirky, Clay. 2010. *Cognitive Surplus: Creativity and Generosity in a Connected Era.* New York: Penguin.

Siebers, Hans. 2019. "Are Education and Nationalism a Happy Marriage? Ethnonationalist Disruptions of Education in Dutch Classrooms." *British Journal of Sociology of Education* 40 (1): 33–49.

Silver, Hilary. 2007. "Social Exclusion: Comparative Analysis of Europe and Middle East Youth." *Middle East Youth Initiative Working Paper* 1. Wolfensohn Center for Development and Dubai School of Government.

Singerman, Diane. 2007. "The Economic Imperatives of Marriage: Emerging Practices and Identities among Youth in the Middle East." *Middle East Youth Initiative Working Paper* 6. Wolfensohn Center for Development and Dubai School of Government.

Smith, Linda T. 1999. *Decolonizing Methodologies: Research and Indigenous Peoples.* London: Zed Press.

Standing, Guy. 2011. *The Precariat: The New Dangerous Class.* London: Bloomsbury.

Standing, Guy. 2014. "Why the Precariat Is Not a 'Bogus Concept'." *openDemocracy,* March 4, 2014.

Standing, Guy. 2016. *The Corruption of Capitalism: Why Rentiers Thrive and Work Does Not Pay.* London: Biteback Publishing Ltd.

Starrett, Gregory. 1998. *Putting Islam to Work: Education, Politics and Religious Transformation in Egypt.* Berkeley: University of California Press.

Stenberg, Leif. 1996. "The Islamization of Science: Four Muslim Positions Developing an Islamic Modernity." PhD Dissertation in History of Religions, Lund University, Stockholm.

Stoler, Ann, and David Bond. 2006. "Refractions of Empire: Untimely Comparisons in Harsh Times." *Radical History Review* 95: 93–107.

Sukarieh, Mayssoun, and Stuart Tannock. 2015. *Youth Rising? The Politics of Youth in the Global Economy.* New York: Routledge.

Tadros, Mariz. 2014. *The Muslim Brotherhood in Contemporary Egypt: Democracy Redefined or Confined?* London: Routledge.

Tapscott, Don. 1998. *Growing Up Digital: The Rise of the Net Generation.* New York: McGraw-Hill.

Tapscott, Don. 2009. *Grown Up Digital: How the Net Generation Is Changing Your World.* New York: McGraw-Hill.

Tawil, Hani A. 2001. "al-Ghazali (1058–1111)." In *Fifty Major Thinkers on Education: From Confucius to Dewey*, edited by Joy Palmer, Liora Bresler, and David Cooper, 29–33. London and New York: Routledge.

Tharoor, Ishaan. 2011. "From Europe with Love: US 'Indignados' Occupy Wall Street." *Time*, October 5, 2011.

Torres, Carlos. A. 2002. "Globalization, Education, and Citizenship: Solidarity versus Markets?" *American Educational Research Journal* 39: 363–378.

Toussaint, Eric. 2012. "The International Context of Global Outrage, Part 3: From The Arab Spring to the Indignados Movement to Occupy Wall Street." *Committee for the Abolition of Illegitimate Debt*, January 10, 2012.

Twenge, Jean, and Keith W. Campbell. 2009. *The Narcissism Epidemic: Living in the Age of Entitlement.* New York: Free Press.

United Nations Educational, Social and Cultural Organization. 2006. *Decentralization of Education in Egypt.* Paris.

United Nations. 2007. *World Youth Report 2007: Young People's Transition to Adulthood: Progress and Challenges.* New York: United Nations Press Release.

United Nations. 2015. "Security Council, Unanimously Adopting Resolution 2250 (2015), Urges Member States to Increase Representation of Youth in Decision-Making at All Levels." Press Release. https://www.un.org/press/en/2015/sc12149.doc.htm

United Nations Department of Economic and Social Affairs 2005. *World Youth Report 2005: Young People Today, and in 2015.* New York: UNDESA.

United Nations Development Programme (UNDP). 2002. *Arab Human Development Report 2002: Creating Opportunities for Future Generations.* New York: United Nations Publications.

United Nations Development Programme (UNDP). 2003. *Arab Human Development Report 2003: Building a Knowledge Society.* New York: United Nations Publications.

United Nations Development Programme (UNDP). 2005. *Egypt Human Development Report: Choosing our Future: Towards a New Social Contract.* Cairo, Egypt: UNDP and the Institute of National Planning.

United Nations Development Programme (UNDP). 2015. *Arab Human Development Report 2015: Work for Human Development.* New York: United Nations Publications.

United Nations Development Programme (UNDP). 2016. *Arab Human Development Report 2016: Youth and the Prospect for Human Development in a Changing Reality.* New York: United Nations Publications.

United Nations Office for West Africa. 2005. *Youth Unemployment and Regional Insecurity in West Africa.* Dakar, Senegal: UNOWA.

United States Department of State. 2009. Middle East Partnership Initiative (MEPI). https://2001-2009.state.gov/r/pa/prs/ps/2002/15923.htm

al-Usra al-Arabiya. 1993. "Wazir al-tarbiya wa-l-ta'lim: al-irhabi fi madrasitna." May 2, 1993.

Vinken, Henk. 2005. "Young People's Civic Engagement: The Need for New Perspectives." In *Contemporary Youth Research: Local Expressions and Global Connections*, edited by Helena Helve and Gunilla Holm, 147–158. Burlington, VT: Ashgate.

al-Wafd. 2001. "Tahaluf al-sahyuniya wa-l-'almaniya did al-tarbiya al-diniya." October 7, 2001.

Waly, Salma G. 2014. "Citizenship Education in Post-revolutionary Egypt: Examining the Curriculum of a Civic Organization." *International Education Journal: Comparative Perspectives* 13 (2): 73–87.

Wasik, Bill. 2006. "My Crowd: or, Phase 5." *Harper's Magazine*, March.

Hans Wehr, 1980. *A Dictionary of Modern Written Arabic*. Librairie du Liban (Third Printing).

Wickham, Carrie R. 2013. *The Muslim Brotherhood: Evolution of an Islamist Movement*. Princeton, NJ: Princeton University Press.

Willis, Paul. 1977. *Learning to Labor*. New York: Columbia University Press.

Wohl, Robert. 1979. *The Generation of 1914*. Cambridge, MA: Harvard University Press.

Wolfensohn Center. 2008. *From Oil Boom to Youth Boon: Tapping the Middle East Demographic Gift*. Washington, DC: The Brookings Institution.

World Bank. 2002. *Arab Republic of Egypt Educational Sector Review: Progress and Priorities for the Future*, Vol. 1. Main Report.

World Bank. 2004. *Unlocking the Employment Potential in the Middle East and North Africa toward a New Social Contract*. Washington DC: World Bank Publications.

World Bank. 2007. *World Development Report 2007: Development and the Next Generation*. Washington DC: World Bank Publications.

World Bank, Harvard University, and OECD. 2020. *Lessons from Education Webinar: Lessons Learned from Egypt during the Pandemic: Implementing Digital Technologies to Support Remote Learning and Student Assessment*, July 9, 2020. https://www.worldbank.org/en/events/2020/07/09/joint-oecd-harvard-hundred-world-bank-webinar-accelerating-modernization-of-education-in-egypt

World Bank. 2009. *World Development Report 2009: Reshaping Economic Geography*. World Bank.

World Economic Forum. 2005. *Women's Empowerment: Measuring the Global Gender Gap*. Geneva, Switzerland.

Yousef, Hoda A. 2013. "Seeking the Educational Cure: Egypt and European Education, 1805–1920s." *European Education* 44 (4): 51–66.

Yousef, Hoda A. 2017. "Losing the Future? Constructing Educational Need in Egypt, 1820s to 1920s." *History of Education* 46 (5): 561–577.

Youssef, N. 2012. *Min dakhil al-Ikhwan al-Muslimin*. Cairo: Dar al-Shorouk.

Zeghal, Malika. 1996. *Gardiens de l'Islam. Les oulémas d'al-Azhar dans l'Egypte contemporaine*. Paris: Presses de Sciences Po.

Žižek, Slavoj. 2004. *Iraq: The Borrowed Kettle*. New York: Verso.

Index

Page numbers in *italic* refer to photos or tables.

al-Azhar University 6, 103, 202n12
Azza, Abla (social worker, Falaki
  School) 23

Badran, Shebl 125
Baha' al-Din, Husayn Kamal: Center
  for Curriculum and Instructional
  Materials 141–42; curricular
  reform 111; Islamist militancy
  99–102, 108, 204n3 (ch. 6);
  Islamization of education 114;
  purge of Islamism in K–12 109–11
al-Banna, Hassan 102–105, *103*, 204n4
Barsoum, Ghada 151, 209n3 (ch. 10)
al-Bashaer School (PIELS) 123–26
Bauman, Zygmunt 182
Bedi, Arjun S. 204n2 (ch. 4)
Begin, Menachem 202n14
Ben Ali, Zine El Abidine 180
Bhattacharya, Manasi 204n2 (ch. 4)
blogosphere 174–76, 177–78, 210n12
Boeck, Filip de 151
British Foreign and Commonwealth
  Office 203n20
British protectorate 5, 201n8
Building the National Character
  (textbook) 208n12
built environments: al-Bashaer School
  124; home economics classroom
  61–65; Ministry examinations
  90; number of classrooms 212n7;
  office decorations 119–20,
  123; power signals 22; private
  schools 139; public high school
  194; renewing of 45–48; seating
  shortages 30; segregated schools
  118–19, 120; territories 27–28, 47
Butler, Judith 184
Butler-Adam, John 197

Camp David Accords 7, 202n14
Carnoy, Martin 207n3

Carter, Jimmy 202n14
CCIM (Center for Curriculum and
  Instructional Materials) 141–42,
  145
Center for Curriculum and
  Instructional Materials (CCIM)
  141–42, 145, 147
cheating 87–89
Chhachhi, Amrita 204n2 (ch. 4)
Christians 31–33, 101, 108, 125–26
citizenship development: counter-
  Islamist measures 109, 205n11;
  counternationalism in Islamic
  schools 113, 115, 120–22, 126,
  139–40; global citizenship
  education 141–46, *143*, 208n9,
  208n10, 208n12; *al-hukm al-dhati*
  21–22, 38; obedience to authority
  144, 164; punctuality 39–41; *tabur*
  (morning assembly) 35–39, 91.
  See also citizenship in digital age;
  hidden curriculum
citizenship in digital age: overview
  11–13, 163; citizen media 174–76;
  civic engagement 13, 159–61;
  cultural revolution 172–74;
  limitations of civic renewal
  181–82; methodology of this study
  169–70; opening frontiers 171–72;
  sociology of generations 166–68;
  wired generation 176–81; wired
  youth 163–66; youth on the rise
  168–69. *See also* Facebook; internet
  use; youth and globalization
civic engagement. *See* citizenship in
  digital age; global citizenship
  education
class dynamics. *See* social class
  dynamics
Cole, Ardra L. 151
communication technologies 159–61,
  164–66, 169–70, 209n7. *See*

educational reforms. *See also*
educational policies; hidden
curriculum
—CURRICULAR REFORM: as counter-
Islamist strategy 111, 141–42;
global citizenship education
141–46, *143*, 208n12;
internationalization 99; social
studies 205n11; social studies,
geography, history 141–42; and
soft power 135, 146–47
—DIGITAL TRANSFORMATION 13–15,
193, 196–99, 212n6, 212n9,
212n10
education and empire: overview
135–36; colonialism and capitalism
207n3; critical approaches to
207n2; decentralization in
schools 137–39; education decade
(1990s) 137; Palestine and Iraq
207n1 (ch. 9); privatization of
schools 139–41; soft and hard
power 146–47. *See also* economic
liberalization; educational policies;
privatization of schools
"Education for All" 135–36
education in Egypt: budget for
education 137; history of 4–8;
methods of this study 2, 9–15,
31–33, 169–70, 206n8, 207n10,
208n1; and national security
99–102; preparatory stage *84*,
204n1 (ch. 2); presecondary
students *198*, 212n10; reach
and place of in society 1; *tarbiya*
and *ta'lim* (upbringing and
knowledge) 2–4, 50–53, 125.
See also discipline in schools;
educational policies; educational
reforms; education and empire;
examinations; future of education;
gender dynamics; Islamism and

education; pedagogic styles;
private lessons; privatization of
schools; school rituals; social
class dynamics; social relations;
teachers; universities; youth and
globalization
education markets. *See* Islamic schools;
private lessons; privatization of
schools
Egypt: budget for education 137;
developmental indices 137,
207n4; emergency law 101,
204n3 (ch. 6); Ministry of
Upbringing and Education 4,
201n5; minorities 6, 31–33, 101,
108; New Administrative Capital
202n19; population growth
68, 197, 212n7; smart cities 13,
202n19; unemployment 149, 150,
209n3 (ch. 10); and United Arab
Republic 201n10. *See also* rights
Egypt Human Development Report
(2005) 138
Egyptian Boy Scouts 104, 105
Egyptian Knowledge Bank (EKB) 14,
198
Egyptian Movement for Change
(Kifaya) 209n7
ElBaradei, Mohamed 178–79, 180–81
Emad, Ustaz (junior science teacher,
Falaki School) 67, 68
Emad, Ustaz (teacher, Falaki School) 33
Emodo 212n9
empire and education. *See* education
and empire
empowerment 185–87
entrepreneurship 189–90
escapism 154–55, 209n4
Esposito, John 150–51
Every Child Connected 212n10
examinations: administration of 89–93,
91, 94–95; cheating 87–89; fail

Socialist Union 101–102
social media: civic engagement 13, 159–61; limitations of 182; prodemocracy movements 169; YouTube 175. *See also* citizenship in digital age; Facebook; internet use; youth and globalization
social relations: connections to get ahead *(wasta)* 158; effects of private lessons 140–41, 208n8; school community as extended family 50–53; solidarity versus competition 185–86. *See also* discipline in schools; gender dynamics; minorities; pedagogic styles; social class dynamics
—PRINCIPAL–STUDENT: Islamic schools 118; principal as parent-in-chief 50–53; principal as role model 40–41; strict disciplinarian 23, 26, 36–37, 38, 39
—PRINCIPAL–TEACHER 43–45
—STUDENT–NON-TEACHING STAFF 39–40
—STUDENT–PRINCIPAL: manners in addressing 23; students' opinions 40–41
—STUDENT–RESEARCHER 30–31
—STUDENT–TEACHER: favorite teachers 72–73; form of address 22; worst teachers 78
—TEACHER–RESEARCHER 26–30, 31, 33
—TEACHER–STUDENT: in past 68
—TEACHER–TEACHER: competition between 86–87; hierarchies 27–28; Islamic schools 118
sociology of generations: overview 166–68; findings 171–81; methodology 169–70; youth on the rise 168–69. *See also* citizenship in digital age; generation terms
socioreligious change 127–32

soft power: use by Muslim Brotherhood 104–105; use by Nasser 5–6; use by United States 135, 146–47
Somalia 188
songs, chants, and slogans 37–38, 106–107, 116–17, 120–22, 205n7
Sorour, Ahmad Fathi 99, 101, 114
Standing, Guy 183–85, 190
STEM (science, technology, engineering, and mathematics) 11
Strengthening Groups (Majmu'at Taqwiya) 212n10
sub-Saharan Africa, religion classes in 141
Sudan 188
Supreme Council for Education 109
Supreme Council of the Armed Forces (SCAF) 164, 209n1
Syria 4, 185, 188, 201n10

tabur (morning assembly): Falaki School 35–39, 91; Islamic schools 117, 120–22
Tapscott, Don 165
tarbiya and *ta'lim* (upbringing and knowledge) 2–4, 50–53, 125
teachers: art of teaching 72–75; corruption of profession 75–80; dissatisfaction of 67–69; downveiling 130–32; earnings from *magmu'at* 84–85; as exam proctors 88–89; Islamists 31; punishment of 80–81, 110–11; recruitment of 116, 124–25; salaries in government schools 69–72, 70, 80, 204n1 (ch. 4); salaries in Islamic schools 116, 120; training 108–109; on Values and Morals course 145–46. *See also* Islamic schools; pedagogic styles; private lessons

Teachers' Syndicate 111
teacher training 108–109
teaching as patriotism 67–69
Terrorism and Kebab (film) 155, 209n5
Thanawiya 'Amma (university entrance
exam): and career options 68;
high stakes of 83–85, 158; private
lessons 140, 194–96, *196*, 208n7,
212n5
"Torture of the Grave" sermon 109,
110
tuition fees: Islamic schools 114–15;
private schools 139
Tunisia 169, 180
Turner, Bryan 167
Twitter Revolution 169, 210n4

ulama (Muslim scholarly class) 6, 111.
See also al-Azhar University
UNDP (United Nations Development
Programme) 186, 211n2. *See
also* educational policies, *AHDR
(Arab Human Development Report)
2016*
UNESCO Regional Bureau for
Science in Arab States 14
United Arab Emirates 4
United Arab Republic 201n10
United Nations agencies 189
United Nations Development
Programme (UNDP) 186, 211n2.
See also educational policies,
*AHDR (Arab Human Development
Report) 2016*
United Nations Global Forum on
Youth Peace and Security 187–88
United Nations Millennium
Development 137–38
United States: aid funds 7, 137–38, 141,
155–56, 205n12; and economic
policies 159; and educational
reforms 135, 141–42, 146–47;

extraordinary rendition 204n3
(ch. 6), 208n14; government-
funded investments 190; hard
power maneuvers 147, 187–88,
208n14; instructional methods
and curricula studies in 105–106;
preoccupation with Muslim youth
149–52; Sayyid Qutb in 105–106;
State Department training for
bloggers 176
universities: connections to get ahead
(wasta) 158; counter-Islamist
measures at 108–109, 205n10;
Islamists in 100–102, 104–105,
107–109, 205n5; unemployment
of graduates 168. *See also* Islamist
militants; Muslim Brotherhood
university entrance exam (Thanawiya
'Amma). *See* Thanawiya 'Amma
(university entrance exam)
upbringing and knowledge (*tarbiya* and
ta'lim) 2–4, 50–53, 125
Upper Egypt: Islamist militants in
schools 107–108, 205n9; massacre
of Christians 101; teacher
transfers to 110
USAID (United States Agency for
International Development)
7, 137–38, 141. *See also* United
States

Values and Morals (al-Qiyam wa-l-
Akhlaq) 136, 142–43, *143*
Values and Respect for the Other 142,
208n12
Vinken, Henk 170
violence: in classrooms 75–80; by
Islamists 99–100, 101, 117, 136;
marital 204n2 (ch. 4); by police
175–76, 179; by states against
citizens 187–88. *See also* discipline
in schools; hard power

CPSIA information can be obtained
at www.ICGtesting.com
Printed in the USA
JSHW030832190322
23980JS00003B/5